Suicide, Self-Injury, and Violence in the Schools

Suicide, Self-Injury, and Violence in the Schools

Assessment, Prevention, and Intervention Strategies

Gerald A. Juhnke,
Darcy Haag Granello,
Paul F. Granello

WILEY

John Wiley & Sons, Inc.

Contents

Preface

Welcome! What an honor to have you peruse our book. Like you, we have skimmed the opening pages of many a book to see if it was worthy of our time or not. We hope you find this book helpful and to your liking. Truly it is an honor to serve you.

The intent of the book is simple. We want to help school counselors and other school professionals devise the very best prevention, intervention, and postventions for students who present risk for suicide or violence. The book also will help you create interventions and postventions for students who have experienced school suicide or violence. No one understands your students like you. You are an expert on your school and your students. You know what works. You understand your students' specific needs. Our intent is not to eclipse your clinical judgment or knowledge. Neither do we intend to tell you what you *must* do. Instead, we wish to *join* you in developing relevant and useful school suicide and violence prevention, interventions, and postvention strategies. We hope that these strategies will empower you, your students, your school, and your community.

This book skips the mundane minutia found elsewhere. Instead, we provide you with the most important information related to school suicide and violence. The book is divided into three parts. Part I is specific to suicide and self-inflicted injury and focuses on what works rather than nebulous, esoteric rhetoric. In this part Dr. Darcy Granello and Dr. Paul Granello provide critical information regarding suicide, suicidal behaviors, and self-inflicted injury specific to children and adolescents. The Granellos are renowned suicide authorities who present nationally and internationally on suicide. Drs. Granello describe important prevention and screening topics for middle and high school counselors. Then they describe suicide intervention and postvention. Their materials will help you gain the confidence and knowledge needed to effectively intervene. Finally, the Granellos discuss the ever-growing and pertinent issues related to nonsuicidal self-injury behaviors. Their discussions are relevant and to the point. If you are a school counselor or mental health professional working with schools or school-age children or adolescents, the information and guidance they provide will be invaluable.

Part II is authored by Dr. Gerald Juhnke and focuses on violence. Dr. Juhnke is a nationally known leader in the counseling field. He has written numerous publications on suicide, family, alcohol and drug behaviors, and violence. He shares his expertise to help readers learn how to effectively conduct face-to-face clinical interviews and utilize the Violent Student Scale with violent and potentially violent students and their parent(s). Multiple mini-case vignettes are used to aid your thorough comprehension of school violence assessment. Next, Dr. Juhnke describes how you can include Systems of Care and the dynamics of "wrap around" to augment your counseling interventions. The intent is to co-empower students and their parent(s) by jointly creating counseling interventions designed to reduce repeat or new violence probability. Dr. Juhnke also describes how to utilize Psychological First Aid and an Adapted Debriefing Model for post-violence survivors.

The third and final part of this book addresses a number of pressing issues of which school counselors and other school professionals must be aware. These include ethical and legal issues that must be considered whenever school suicide and violence topics arise. Specifically, the Ethics and Legal Issues chapter describes an ethical decision-making model that contains a process designed to help school counselors and mental health professionals consider the impact of potential clinical interventions before such interventions are made. Given the potential for litigation related to school suicide and violence situations, the authors also describe the importance of professional liability insurance and consultation with specialized legal counsel whenever issues of suicide or violence are possible. The final chapter wraps things up by discussing the importance of school suicide and violence preparedness. A general template for school counselors is presented as well as promising future interventions.

Again, we thank you for allowing us to serve you. We wish you the very best in your professional efforts of helping America's students and tomorrow's leaders.

GERALD "JERRY" JUHNKE
DARCY HAAG GRANELLO
PAUL F. GRANELLO

WARNING

Suicide and violence risk assessments, prevention programming, and interventions are complex processes. It is literally impossible to identify all persons who will ultimately behave violently or who will complete suicide. Thus, the suicide and violence assessments and face-to-face clinical interviews described or reported in this book should not be used as the sole methods to make a suicide or violence assessment. These assessments and interviews simply provide a "snapshot" in time and suggest potential immediate risk levels that should be continually re-evaluated by an experienced interdisciplinary mental health team. Concomitantly, the suggested or described suicide and violence prevention, intervention, and treatment methods should be viewed merely as partial components to a structured, multi-component, and thorough suicide and violence prevention and intervention process facilitated by a threat or safety committee minimally comprised of experienced and expert counselors, counseling supervisors, legal counsel, and a student ombudsman or advocate. Remember: Always consult with your counseling supervisor, school district legal counsel, professional liability insurance risk management advisor, and professional peers to insure that your assessments and interventions provide the greatest amount of safety for all.

Acknowledgments

Life is filled with abundant blessings and sprinklings of challenges. Throughout the writing process we have been abundantly blessed by many wonderful and supportive family members, friends, and professional colleagues. Specifically, we wish to thank Deborah, Bryce, Brenna, Gerald, and Babe Juhnke; Doug, Terri, Kevin, Kim, Christian, Brian, and Lauren Haag; and Alanna, Victor, Heather, Laura, Matthew, Jodi, and Andrew Granello. Without their support and encouragement, this book would never have been completed. They endured many long absences as we toiled away. Additionally, we wish to recognize Mrs. Meryl Haag, Mr. Leon J. Granello, Mr. Leon V. Granello, and Dr. Nicholas Vacc, whose memories and lives have influenced our writings.

We also recognize our many mentors, professional colleagues, friends, and helpers, including:

Mr. Peter Acosta

Dr. Rick Balkin

Dr. Jeanne Bleuer

Ms. Lisa Bratt

Dr. Brian Canfield

Dr. Kenneth Coll

Ms. Deborah Copeland

Dr. Dan Cruikshanks

Dr. Colette Dollarhide

Dr. Louise Douce

Dr. Rochelle Dunn

Dr. David Fenell

Drs. Phyllis and Jim Gloystein

Dr. Alan Hovestadt

Mr. John Kimmons

Dr. Dana Levitt

Dr. David Lundberg

Mr. Jerry Mitchell

Dr. Joe Olds

Dr. Paul Peluso

Dr. Kathryn Plank

Dr. William Purkey

Dr. Norma Simmermacher

Mr. Robert Staufert

Dr. Michael Sunich

Dr. Garry Walz

Dr. Richard Watts

Dr. Joe Wheaton

Ms. Wendy Winger

Dr. J. Melvin Witmer

Dr. Mark Young

Ms. Fangzhou Yu

Dr. Peter Zafirides

As well, we sincerely thank Ms. Isabel Pratt and the incredible Wiley team who have helped us make this book a reality.

Finally, we thank those who allowed us to serve and counsel you during your times of crisis and overwhelming heartache. Suicide, nonsuicidal self-inflicted injuries, and violence are times of great turmoil, crisis, and emotional confusion. You allowed us to enter your world and learn from your trauma and hardships. Your willingness to allow us into your world has provided the foundation for this book and our training and supervision of professional counselors. We hope that the many things we learned from you will provide our supervisees, students, and professional colleagues a level of respect, courtesy, knowledge, and therapeutic wisdom that will promote healing and speed recovery.

About the Authors

Gerald A. Juhnke, Ed.D., LPC, NCC, MAC, ACS, CCAS, is a professor and the doctoral program director for the University of Texas at San Antonio's Department of Counseling. Prior to his appointment at UTSA, Jerry was a professor and clinical director of the Nicholas A. Vacc Center for Counseling and Consulting Services Clinic at the University of North Carolina at Greensboro's Department of Counselor Education (UNCG). Jerry has authored, coauthored, or coedited 6 books and over 40 refereed scholarly journal articles. He has specialized in the areas of suicide, life-threatening behaviors, and family addictions since 1986. Jerry is an American Counseling Association Fellow and a former president of two counseling associations, the International Association of Addictions and Offender Counselors and the Association for Assessment in Counseling. He is a former editor of the *Journal of Addictions and Offender Counseling* and is a former co-chair of the American Counseling Association's Council of Journal Editors. Jerry has received numerous professional counseling awards, including the American Counseling Association's Ralph E. Berdie Research Award, the International Association of Addictions and Offender Counselors' *Journal of Addictions and Offender Counseling* Research Award, and the International Association of Addictions and Offender Counselors' Addictions Educator Excellence Award. He has provided counseling services and supervised counselors in diverse settings, including independent practice, community mental health, corrections, and universities. Jerry has served as a lecturer-consultant to the U.S. Army's Soldier and Family Support Branch as well as to the University of Texas Health Science Center Division of Community Pediatrics, school districts, psychiatric hospitals, courts, and municipalities. He is a former North Carolina Governor's Institute Faculty Fellow and former Fellow of UNCG's Center for the Study of Social Issues, Division on Youth Aggression and Violence.

Darcy Haag Granello, Ph.D., LPCC-S, is a professor and coordinator for the Counselor Education Program at The Ohio State University (OSU). Darcy has coauthored 3 books and over 70 refereed scholarly journal articles. She has made over 150 international, national, and state presentations and has secured over $750,000 in grants. Darcy conducts research in several aspects of counseling and counselor education, including cognitive development of counselors, counseling supervision, multicultural counseling, and attitudes toward persons with mental illness. She has been working in the area of suicide prevention since 2002. In 2006 and again in 2009, she received grants from Substance Abuse Mental Health Services Administration to develop comprehensive suicide prevention programs for the OSU campus. Darcy's service to the counseling profession has included editorial board membership on three journals (*Counselor Education and Supervision, Journal of College Counseling*, and *Counseling Outcome Research and Evaluation*). She served two terms as the first associate editor for quantitative manuscripts for the *Journal of Counselor Education and Supervision*. She is a past president of the Ohio Association for Counselor Education and Supervision and creator and list owner for COUNSGRADS, the national counseling student listserv. Darcy received the American Counseling Association's 2003 Research Award. She also received the Ohio Counseling Association's Research & Writing Award in 2002, a research award from the Association for Counselor Education and Supervision in 1999, and a senior faculty research award from the OSU College of Education in 2001.

Paul F. Granello, Ph.D., LPCC-S, is an associate professor and coordinator of clinical placements for the Counselor Education Program at The Ohio State University (OSU). Paul is a founding partner with the Ohio Department of Mental Health in establishing the Ohio Suicide Prevention Foundation. He is the recipient of the $2.3 million in federal and state funds for suicide prevention. Paul has coauthored 3 books on suicide and has presented and trained on the topic of suicide in over 100 workshops nationally and internationally. He has published more than 30 refereed scholarly journal articles and 9 book chapters. He is a Question-Persuade-Refer (QPR) and Suicide Prevention Resource Center (SPRC) certified instructor for suicide gatekeeper trainings, an SPRC trainer for clinical assessment in suicide, and a Red Cross–certified mental health responder. Paul conducts research in suicide, psychotherapy outcomes, and the psychological and social characteristics of individual well-being. He is also very interested in technology in counseling and has published 2 DVDs on counseling. He is dedicated to the local community and has provided numerous workshops on health and wellness topics for both the Ohio State and Columbus communities. He currently is a member of The Ohio State University Campus Wellness Collaborative and has authored a white paper and action plan for the OSU president on the topic of wellness. Paul received the David Brooks Award for Meritorious Service from the Ohio Counseling Association in 2002, the Ohio Association for Counselor Education Award for professional service in 2006, and the Ohio University Distinguished Alumni Award in 2007.

Suicide and Self-Injurious Behaviors

1

Suicide in Children and Adolescents

SUICIDE IN CHILDREN AND ADOLESCENTS

Children and adolescents are among the most susceptible to suicidal thoughts and behaviors. They lack adult perspective and experience, and many have not yet learned to handle life's challenges. Today, children and adolescents often face situations or exposure to information that is developmentally beyond their capacity to understand. It is easy for adults to minimize suicide risk in young people and assume that childhood is a carefree time with little worry or responsibility. In truth, childhood and adolescence can be a tumultuous period that can elicit thoughts and emotions that are extremely different to manage. Children and adolescents often have little control over situations at home and at school, and they may not have the coping skills or knowledge to seek help when they need it the most. In this chapter, we discuss some of the most salient issues relating to child and adolescent suicide, including methods to identify young people who may be at risk for suicide or other self-injurious behaviors.

Putting It Into Perspective

In 2009, suicide was the 11th leading cause of death for all ages in the United States. For people between the ages of 10 and 24, suicide is the third leading cause of death, accounting for nearly 4,500 deaths in this age bracket each year. That is equivalent to 12 suicides per day, or 1 suicide every 2 hours. Although suicide deaths represent just 1.3% of all deaths in the United States

---

With contributions from Karen Michelle Hunnicutt Hollenbaugh and Alexis M. Rae each year, suicide accounts for 12.3% of all deaths among 15- to 24-year-olds. That is because young people are far less likely to die than older adults. But when young people do die, it is far more likely to be by their own hand.

However, the 10- to 24-year age group represents a wide developmental continuum, and as might be expected, there are large variations in suicide completion rates, attempts, and methods within this group. For example, suicide rates are nearly six times higher in the 15- to 19-year age group (8.2 deaths per 100,000 in the population) than in the 10- to 14-year age group (1.3 deaths per 100,000). Those in the 20- to 24-year age group have even higher rates (12.5 per 100,000). Further, while older adolescents tend to use firearms (46%), suffocation (39%), and poisoning (8%) as methods for completion, children are far more likely to die by suffocation (66% of suicide deaths).

Suicide deaths, however, represent only one extreme end of the continuum of suicidal thoughts and behaviors. In the 10- to 24-year age group, there are more suicide attempts for every suicide completion than in any other age group. Among young people, there are as many as 100 to 200 suicide attempts for every completion, or as many as 900,000 attempts each year. Most of these attempts have low lethality, and many do not require medical attention. Nevertheless, every year, approximately 149,000 youth in this age group receive medical care for self-inflicted injuries at emergency departments across the United States (National Center for Injury Prevention and Control [NCIPC], 2008).

National surveys of high school students (grades 9 to 12) in public and private schools consistently find high levels of suicide ideation and behaviors. Each year, about 17% of high school students seriously consider suicide, 13% create a suicide plan, and about 7% report trying to take their own life (Centers for Disease Control [CDC], 2008; NCIPC, 2008). Other surveys have found annual rates of suicide attempts in high school students closer to 10% (Aseltine & DeMartino, 2004). Regardless of which survey is more accurate, the reality is that suicide ideation and suicide behavior represent a very significant public health problem among the nation's young people.

Perhaps more than in any other age group, suicide in young people represents a loss of potential that is hard to accept. In fact, one of the ways that suicide is represented in government statistics is through something called "Years of Potential Life Lost." Each year in the United States, we lose 270,000 years of potential life through child and adolescent suicide. When young people die by suicide, it is hard not to think of all that potential, of all that the future could have held, and of all the possibilities that will never come to fruition. Clearly, this loss of potential is the impetus behind child and adolescent suicide prevention efforts. In reality, suicide rates (as measured by number of suicide deaths per 100,000 people in the population) are much higher in other age groups. For example, among white males older than age 65, the suicide rate is 31 per 100,000 (and 48 per 100,000 among white males older than age 85). Nevertheless most efforts in suicide prevention are aimed toward children and adolescents.

Although suicide is a public health problem across all young people, some groups within the 10- to 24-year age group are at a higher risk than others. Boys are four times more likely to die from suicide than girls. This male-to-female ratio is remarkably consistent across all ages in the U.S. population. Although males complete suicide more often, females attempt suicide two to three times as often as males (CDC, 2007). These differences are due primarily to the lethality of the method used to attempt suicide. Males tend to choose more lethal means such as firearms, where females are more likely to choose pills or poisons.

In general, Caucasian males account for the majority of suicide completions among all age groups, representing about 74% of all suicide deaths. However, there are some cultural variations in suicide risk among children and adolescents. For example, rates of completed suicide are higher among American Indians and Alaska Natives. Hispanic children and adolescents have higher rates of suicide attempts than their Caucasian counterparts. Preliminary research indicates that suicide is the leading cause of death among gay, lesbian, bisexual, and transgender (GLBT) youth and is considerably higher than that for heterosexual youth. In fact, it appears that GLBT youth are two to three times more likely to complete suicide and may constitute as many as 30% of all adolescent suicides (McWhirter, McWhirter, McWhirter, & McWhirter, 2007).

As troubling as all these statistics are, they are probably low. Many suicides are ruled accidental deaths and are not reported. Often these accidents are associated with recklessness and/or alcohol use, which are also suicide risk factors. Drug overdoses, for example, are often recorded as accidental deaths and could be unrecognized suicides. Some researchers have suggested that suicide rates may be underreported by as much as 50%.

In our work with training school personnel and other professionals about suicide, we have found that the data and statistics quickly can become overwhelming. You may be feeling that sense of dismay as well.

The sad truth is that suicide rates among young people are increasing. Suicide rates for children ages 10 to 14 have increased by 50% in the last 20 years. Suicide rates among adolescents have doubled since 1950. Perhaps, then, it should come as no surprise that when we are exposed to these figures, our natural tendency is to feel helpless. The frustration and fear that we all have around the topic of child and adolescent suicide is clearly indicative of the concerns we all have about larger social problems that face today's youth. And although the information can be overwhelming, it is important to take some time and reflect on the implications this has for all of us as individuals, whether we are counselors, educators, or family members and friends. Each of us can do something to help prevent suicide. If we become educated and informed and willing to educate others, intervene when needed, and seek help when appropriate, we can help make a difference.

MYTHS ABOUT CHILD AND ADOLESCENT SUICIDE

D. H. Granello and P. F. Granello (2007) reported many myths about childhood suicide, including:

- **Childhood is a relatively carefree time in life**. Childhood actually can be a difficult time in which children experience many of the emotional stressors adults face without the requisite skills or experience to manage them. Today's children often are exposed to material or decisions that are beyond their developmental capacity to manage.
- **Children do not understand the finality of death**. It is difficult to make sweeping generalizations about what *all* children may or may not understand. However, there is a growing body of evidence that many children in elementary school understand the finality of death. In our work, we have seen very young children who have made suicide attempts with the full intention to die.
- **Children do not complete suicide**. In truth, research shows that children have some concept of the idea of taking their own lives, and many deaths that have been ruled as accidents may in fact be suicide.

There are also many myths regarding adolescent suicide:

- **Talking about suicide to adolescents increases suicide risk**. This is a particularly dangerous myth that has been thoroughly discredited through research. The problem is that the myth keeps adolescents from discussing suicide, mental health, or their own thoughts of death with reliable adult resources. In fact, educating students about suicide and appropriate help-seeking behaviors can help prevent suicide, as adolescents are more likely to tell peers than adults about suicidal thoughts.

- **Most adolescents who attempt suicide wish to die.** Most people who die by suicide are actually ambivalent. It is not so much that they want to die as they simply want the pain they are experiencing to end. Often adolescents simply do not see another way out of their current situation.
- **Adolescents only use the word "suicide" for attention.** The word "suicide" should always be taken seriously. Even if it is discovered the adolescent used the term to elicit attention, talking about suicide remains a plea for help and an extremely important risk factor that can lead to suicide attempts and completion.
- **Every adolescent who completes suicide is depressed.** Most people (as many as 90%) who die by suicide have some type of mental disorder at the time of their death, although not necessarily depression. Unfortunately, that disorder often is either undiagnosed or untreated. In fact, research demonstrates that only about 20% of depressed adolescents ever receive any intervention and only about 1% of adolescents who completed suicide were receiving mental health treatment at the time of their death. Adults may not recognize depression in young people, where depression may manifest as anger or irritability rather than sadness.
- **Current prevention programs are sufficient to prevent teen suicide.** Research has shown that current prevention programs have done little to reduce teen suicide rates, primarily because few states require suicide prevention programming in schools and most schools have very little prevention programming in place. The good news is that there is increasing evidence that primarily prevention programming in schools has positive effects.

Which of these myths have you heard before? Are there others? What implications do you think these myths have for school personnel as they work with children and adolescents?

RISK FACTORS FOR SUICIDE

Suicide is an extremely complex phenomenon. A dangerous pitfall that many people make after a young person dies by suicide is looking for easy answers. Maybe it is our innate desire to try to make sense of something so senseless, but the answers to understanding suicide are never that simple.

Our work with suicide prevention has brought us into contact with many people who have lost children or students to suicide. For example, we think about our work with a high school baseball coach who lost one of his students to suicide. The young man was sent home from baseball practice because he had a wad of chewing tobacco in his mouth, which violated school rules. When he arrived home in the middle of the afternoon, he found his father's gun and shot himself. Another colleague from a local high school tells a story of a high school senior who killed himself the day the school posted the names of the colleges that all the seniors would be attending. The young man did not get into the college of his choice. A local volunteer for suicide prevention efforts lost his daughter to suicide. She was a freshman in college when she called home to ask permission to use her parents' credit card to purchase a pizza. Her mother told her that they had already paid for the school's meal plan service, and she should eat at the cafeteria. The young woman killed herself later that evening.

These stories represent three terrible tragedies. But if we were to look only at the surface, it might be easy to get the wrong message. Being sent home from baseball practice, facing your friends when they know you did not get into the college of your choice, not getting to eat pizza for dinner—none of these events was the reason behind a suicide. Each of these stories represents only the last little bit—the *precipitating event*—the proverbial straw that broke the camel's back. Each of these young people got to a place of suicide crisis through very different paths, and if we tell only this little part of their stories, we miss the point.

Suicide risk is extremely complex, and everyone's pathway to a place of suicidal crisis is different. Suicide risk factors can help us understand some of the major concerns that many suicidal people share, but they are useful only to the extent they help us understand the problem of suicide as it affects segments of our population in general. Knowing which groups of individuals are at highest risk for suicide can help school personnel as they make decisions about prevention programming and intervention needs, but they do not do much to help us understand individual risk. Risk factors are based on aggregate data. That is, researchers review all suicide deaths in a particular age group in order to understand what commonalities exist. That information can be extremely useful, but only if it is used appropriately.

To underscore the complexity of suicide risk, more than 75 different child and adolescent suicide risk factors have been identified in the literature (Granello, in press b). In fact, there are so many different child and adolescent risk factors that understanding them all becomes challenging. Therefore, only the most prevalent and well-researched risk factors will be mentioned here. It should be noted that the term "risk factor" refers to any aspect of an individual, either biological or environmental, that may increase the probability of suicidal thoughts or behaviors. Children and adolescents can exhibit some of these factors and not be suicidal; conversely, they can exhibit factors that have not been listed here and have thoughts of suicide. The important thing is to be aware of the risk factors and the resources available and to be willing to have an open discussion with any child or adolescent who may be at risk.

Biological Risk Factors

Family history is a prevalent risk factor for suicide attempts. Adolescents and children are more likely to attempt suicide if other members of their family have completed suicide in the past. This risk increases if the suicide was recent, especially within the past year (Kiriakidis, 2008). Of course, it is difficult to know whether this connection is due to biological links or to the effects of modeling. We know, for example, that young people who are exposed to suicide *in any form* (through school, friends, celebrity, media reports) can be at increased risk for copycat suicide, particularly if the aftermath of the suicide is handled poorly. Nevertheless, genetic aspects have been identified as risk factors for suicidal thoughts and attempts. For example, a study of twins found that monozygotic (from the same egg) twins were more likely to have correlations in suicide risk factors such as substance abuse, depression, and aggression than their dizygotic (two different eggs) counterparts (Cho, Guo, Iritani, & Hallfors, 2006). In fact, there is ample evidence that certain mental disorders (e.g., depression, bipolar disorder, anxiety disorders, schizophrenia) run in families, and 90% of people who die by suicide have some underlying mental disorder(s). Some research also suggests that environmental risk factors manifest themselves differently based on gender. Female children who died by suicide were far more likely to have reported interpersonal stressors than male children (Ang, Chia, & Fung, 2006).

Emotional Risk Factors

In general, children and adolescents at risk for suicide have high rates of psychological distress. For some young people, suicide attempts and nonsuicidal self-inflicted injuries are a way to express severe emotional pain. In general, children and adolescents diagnosed with mental health disorders have drastically higher rates of suicidal thoughts and behaviors than those without. Specifically, young people diagnosed with bipolar disorder, depressive disorders, schizophrenia, substance use disorders, and conduct disorder are at an even higher risk than those who have mental health diagnoses. As noted earlier, many of these mental health disorders go undetected and untreated in young people, which underscores the importance of appropriate mental health care as an important component of suicide prevention.

Hopelessness is an important risk factor in all suicides, and the combination of depression and hopelessness is particularly troubling. People with severe depression who believe *it will never get any better* are at significantly elevated risk. Remember, suicide is not about death. People who are suicidal are in tremendous psychological pain. Edwin S. Shneidman, the "father of suicidology," calls this pain "psychache"—a strong word to reflect the severity of the pain. People who are hopeless believe that they will always feel this bad, and they cannot imagine a lifetime of pain.

Impulsivity is an emotional risk factor that is significantly different in children and adolescents than it is in adults. Children are far more likely than adults to have impulsive suicides, and in general, they are less likely to spend time planning a suicide attempt. Children with high levels of impulsivity may have difficulty coping with stressful situations, may be aggressive, and could have diagnoses of brain damage and Attention Deficit Hyperactivity Disorder (ADHD). These diagnoses have been linked to higher levels of suicide attempts in children (Stillion & McDowell, 1996). Even among adolescents, impulsivity continues to be a significant risk factor for suicide. A 2001 study found that among nearly lethal suicide attempts of young people (ages 13–34), almost one-quarter (24%) of the attempts occurred with less than 5 minutes between the decision to attempt suicide and the actual attempt (Simon et al., 2001). Perhaps as many as 50% of completed adolescent suicides could be classified as impulsive (fewer than 5 minutes between decision and action) (O'Donnell, Farmer, & Catalan, 1996). For these individuals, the suicide appears to be a method for handling crisis and conflict rather than a depressive desire to die.

Cognitive Risk Factors

Children and adolescents who have poor coping and problem-solving skills are at higher risk for suicide. In general, children and adolescents tend to engage in more black-and-white/right-or-wrong thinking than adults. When they are in psychological pain and do not want to continue, they may decide that suicide is a way to alleviate the pain. Once they come up with that "solution," they quit trying to find other ways to solve their problems. Of course, these "cognitive blinders" can occur at any age, and one of the symptoms of clinical depression is rigid thinking styles. Perhaps, then, it is no surprise that depressed children are even *more likely* than depressed adults to have poor coping and an inability to problem-solve.

A second significant cognitive risk factor among young people is perfectionism. You may have heard stories of children or adolescents who appeared to have it all. They were good students, popular, and future-oriented. When they were faced with a crisis, however, they were unable to handle it. Highly perfectionist children and adolescents can be at increased risk for suicide. Perfectionism, which can be adaptive when used appropriately for goal orientation, can be extremely maladaptive when people set standards for themselves that are so high, they cannot be attained. When they cannot fulfill their own expectations of themselves, they find that they have not developed the coping skills to manage. When this occurs, suicide starts to seem like the only way out. It is important that we never assume that a student would not have suicidal thoughts based on our ideas about his or her situation.

Behavioral Risk Factors

Impulsive behaviors and substance abuse in children and adolescents can be coupled with reckless or risk-taking behaviors that can lead to serious injury or death. Examples of high-risk behaviors range from extreme sports, to driving under the influence, gambling, unprotected sex, and street racing. Predisposing factors to high-risk behaviors include low self-esteem, poor parental supervision, and school failure. Research shows that Russian roulette remains a significant modality of death by extreme risk taking, particularly among young males (Shields, Hunsaker, & Stewart, 2008). Another high-risk activity, autoerotic asphyxiation, is a method to intentionally cut off oxygen to the brain in order to intensify sexual arousal. Various methods are used to achieve the level of oxygen depletion needed, such as plastic bags over the head, strangulation, or the use of gas or other solvents. Although most individuals who participate are not suicidal, serious injury or death can occur. In fact, it is estimated that autoerotic asphyxiation results in 1,000 deaths per year in the United States, primarily among young males (Downs, 2005). In the choking game, which differs from autoerotic asphyxiation, participants attempt to gain a "high," or euphoric feeling, by depriving the brain of oxygen. This is done by applying pressure with a person's hands or with belts, neckties, or other devices. Another variation involves one person taking a deep breath and holding it while a second person hugs him or her from behind until the first person feels dizzy and passes out. Fewer deaths occur with the choking game than with autoerotic asphyxiation. Nevertheless, deaths and brain injury can occur. A study of eighth graders in Oregon found that 36% had heard of the choking game, 30% had heard of someone participating, and about 6% had participated themselves. Rural youth (7%) were slightly more likely to have participated than urban youth (5%). Youth with mental health problems and substance abuse were nine times more likely to participate in the choking game than children with neither predisposing risk factor (CDC, 2010).

Warner (2009) identified these warning signs for the choking game:

- Strange bruising or red marks around the neck
- Bloodshot eyes
- Bed sheets, belts, T-shirts, ties, or ropes tied in strange knots and/or found in unusual places
- Visiting Web sites or chat rooms mentioning asphyxiation or the choking game
- Curiosity about asphyxiation (asking questions like "How does it feel?" or "What happens if . . .")
- Disorientation and/or grogginess after being alone
- Locked or blocked bedroom or bathroom doors
- Frequent, often severe headaches
- Changes in attitude; becoming more aggressive
- Wear marks on furniture (bunk beds or closet rods)

Other behavioral risk factors have been correlated with increased suicide risk. These include high-risk sexual activity (multiple partners, unprotected sex), binge drinking, and violence. Youth who come into contact with law enforcement, particularly those in juvenile detention centers, are at escalated risk. Finally, nonsuicidal self-inflicted injury (such as cutting or burning) has been linked to increases in suicide risk. Because of the risks associated with self-harm, Chapter 4 is dedicated to the topic.

Environmental Risk Factors

Environmental risk factors can play a significant role in child and adolescent suicide. Specifically, the role of shame and/or embarrassment appears to be salient for young people. Adolescence is a time of belonging. Young people appear to be particularly vulnerable to peer pressure, to needing the acceptance of others, and to wanting to belong with a peer group. When faced with stressors that will bring them shame or embarrassment in front of their peers, they may be unprepared to manage the consequences and unwilling even to try. We often hear of young people having a suicide attempt or completion after a public breakup of a relationship; after they are "outed" as gay, lesbian, bisexual, or transgendered; or after they are ridiculed (or perceive that they have been) in front of others.

Isolation and withdrawal are suicide risk factors for all age groups but may be particularly important for young people. The necessity of belonging, of fitting in, is so strong in adolescence that social isolation can be devastating. Young people who start to withdraw (especially those who previously had strong social relationships) can be sending clear warning signs to others that they are at risk.

Two other significant environment risk factors for children and adolescents are history of abuse and family dysfunction. Physical, sexual, and emotional abuse can be highly correlated with suicidal thoughts and behaviors. Children who are abused have higher rates of depression and hopelessness than nonabused children, with a resulting elevated risk for suicide. Family dysfunction can include having family members with substance abuse issues, high levels of conflict, or high medical or mental health needs. All of these factors have many implications for mental health. Clearly, all of these factors are interconnected, and the more risk factors, in general, the higher the suicide risk.

Finally, being in a lower income bracket is associated with higher levels of stress and lower levels of support, which are linked to increased suicide risk. Research also shows that individuals in rural areas are at higher risk for suicide than those in urban areas, but it should be noted that this could be due to correlation with other variables, including drug and alcohol problems, lack of mental health resources, and socioeconomic status.

Triggering Conditions

Triggering conditions are personal or environmental stressors that put youth at higher risk for suicide. Any significant stressor in the life of a young person could be considered a suicide triggering condition, even if those stressors not directly mentioned here. Remember, what constitutes a "significant stressor" is unique to the individual. In the case of young people, it is tempting for adults to look at a situation and think it is not very serious, but for the person involved, it may seem like the end of the world. When we talk to professionals about suicide risk in adolescents, we often ask them to think back to when they were young teenagers. "Do you remember how serious everything seemed? How the reactions of friends meant everything? How a casual hello—or even a look—by a certain someone could make your day (and conversely, a snub or rejection by that person) could be the worst thing ever?" Adults have more perspective, more experiences to draw on, and generally are less emotion based in their behaviors. That is why well-meaning adults tell adolescents things like "There are other fish in the sea." From an adult perspective, we have all come to realize that the "love of our life" at age 13 probably will not end up being our life partner. But such comments are seldom helpful to the teenager involved. In fact, they can feel minimizing and dismissive and can end up making the situation worse (e.g., "Not only does the person I love ignore me, but my friends and family don't understand how terrible I feel! I am truly alone, and nobody cares!")

There have been many different triggering conditions for suicide identified in the literature (e.g., Capuzzi & Gross, 2004; McEvoy & McEvoy, 1994). Examples include:

- Difficult transitions times (e.g., parental divorce, breakup of romantic relationship, move to a new school, graduation)
- Significant social embarrassment or failure
- Bullying or other victimization
- Social isolation
- Intense conflicts with friends, family, school officials, or the law
- Onset of a severe illness in self or family member
- Serious alcohol or substance abuse
- Suicides by peers or celebrities
- Anniversary date of significant trauma or painful life event

- Confirmation of an unwanted pregnancy
- Conflict over an emerging sexual identity
- Being forced to assume significant responsibilities while lacking the emotional resources and skills to do so

Warning Signs

Warning signs are specific behaviors that suicidal individuals display that may help others recognize that they are at increased risk for suicide. For example, a typical path for a person who has specific risk factors for suicide (e.g., depression, hopelessness, substance abuse) might include the occurrence of one or more triggering conditions (e.g., breakup of relationship, legal involvement), and he or she then demonstrates warning signs that indicate that movement toward increased risk for suicide. Of course, not all suicidal individuals follow this path, but having a general idea of the progression toward elevated risk can be useful for school personnel to help identify at-risk youth.

There are many warning signs for child and adolescents suicide (Lazear, Roggenbaum, & Blase, 2003). Some of the more commonly occurring ones are:

- Threatening to hurt or kill oneself or talking about wanting to hurt or kill oneself. (Eighty percent of adolescents who die by suicide tell someone that they want to die or plan to kill themselves prior to their death.) This can be through indirect comments, such as "I won't be a problem for you much longer," "Nothing matters," "It's no use," and "I won't see you again."
- Looking for ways to kill oneself, seeking access to firearms, pills, or other means.
- Talking or writing about death, dying, or suicide, particularly when these actions are out of the ordinary for the person.
- Withdrawal from friends and family.
- Marked personality change or severe mood swings.
- Exhibiting impulsivity, such as violent actions, rebellious behavior, or running away.
- Difficulty concentrating.
- Trouble in school (declining schoolwork, loss of interest).
- Refusing help, feeling "beyond help."

- Feeling rage, uncontrolled anger, or seeking revenge.
- Feeling trapped, as if there is no way out.
- Feeling anxious, agitated, or unable to sleep, or sleeping all the time.
- Giving away prized possessions.
- Making a will or writing letters of good-bye.
- Seeing no reason for living or having no sense of purpose in life.

Protective Factors

Protective factors reduce the risk of suicide. They enhance resilience and serve to counterbalance risk factors. They are not just the opposite of risk factors, but they are circumstances that, even in the presence of considerable risk, can act preventively to help reduce suicide. The role of protective factors in reducing suicide risk is uncertain, as they have not been studied as extensively as risk factors. Nevertheless, it appears that protective factors can help buffer individuals from at least some of the thoughts and behaviors associated with suicide. Protective factors for children and adolescents that have been identified by the National Strategy for Suicide Prevention (2001) include:

- Effective clinical care for mental, physical, and substance abuse disorders
- Easy access to a variety of clinical interventions and support for help seeking
- Restricted access to highly lethal means
- Family and community support
- Support from ongoing medical and mental health care relationships
- Skills in problem solving, conflict resolution, and nonviolent ways of handling disputes
- Cultural and religious beliefs that discourage suicide and support instincts for self-preservation

To the degree that school personnel can help young people develop these protective factors, they may be able to help reduce suicide risk. However, very little research has been conducted on the role of protective factors in prevention. To date, self-esteem and family support have been linked to decreases in suicide, suggesting that interventions that teach self-esteem enhancement and strategies to mobilize support may be productive, although this will require more research (Sharaf, Thompson, & Walsh, 2009).

BULLYING, CYBERBULLYING, AND THE INTERNET

Bullying is a serious issue in schools across the United States that can result in victims becoming depressed and suicidal. More recently, the issue of cyberbullying has become more prevalent with the increase in Internet use by children and adolescents. Bullying and cyberbullying can have a profound effect on a young person's wellness and is a major risk factor for suicide.

Bullying

Research has increasingly shown that children and adolescents involved in bullying behaviors are at higher risk for suicidal behavior (Kim & Leventhal, 2008; Kim, Leventhal, Koh, & Boyce, 2009). The term "bullying" includes any physical or emotional abuse that a child or adolescent may endure in or outside of school. Often students who stand out as different, or have fewer friends, are targets for bullying. For example, gay and lesbian youth are at particular risk. Higher rates of suicidal thoughts and behaviors have been found among this population, and research has shown this can be precipitated by bullying.

Bullying is remarkably common. A large-scale study found 16% of U.S. children in grades 6 to 10 say they have been victims of bullying during the current academic term, and 13% of students said they bullied other children (National Institutes of Health, 2001). Unfortunately, the long-term effects of bullying can be profound. Victims are more likely to suffer from depression and low self-esteem well into adulthood. Bullies themselves are more likely to engage in criminal behavior later in life. Often adults minimize these behaviors, thinking of bullying as a rite of passage or with a kids-will-be-kids approach. However, recent research has linked bullying to suicide risk, underscoring the serious nature of school-based bullying. A study linking bullying to suicide in countries around the world found victims of suicide were between two and five times more likely to report having suicidal thoughts and suicide attempts than were nonvictimized children. Importantly, the bullies themselves were also at higher risk for suicide, particularly among males (Nock, 2009).

Cyberbullying

Cyberbullying can consist of any number of aggressive activities toward another in an online environment, including harassment, denigration, impersonation, trickery, and exclusion. In addition, cyberthreats can include direct threats or distressing material that harms the victim psychologically (Willard, 2007). A widely publicized occurrence of cyberbullying that made the headlines ended tragically in the suicide of a 13-year-old girl. The girl was tricked into believing that the mother of a classmate was really a 16-year-old boy who was interested in her on the popular social networking site MySpace. The "boy" later turned on her, telling her "the world would be a better place" without her. The girl hanged herself with a belt in her home shortly afterward (Cable News Network, 2009). This example illuminates the seriousness of the potential for abuse on the Internet and the heartbreaking consequences.

Victims of cyberbullying exhibit lower self-esteem and higher overall psychological problems than their nonvictimized peers (Campfield, 2009). Sadly, victims of cyberbullying may not seek out the help they need. In one study, 25% of children reported that they would not tell anyone if they were cyberbullied, and 47% of respondents reported that they would tell peers and others but would not confide in school personnel, either for fear of consequences (retribution by the bully, limitation of Internet use by parents, etc.) or belief school officials simply could not do much to stop the problem (Cassidy, Jackson, & Brown, 2009).

Children and adolescents perceive cyberbullying to be a serious problem, made even more threatening by the perceived anonymity of the Internet, whether the actions actually were done anonymously or not (Mishna, Saini, & Solomon, 2009). This fact raises important questions about why adolescents perceive their Internet interactions as anonymous, even when they fully disclose their identity. It may be related to the situation in which they are engaging in these interactions, such as in the privacy of their own home, without actual physical or verbal contact.

Statistics on cyberbullying vary greatly. One study conducted by the National Crime Prevention Council reported that 43% of children and adolescents surveyed reported being victims of cyberbullying at least once (2007). Another study reported that at least 69% of students surveyed reported engaging in or being a victim of cyberbullying in some form (Campfield, 2009). Regardless of the actual percentages, it is clear that cyberbullying is an increasing problem with significant implications for the wellness of children and adolescents. Preliminary research also suggests that students who are bullied in school are more likely to be bullied over the Internet (Katzer, Fetchenhauer, & Belschak, 2009).

Internet Suicidal Behaviors

In November 2008, a young man completed suicide on live video over the Internet while countless other members of the public online forum did nothing to warn authorities. At times during the drama that played itself out online, individuals even encouraged him to complete the act. There are several Web sites available that support suicide, discuss methods for completion, and offer tips on writing suicide notes. Although there is evidence that some suicidal individuals seek out pro-suicide Web sites and find support for suicidal behaviors in online chat rooms and forums, it is equally clear that many highly suicidal individuals find beneficial support, connections and belonging, and information that helps reduce their suicide risk online (Harris, McLean, & Sheffield, 2009).

Thus, the role of the Internet in suicide prevention and suicide risk is poorly understood. Nevertheless, it is clear that many suicidal youth are discussing their suicidal thoughts online. In our work, we often connect with students who tell us that they learned of a peer's suicidal thoughts or behaviors from online discussions or posts. Clearly, monitoring Internet communications is a facet of suicide intervention and prevention that schools can emphasize with parents. In addition, children and adolescents should be educated on cyberbullying, including what to do if they are bullied online (Willard, 2007).

CHAPTER SUMMARY

In the last 50 years, the risk for child and adolescent suicide has increased. School personnel must understand the risk factors, triggering conditions, warning signs, and protective factors that can help them identify suicide risk. Children and adolescents are particularly vulnerable to suicide because of their lack of experience and perspective, their lack of fully developed coping skills, and the high levels of stress and emotions that many of them experience. The best approach to reducing suicide is always prevention, and schools are a natural place for suicide prevention and education programming, which is the focus of the next chapter.

2

School-Based Suicide Prevention Programming

The nation's schools play an essential role in youth suicide prevention. School-based suicide prevention programming has the potential not only to save the lives of students who may be at immediate risk but to instill values of help-seeking and prosocial behaviors in all young people that can last a lifetime. A positive and proactive school environment helps keep children and adolescents safe from self-harm not just by identifying warning signs and intervening with at-risk youth but by providing programs and resources that are responsive to students' personal and social-emotional needs. At school, students can learn about the role of stigma in mental health, healthy help-seeking behavior, how to intervene if they fear a friend may be at risk, and protective skills that can help minimize risk. Students at risk benefit from immediate contact with multiple helpers, such as teachers, counselors, coaches, staff, and classmates, who all have the potential to intervene. When suicide prevention programming is part of a larger effort to promote student mental health, the results can be dramatic (e.g., Aseltine & DeMartino, 2004). Unfortunately, without suicide prevention programming and education, schools can become places where students keep secrets, teachers are uncertain about what to say if they see problem behaviors in their students, and common myths and misunderstandings about suicide become the norm.

D. H. Granello and P. F. Granello (2007) identified some particularly dangerous myths that often exist within school systems.

- MYTH: Suicide prevention has no place in schools.
    - FACT: Our nation's schools, in partnership with communities and families, are the obvious places to identify suicidal youth and to

provide information to all children and their families. The 1999 Surgeon General's Call to Action, the 2001 National Strategy for Suicide Prevention, and the 2003 New Freedom Commission on Mental Health all call on schools to be active partners in supporting and maintaining the mental health of young people. Several key reasons have been identified for schools to be the primary place for primary prevention (Lazear, Roggenbaum, & Blase, 2003):

- In schools (rather than home or community), students' problems with academics, peers, or other issues are more likely to be evident.
- Suicide warning signs may appear with greater frequency at schools than at home.
- At schools, students have the greatest access to many different resources, such as teachers, counselors, nurses, and classmates, who have the potential to intervene.
- Students who feel connected to their schools (e.g., they believe teachers like and care about them, feel close to other students, feel part of the school) are less likely to engage in suicidal behaviors.
- Research has found that schools are the ideal place for primary and secondary prevention activities.

- MYTH: Talking about suicide will cause suicide.
  - FACT: This is a particularly dangerous myth. Promulgating this myth is not only irresponsible but actually harmful to students and to school-wide suicide prevention efforts. The reality is that talking about suicide and the feelings surrounding suicide can greatly reduce the distress of a suicidal person. Talking to people about suicide helps them understand that we care—that they are not alone. A study of more than 2,000 teenagers found that not only were depressed teenagers not more likely to consider suicide after it was brought up in a class, depressed teenagers who had attempted suicide in the past reported that they were, in fact, *less likely* to be suicidal or upset after the discussion (Gould et al., 2005). Additionally, there are more than 30 years of crisis hotline experience and more than 20 years of school-based suicide prevention programming with *not one single documented case of stimulating suicidal behavior through discussion of the topic* (Kalafat, 2003). The

fact is, we do not give people morbid ideas if we bring up the topic. In reality, most people consider suicide, at least fleetingly, at some point in their lives. Giving permission to talk about those feelings and find solutions other than suicide can be extremely beneficial. Of course, if by talking about suicide you mean simply discussing methods of completing suicide or providing Web sites with how-to directions for suicide, then yes, this kind of talk can be dangerous to persons at risk. But, of course, that is not the kind of talk we are promoting through primary prevention programming.

- MYTH: Schools can be sued if they have a suicide prevention program.
  - FACT: Actually, the opposite is true. Schools can be sued successfully if they ignore this important component of student life. In fact, two important court cases set legal precedent for the role of schools in suicide prevention. In *Kelson v. The City of Springfield, Oregon* (1985), a judge ruled that an inadequate response of the school staff resulted in the death of a 14-year-old student. This case established the precedent that parents of a student who completes suicide can *sue the school* if the death allegedly resulted from inadequate school-based prevention. Further, the findings in this case demanded that *all school staff* (e.g., janitors, lunchroom personnel, secretaries), not just teachers and administrators, are responsible for protection of the student. In the second case, *Wyke v. Polk County School Board* (1997), the court found that a school that did not have a fully developed suicide prevention policy in place was negligent when it failed to notify parents of suicide attempts of a 13-year-old student. The judgment in this case is significant because it indicates that school administrators and teachers can be held liable for not recognizing and reporting a student who is at risk for suicide, which has clear implications for staff training in suicide risk.
- MYTH: Suicide programs lead to contagion and "copycat" suicides.
  - FACT: Copycat suicides do occur, and if someone is already vulnerable (e.g., depressed, showing warning signs, has made a previous attempt), then one suicide in a school system can trigger another. However, it is not the primary prevention programming that leads to copycat suicides—it is the existence of other

completed suicides in a young person's life (either in the school system or elsewhere in the community). Thus, primary prevention programming is intended to mitigate the *already existing danger* of copycat suicides in the schools.

These myths (and others) can have serious negative consequences for the school climate, and they underscore the importance of a school-based suicide prevention program to help promote a healthier environment. A suicide prevention program provides screening, education, and skill-based training for all students, parents, teachers, and staff. This broad-based approach has its roots in new advances in mental health in which prevention is classified into three levels: universal, selective, and indicated.

Levels of School-Based Prevention

Three levels of school-based prevention exist.

1. **Universal interventions are directed at an entire population in a school.** Such interventions may include:
   a. Training and education for the entire school (students, parents, staff, teachers) regarding suicide risk, including warning signs and risk factors, how to ask for help, and how to respond to potentially suicidal students or peers.
   b. Efforts to reduce stigma and increase help-seeking and supportive responses among the entire school.
   c. Teaching of generic coping skills and other protective factors.
   d. Methods to enhance a sense of connection and participation among members of the school community.
   e. Screening of entire school population to determine suicide risk or mental health concerns.
2. **Selective interventions are targeted to subpopulations that are characterized by certain risk factor(s).** Students in transition periods, students with poor coping skills, and students who have been exposed to a suicide are examples of targeted populations. Such interventions may include:
   a. Psychoeducational groups to increase coping skills.
   b. Programs to increase resilience and help seeking.
   c. Targeted assessments or screenings.
   d. Linkages to community resources or referrals.

3. **Indicated interventions are targeted to specific individuals who have been identified as at risk for suicide through some screening procedure.** Such interventions may include:
   a. Comprehensive and ongoing suicide risk assessments.
   b. Linkages to community resources or referrals.
   c. Ongoing and open communication among school personnel, parents, and mental health providers.
   d. Protocols for monitoring risk during school hours and established procedures for managing escalation.

The strategies discussed in this chapter fall within the universal intervention category. That is, they target all students in the school, regardless of risk. Universal approaches provide education, training, and screening to the entire population of the school and promote school-wide improvements in mental health. Specific suicide prevention programs often are embedded within broader mental health education programs, focusing on the development and enhancement of healthy coping and other positive social and emotional life skills. Universal approaches may be particularly important in schools because:

- Most suicidal youths confide in their peers more than adults.
- Without training and education, some adolescents, particularly males, may not respond to their troubled peers in empathetic or helpful ways.
- As few as 25% of peer confidants tell an adult when they know of a suicidal peer.
- School personnel are consistently among the *last* choices of adolescents for discussing personal concerns.
- The inaccessibility of and reluctance of adolescents to seek out helpful adults is considered to be a *risk factor* that contributes to destructive outcomes.
- Conversely, research has shown that contact with helpful adults may be a *protective factor* for many troubled youth.
- There is evidence that *providing help* can be beneficial for adolescents. Participation in helping interactions can shape prosocial behaviors and reduce problematic behavior (Granello & Granello, 2007).

Schools are a natural place to provide universal approaches to suicide prevention. Schools are the institutions within a community that have responsibility for the education and socialization of youth. Increasingly, schools have responsibility for socialization and protection of youth coming from homes with family disintegration, substance abuse, interpersonal violence, and risky sexual behavior, all of which have been linked to increased suicide risk (Kalafat, 2003). With so many students in need, school counselors and school psychologists are increasingly being asked to move away from an individualized service delivery model to a more population-based public health approach within schools (Doll & Cummings, 2008). The central characteristic of any public health model is its proactive emphasis on prevention, which fits naturally with the universal approach to suicide prevention. Using a public health approach for school-based suicide prevention is on the national agenda, and the 2001 National Strategy for Suicide Prevention (NSSP) framework includes guidelines for universal approaches in schools. The framework calls on schools to (a) implement suicide prevention awareness and education programs; (b) train students, staff, and parents to identify at-risk youth and refer them to services; and (c) engage in effective school-based suicide screening programs. These three essential components form the foundation of comprehensive school-based universal prevention programs.

Although schools are a natural setting for suicide prevention programming, many schools do not provide this service to their students and staff. The Centers for Disease Control's 2000 report on School Health Policies and Programs indicated that fewer than half of states mandated suicide prevention in at least one grade. Further, although education and training programs are being developed across the country, there continues to be strong debate and controversy over how, or even whether, they should be implemented. Critics argue that it is inappropriate for mental health matters to fall under the purview of schools, that suicide prevention is expensive, that these efforts could violate the rights and privacy of students and families, and that schools should focus on the fundamentals of education. Proponents of school-based suicide prevention efforts argue that these programs have the potential to save lives and alleviate suffering, that parental rights are not violated because participation in all activities is voluntary and schools are required to obtain parental consent for screenings, and that providing skill sets for help seeking has lifetime benefits for participants. Nevertheless, the controversy continues, and school personnel who engage in suicide prevention activities must be prepared to counter criticism with facts and data.

The three major types of universal prevention activities—suicide prevention awareness and education, skills training to identify and refer at-risk youth, and screening programs for suicide and mental health concerns—each represents an important component of school-based suicide prevention. In the sections to come, we discuss each of these strategies in greater depth, with examples from our own work to help illustrate these universal prevention activities.

SUICIDE PREVENTION AWARENESS AND EDUCATION

A 2001 study (Washington County Department of Public Health & Environment, 2001) asked teenagers what they would like to see in school-based suicide prevention programming. The teenagers in the study said they wanted education programming that would:

Teach teens that depression is a form of illness that can be treated	65%
Inform teens how common depression is	56%
Teach teens how to tell if someone is really depressed, or just in a bad mood	68%
Teach teens how to recognize depression in oneself or others	74%
Teach teens where to go for help if you or a friend is depressed or suicidal	73%
Teach teens how to talk to a friend who is depressed or considering suicide	81%

Teenagers in the study said that they want to learn this information through the use of guest speakers (93% ranked this as one of their top-three choices for a source of information), on television (60%), from a caring adult (54%), or through peer education (53%). When asked what adults could do to help, the overwhelming response from teens was nothing complicated or expensive. By far, the most common response was "talk and listen to youth."

Students need information about suicide, depression, and mental health. Large-scale studies of student populations consistently demonstrate high levels of suicide ideation, suicide behaviors, and depression among student populations. About 18% of sixth graders have considered killing themselves in the last 12 months (Whalen et al., 2005). Among high school students, the rates are even higher. A 2007 national survey of more than 15,000 high school students found that over the last year, 28% of high school students met criteria for depression, 17% had seriously considered suicide, 13% had a suicide plan, and 7% attempted suicide (Centers for Disease Control and Prevention, 2008). Other studies find that the incidence of suicide attempts by adolescents may exceed 10% annually (Aseltine & DeMartino, 2004). Put another way, in a typical high school classroom of 33 students, 1 male and 2 female students attempt suicide each year.

In spite of the high levels of depression, suicidal thoughts, ideations, and behaviors, it is clear that most children and adolescents do not seek out appropriate mental health assistance. In fact, fewer than 20% of depressed adolescents receive any intervention (American Academy of Child & Adolescent Psychiatry, 2005). The most common scenario is for troubled young people to turn to each other for help. Adolescents in particular may be disinclined to seek help from adults, given their developmental needs for autonomy and dependence. Research demonstrates that suicidal children and adolescents are far more likely to confide in a peer than they are to talk with an adult. Among students with a previous suicide attempt, only 18% say they would talk with an adult if they needed help, compared with 38% of students with no previous suicide attempt who say they would seek adult assistance if they were in distress (Wyman et al., 2008). What is perhaps most alarming is that studies consistently demonstrate that only 25% of teens say they would tell an adult if they knew a friend was suicidal (Kalafat, 2003).

Given the existing levels of depression, suicidal thoughts, ideation, and behaviors in schools and the reluctance of young people to turn to adults for help, it is clear that adolescents need education and training about appropriate help-seeking behaviors. One of the most dangerous myths surrounding suicide prevention education in schools is that talking about suicide will put the idea in someone's head. School personnel who believe this myth may be reluctant to engage in educational programming. This myth is *not true*, and perpetuating the myth is *harmful* to students. The research is clear. Students are thinking about and talking about mental health, depression, and suicide. What is also clear is that young people want more information. In one study with more than 1,500 high school students, 87% stated that depression and suicidal thoughts and attempts were a problem among teenagers, and 73% said that they needed more information on where to go for help if they felt depressed or suicidal (Washington County Department of Public Health & Environment, 2001).

In the absence of accurate information, teenagers will look for answers wherever they can find them. They will consult with other peers, attempt to make up answers for themselves, or, as is more and more the case, use the Internet to look for information. Suicide information is easily accessible over the Web, as are special chat rooms for discussions with likeminded people. Chat room visits are typical of adolescents and young adults, a group at the highest risk for imitative suicidal behavior. The quality of information offered in these chat rooms is highly variable, ranging from encouraging people to seek help to teaching clear methods for suicide completion or advice on writing a suicide note. There are anecdotal reports of teenagers attempting suicide after visiting chat rooms and other Internet forums (Becker & Schmidt, 2005).

Student classroom activities, or classroom guidance activities for younger students, represent an appropriate model for suicide prevention education. Typically, these sessions are situated within larger modules on mental health, problem solving, decision making, conflict resolution, and help seeking. These types of programs clearly fit within a school's resources and culture because they have an educational rather than clinical focus; they are taught by school personnel, such as teachers or counselors; and they fit within the existing curriculum structure.

Younger students, such as those in elementary grades, may benefit most from classroom guidance activities that lay the foundation for healthy behaviors rather than from specific discussions on suicide risk and warning signs. Developmentally appropriate education that focuses on protective factors, such as coping skills, emotional regulation, and reaching out to caring adults, can be useful. Programs that help children feel connected to the school, to family, and to the community and provide opportunities to participate and make contributions also are important in developing strong protective factors. However, this type of training alone cannot mitigate suicidal behaviors. Supportive environments and education in protective factors may help attenuate the development of some psychopathology, but the reality is that many children with significant mental health concerns go undetected within schools (Kalafat, 2003). Suicidal young children must be identified by trained adults within the school and sought out for more advanced behavioral health interventions.

In grades 8 to 12, classroom activities should include more direct education in suicide, depression, and mental health. Often these sessions consist of several class periods, typically included in the health curriculum. These types of classroom activities represent a valuable method of communicating to a large number of students without extensive staff time. A suicide prevention classroom activity can include information about suicide risk factors and warning signs, the dispelling of suicide myths, how to recognize warning signs in others, where to go for resources to help, and how to respond to a troubled friend. Often classes involve the use of stimulus media, peer-led discussion, or role-plays. An important focus of classroom guidance activities for adolescents is to lessen the stigma regarding help seeking and to stress the importance of discussing a fellow student they may be concerned about with a school counselor, nurse, or administrator (Kalafat & Elias, 1995). Further, students should be helped to see that suicidal thoughts and feelings may be part of a mental illness, such as depression or bipolar disorder. We have found that it is very important to help adolescents understand that mental illness is an illness that needs to be treated, not a sign of character weakness. Finally, adolescents need to understand that feeling sad and even fleeting thoughts of suicide are normal (and that thinking about suicide does not mean that a person has a mental illness) *but acting on those suicidal thoughts is not okay.* In other words, the point is to emphasize that many people feel frustrated and overwhelmed, but that does not mean they kill themselves.

In general, classroom activities are intended to destigmatize seeking adult help for oneself or for a peer. Adolescents may have a misplaced sense of loyalty to their friends, believing that keeping a peer's suicidal intent secret is the "right" thing to do. In one of our trainings with a group of high school boys, we reinforced the importance of telling an adult if they believed a friend was suicidal. Midway through the training, a young man raised his hand and said, "I think I understand what you are telling us. It's better to lose a friendship than to lose a friend!"

Suicide education curricula should take care to emphasize the complexity of suicide. There are no easy answers to understanding suicide, and simplistic explanations can send the wrong message to students: that suicide is somehow a "solution" to life's problems. Education programs also must help students understand that although it is important for them to reach out and tell an adult if they think a friend is suicidal, *they are not responsible for keeping anyone else alive and should never be put in a position of feeling responsible for another's safety.* Many students will know someone who has completed suicide or made an attempt, and they must not be made to feel responsible for that person's decision. Always include a list of crisis intervention resources and hotline numbers in every training. Make sure someone is available to talk with students individually after the training if they need to process the material with an adult. Finally, there are specific curricular choices that are important to avoid, as research demonstrates that they may increase the potential for copycat suicides. Never talk about suicide as a reaction to stress. Never talk about suicide as a way to end pain. Avoid presentations (in person or via media) of other young people who have made a suicide attempt or media depictions of suicidal behaviors, in case students overidentify with the person or model the behavior.

Of course, it does not make any sense to tell young people that they need to tell an adult if they believe a friend is suicidal if the adults in their world do not know what to do with that information. For this reason, it is *absolutely essential* that all adults within the school system be trained in suicide prevention education *before training occurs with students*. When students are given information about suicide prevention, they may realize that a friend is at risk and turn to adults for assistance. If school personnel have not been trained to answer these student concerns, their interventions may be inappropriate and/or actually escalate risk. Furthermore, it is essential to train *all* adults in the school building. All too often, janitors, bus drivers, lunch assistants, and other staff are overlooked in this training, but for some students, these staff people represent a real lifeline. Additionally, parents need information and education. Whether that training occurs face-to-face at parent meetings or through information in newsletters or parent updates, it is important that parents know what to do if their child tells them about their own or another student's suicidal thoughts or behaviors.

In our own work with suicide prevention education and schools, we use the model discussed in the following education sessions.

Staff Education

Before the start of the school year, we train all staff in an afternoon-long education session that includes information on suicide risks and warning signs, suicide myths, depression and mental health, protective factors, and ways to reach out to at-risk students. This information is included in a suicide gatekeeper training, which is discussed later in the chapter.

Although all staff must have minimum competencies in suicide prevention, we know that not all school staff feel equally comfortable in this role. Students must be able to approach any adult in the school with their concerns. Nevertheless, there are some people who will really respond to the training and will want to communicate to students that they are available and willing to help. To recognize this, we distribute certificates at the end of the staff training for all participants to display in their offices or classrooms. We have found that those who wish to be proactive and communicate to students that they are approachable are quick to put up their certificates. Thus, it is important that the certificate be written in a way that communicates to students that this adult is willing to engage in difficult discussions. A certificate that reads "This Certifies that Mr./s. XX has completed a 3-hour Training in Identifying Distressed Students" misses the mark. In our experience, having a small group of faculty and administrators (and perhaps students) develop a certificate that is meaningful to students within the culture of that school is much more appropriate. We have seen certificates that read "You Can Talk to Me" or "I Am Here to Help" or "I Specialize in 'Difficult Conversations.'" The point is to find a message that resonates with the students (and that students can learn to identify when they go through their own suicide prevention education programs).

Parent Education

In some schools, we have access to parents though face-to-face meetings, although this is quite rare and never includes all parents. In other schools, we have access through newsletters and Web sites. We have found that it is essential to give information to parents periodically and in as many different formats as available. Face-to-face trainings can be similar in format and style to staff education and training, with additional emphasis on the importance of means restriction in the household (e.g., locking up guns and limiting access to pills or other potentially lethal methods). Information for newsletters and Web sites needs to be provided in engaging, short, and readable news briefs. Some schools offer a column on student mental health in every newsletter. Other schools offer information only periodically. We encourage schools to include information on mental health and suicide prevention in newsletters or other communications that go out during particularly stressful times for students, such as during exams, when college acceptance letters are being received, or before graduation. School Web sites should have an ongoing resource page for mental health. Regardless of the format, parents need to be given reliable and accurate information about suicide risk, mental health, and protective factors for their children.

Parents in particular need information about suicide myths, what they can do if they think there is a problem with their child, referral resources for assistance, and what kind of assistance is available. Just as with training for staff and students, parents need to be reminded that the most important thing they can do is *ask the question* and then *listen to the answer*.

Sometimes when we work with schools, we hear from school personnel that they do not have time to write these news briefs. Fortunately, there is a lot of excellent information from reputable sources available on the Internet. At the end of this chapter, we provide a listing of Web sites that offer suicide prevention information in ways that can easily be adapted for parent newsletters or school Web sites.

Once parents have been given information, they will need to be alerted right before the suicide prevention education of their children occurs. We give parents a heads-up that children may come home with questions or concerns after the training or may want to talk with parents about a peer whom students believe may be at risk. Of course, the notice about the upcoming education also provides parents with informed consent so they know their children will have exposure to this topic. In general, the goal is to keep all lines of communication open.

Student Education

Our general approach to training high school students is easily and quickly adapted to the specific needs of a school or age group. First, universal approaches emphasize the importance of training all students. Therefore, finding a class or time that includes all students is essential. However, suicide education training *should never occur* in the context of a large school assembly. Students need time and space to process these difficult topics, and smaller classroom settings are much more appropriate. We recommend training an entire grade level during the course of weeklong effort. Typically, there is an initial training in grade 8 or 9 with a shorter booster session for later grades. For example, a school might decide to train all ninth graders in health class through a series of education sessions. During the same week (or at a similar point in the school calendar), all tenth, eleventh, and twelfth graders might get several shorter trainings.

Second, we do not participate in "one-shot" trainings. A single session does not allow students time to reflect and ask questions. If they are left with concerns or unanswered questions, they do not have time for follow-up. We have found that a suicide prevention education program, within the context of a health class or other curriculum that includes discussion of mental health, works best. Our typical trainings are Monday/Wednesday or Tuesday/Thursday. This two-shot approach allows students to go home with some information after the first day, spend some time thinking about what they have learned, and get any questions answered on the second day. It also prevents us from doing education in the topic on Friday and sending students home to wait over the weekend to have their questions answered.

Third, we believe it is important to have a mix of approaches within the education session and to present information about suicide risk within the context of mental health. For example, we use discussion, media, and role-play in all our education sessions. We also help students recognize the role that depression and mental illness plays in suicide risk. We have found that helping students differentiate between depression and sadness is particularly important. In the United States, we often use the word "depressed" when we really mean sad. For example, you might hear a student say "I failed my test—I'm so depressed." But, of course, clinical depression is a significant mental illness and not the same as feeling sad. In our experience, students often do not understand that distinction, and it clouds their understanding of the role of depression in suicide. Thus, helping them differentiate between the two has been a critical component of training.

Finally, we are clear that the suicide prevention education curriculum is not intended to address suicidal feelings or behaviors directly. Rather, these sessions emphasize help-seeking skills and resources and are designed primarily for students who come into contact with distressed peers. We recognize that there will be students in the room who are in distress themselves, and we are careful to provide resources and referrals for students, but we do not engage in counseling during the training.

Day 1 (1 hour)

Introduction to the topic

Suicide myths, risk factors, warning signs

Brief presentation of statistics, general information for their age group

Discussion of protective factors

Role-play: What is the difference between feeling sad and feeling depressed?

Handout: Send them home with information that can be shared with parents.

Day 2 (1 hour)

Hand out questionnaires that ask:

What is one thing you learned during the last session?

What is one thing you learned that surprised you?

What is one thing you learned that you already knew?

What questions or concerns do you still have?

(Once these questionnaires are collected, we have found it is particularly helpful to have one of the class presenters read through the cards while another person continues with the class. Before the class is over, all concerns listed on the cards should be addressed.)

Review information from previous day, clear up any confusion or concerns

Discussion (with video clips, if available)

Depression

Anger and stress

Role-play: How to reach out to a friend

More role-plays: This time in pairs, how to help a friend

Generate list: What adults could you tell if you or a friend felt suicidal?

Generate specific names from the school and community.

If the school has adopted a particular slogan or logo for adults who are open to these difficult discussions, this is the time to tell students to look for the slogan "You Can Talk to Me" (or whatever the school-specific slogan might be) on the walls of teachers and staff who encourage these conversations.

Make sure all questions are answered before the students leave class.

Provide all students with phone numbers for local suicide help and hotline. Cards with the national number are available from the Suicide Prevention Resource Center (SPRC.org), but you can make cards with the local number by running business card stock through a printer. It is particularly helpful to tell all students to take out their purses/wallets and put these cards in them during the class. That way, no stigmatizing effects differentiate students who make a visible effort to keep the cards versus those who throw them away.

In our work with schools, we have found that students respond well to this general format. Evaluations of the program are consistently positive at the end of training. Sample comments from participants appear next.

1. What is one main point or message that you have taken from these two presentations?
   - Suicide is never the answer.
   - We have to actually do something if a friend confronts us with suicide and not to keep it bottled up.
   - Suicide has so much effect on others.
   - You should talk to people close to you when they seem to be going through a tough time or have not acted normally.
   - Talk to others about your feelings.
   - That suicide is a large problem but I have the power to help.
   - That you always have someone to turn to; you can always get help.
   - Suicide is a permanent solution to a temporary problem.
   - That no matter what, you need to tell adults.
   - Suicide is not worth it. You can always get help.
   - Get help for yourself, and get help if you need it.
   - It takes a strong person to help a friend thinking about suicide.
   - Communication is probably the most important suicide prevention activity to do.

2. Do you think, because of these presentations, you view suicide/depression or anyone dealing with suicide and/or depression differently? How?
   - Yes, I need to act quickly and take every word seriously if a person says he or she will commit suicide.
   - Yes, I feel after being presented with some of these statistics that I would like to change them for the better.
   - No, I have always been willing to help those dealing with these issues and myself have been diagnosed with manic depression.
   - Yes, because I know to be quick in getting help for someone considering suicide. I know not to keep it a secret.
   - I don't think those people are weird anymore. They are normal kids. This could happen to anyone.

- Yes, I used to think they were crazy and they actually wanted to die, but now I know that they just want help. I should help them. Now I know how.
- Yes, I see that suicide is preventable if you look for the warning signs.
- Yes, I learned that depression is a disease that you can recover from.
- Yes. I know it is very important to be open about this topic.
- Yes. Having examined the idea, it seems less likely that suicide is an answer.

It is important to note, however, that this type of suicide prevention education has not been subject to rigorous evaluation. In fact, universal suicide education in general suffers from lack of empirical validation, although several programs and models are emerging as best practices. Notably, Signs of Suicide (SOS) and Lifelines are two universal education programs that are included in the Suicide Prevention Resource Center (SPRC) Best Practice Registry. SOS is a suicide prevention curriculum that educates students on the signs of depression and suicide in others as well as themselves. Students are then taught to ACT: Acknowledge the signs of suicide, Care about the suicidal person and offer help, and Tell a responsible adult. A 2004 evaluation of SOS with 2,100 students in five high schools found significantly lower rates of suicide attempts and greater knowledge and more adaptive attitudes about depression and suicide among students in the intervention group. This makes SOS the first and to date only school-based suicide prevention education program to demonstrate significant reduction in self-reported suicide attempts among high school students (Aseltine & DeMartino, 2004).

SUICIDE GATEKEEPER TRAINING: SKILLS TRAINING TO REFER AT-RISK STUDENTS

Among children and adolescents, many suicide attempts and completions are the result of both unrecognized and untreated mental health and substance abuse disorders. Consequently, *an important key to suicide prevention is to gain the ability to detect and treat people who are exhibiting signs of mental and emotional distress at the earliest possible occasion and to take action to get them help.* This is the goal of suicide prevention gatekeeper training. Gatekeeper training teaches specific groups of people to identify others who are at high risk for suicide and then refer them for assistance. Gatekeeper training in schools is based on the premise that many students at risk for suicide do not reach out and seek appropriate help on their own. In schools, this training involves training school staff, including teachers, counselors, coaches, and others who are in direct contact with children. Gatekeeper training incorporates all of the information in the typical suicide prevention education programs but includes more specific training and focuses on how to intervene with potentially suicidal individuals. At present, suicide gatekeeper training typically is not offered to all students in the schools; the approach is aimed primarily at adults and perhaps student leaders within the school.

Most suicidal adolescents demonstrate clear warning signs before a suicide attempt. In fact, more than 80% of adolescents *tell someone in the week prior to their attempt,* and more than 90% of suicidal young people demonstrate clear warning signs (Granello & Granello, 2007). In fact, the great tragedy of youth suicide is that it takes place despite the suicidal youth giving out clear distress signals. Suicide gatekeeper training is designed specifically to teach school personnel to be on the lookout for those warning signs and other forms of suicidal communications from students.

We have found that it takes approximately 90 minutes to complete gatekeeper training in schools. Although there is no research regarding the need for follow-up training, Kalafat (2003) recommends a "booster training" approximately every two years, and that seems to fit with our experience. We have found that role-plays that mimic difficult conversations with students are particularly helpful. We encourage gatekeepers to be "gently persistent" when they engage with troubled students. That is, if the gatekeeper approaches a student and asks if he or she is okay or would like to talk, the gatekeeper should not accept the first "no" or "I'm fine" but instead gently continue the conversation and encourage the student to seek help. Many school staff members find encouraging discussion without being overly intrusive a difficult balance. Thus, role-playing and other opportunities for practice are essential components for gatekeeper training.

Recent research on gatekeeper training in schools has begun to demonstrate effectiveness in improving skills, knowledge, attitudes, and appropriate referrals. Two published studies have examined effectiveness of these programs in K–12 schools. Both found that school teachers and counselors trained as suicide gatekeepers reported greater knowledge of suicide risk factors, increased confidence in working with suicidal students, and greater involvement with suicidal students than those who did not receive training. As might be expected, improvement in knowledge were greatest among staff members who had low baseline knowledge. All staff members appear to have benefited equally regarding improvements in confidence and commitment to intervening with potentially suicidal students. In both studies, however, actual referrals of students in the months following training varied greatly among staff members trained, suggesting that gatekeeper training needs to focus more clearly on helping staff members with the skills they need to make the necessary referrals (Reis & Cornell, 2008; Wyman et al., 2008).

SUICIDE AND MENTAL HEALTH SCREENING PROGRAMS

A third and final strategy for universal prevention in schools is mental health screening, which involves voluntary assessment of all students' risk for suicide or other mental health problems. The goal of these screenings is to identify students early so that appropriate interventions can occur before problems worsen. In addition to identifying high-risk students, suicide screening programs may have the potential to increase overall help-seeking behaviors in students. Perhaps the largest potential benefit of school-based screening is the ability to identify at-risk students not already known to school professionals.

Given the multiple demands on school personnel, it would be impossible for these individuals to identify all students with mental health needs. Suicide prevention education and gatekeeper training can be effective if peers or gatekeepers recognize warning signs in others, but they cannot reach all at-risk students. Because of the potential for saving lives, screening for suicidality in schools has been called for by the President's New Freedom Commission on Mental Health (2003) and the Children's Mental Health Screening and Prevention Act (2003). This type of screening may be particularly useful for adolescents, as research demonstrates they are more likely to report stigmatizing behaviors in a self-administered instrument as opposed to a face-to-face interview (Scott et al., 2009) and adolescents tend to answer honestly about suicidal thoughts and behaviors when asked (Miller & DuPaul, 1996).

Programs typically involve class- or school-wide self-report screenings to identify potentially suicidal adolescents. Those who score in the high-risk range then are interviewed individually to get a more accurate risk assessment. High risk generally is determined by recent suicide ideation, history of suicide attempt, multiple significant emotion-related impairments (such as sadness, social withdrawal, anxiety, irritability, substance abuse), or self-identification as needing help in any of these domains (Scott et al., 2009). Parents of any student who requires further assistance or intervention are given referrals to appropriate local resources. Of course, screenings should not be done until there is a protocol for addressing high-risk students and appropriate referral resources are available.

Suicide screening can be controversial. Opponents argue that screening for mental health can be expensive, particularly at a time when schools are encountering budget cuts. Further, there is a concern that screening might violate student and family privacy and that schools should not be involved in student mental health. Finally, opponents have argued that screening programs can overestimate the number of children and adolescents who need help, with too many false positives using up staff resources and time.

Schools that implement suicide screening programs must be aware of these concerns and be prepared to counter them with research and data. Perhaps the most important way to counteract the concerns of the critics is to use an empirically validated screening program. Columbia TeenScreen is an example of an empirically validated screening program that is included in the Evidence-Based Practice Registry of the Suicide Prevention Resource Center (SPRC.org). The TeenScreen program is an 11-item self-report questionnaire about suicide risk and mental health concerns. Positive responses on items lead to follow-up questions that rate problem severity, willingness to seek help, and current help-seeking behavior (Shaffer et al., 2004). TeenScreen currently is conducted at more than 450 sites across the nation and was identified by President Bush's New Freedom Commission on Mental Health as a model for early suicide prevention intervention (Hinawi, 2005). TeenScreen has a strong track record of identifying adolescents at risk for suicide. In their research with adolescents in grades 9 to 12, Shaffer and colleagues (2004) found that 100% of adolescents who met criteria for suicide risk were identified by the TeenScreen instrument.

As noted earlier, a major goal of any suicide screening is to identify at-risk youth who previously have not come to the attention of school professionals. Initial research is promising. Scott and colleagues (2009) screened

1,729 high school students using TeenScreen and found that the majority of students who screened positive had not previously been identified as at risk. Among students with the highest risk for suicide (e.g., current ideation and a current mood, anxiety, or substance use disorder), TeenScreen classified an additional 37% of students who had not been identified previously by school personnel. In other words, in the absence of a screening, more than one-third of students in the highest-risk category would never have come to the attention of the school.

Before implementing a suicide screening program, schools will need to consider some basic logistical considerations. For example, will the entire school be screened? Or will screening focus on some group, such as a particular grade? What screening instrument will be used, and is the instrument developmentally and culturally appropriate for the population? Does the instrument have sufficient psychometric qualities, including appropriate sensitivity and specificity in screening for suicide? What are the criteria for a positive score? What staffing is necessary to complete the screening and the follow-up face-to-face interviews? What referrals are available for children who screen positive? How will the screening program be monitored to ensure that protocols are followed? How will informed consent be obtained from parents? (For a more complete listing of logistical questions to be addressed before beginning a screening program, see Joe and Bryant, 2007.)

In our work, we have implemented large-scale screening efforts in middle and high schools using the suicide screening program described next.

Suicide Screening Program in Ohio

Ohio's Adolescent Mental Health Screening Program was funded through the Substance Abuse Mental Health Services Administration (SAMHSA) to screen middle and high school students in Ohio. Over the course of a three-year period, nearly 14,000 students were screened using Columbia's TeenScreen.

Step 1: Active Parental Consent

In order to address any concerns about parental consent and privacy, we opted to use an active consent process. That is, parents or guardians must actively consent to the screening through a signed permission slip in order for their child to be screened. Not all suicide screenings use this method. Scott and colleagues (2009) used passive consent, in which letters describing the screening were mailed to students' homes and sent home with students. Parents who did not

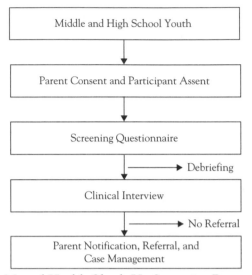

Figure 2.1 Ohio's Mental Health Check-Up Screening Process

want their children to participate in the screening had to opt out. If no request to opt out was received, consent for participation was assumed. Whether using active or passive parental consent, all screening programs also require student assent. In other words, in order for the program to screen students effectively, the students themselves must agree to participate.

Using the active consent process, we were able to screen 13,964 students (in more than 100 sites) in the first three years of the project. This represents a 33% participation rate. In other words, approximately 33% of the students who were offered screening actually participated in the screening. This is lower than the participation rate that Scott et al. (2009) were able to achieve using a passive consent procedure. They were able to screen 67% of those initially offered the service, meaning that a passive consent yields double the rate of participation as active consent. However, given the controversial nature of screening, we chose active consent, even though it meant a lower participation rate.

Step 2: Implementation of the TeenScreen Questionnaire

Students who had been given parental consent and who gave their own assent then were given the TeenScreen questionnaire, which is available either via computer or paper-and-pencil versions. Students who do not score positive are given the opportunity to talk with a mental health professional, if they so desire, and are handed printed information about mental health services and referral resources.

Step 3: Clinical Interview

Students who score positive on the instrument are given a 30-minute interview with a mental health professional for a more complete assessment. The goal is not to make a clinical diagnosis but only to determine whether a more intensive and comprehensive clinical assessment would be beneficial. In our project, approximately 24% of students scored positive (about 2,900 students). This is consistent with other research using the TeenScreen, which typically has a positive hit rate of between 23% and 28%.

Step 4: Parental Notification and Referral

Of course, not all students who receive a clinical interview require further intervention. In fact, one of the criticisms of all suicide screening instruments is the high rate of false positives (students who are identified through the instrument as at risk but who are not at high risk for suicide or other mental health concerns). In our study, about 59% of those who received a clinical interview required follow-up interventions. In this step, parents are notified of the concerns, are encouraged to meet with school personnel regarding the screening results, and are given a follow-up appointment with a mental health professional for a more intensive assessment and necessary interventions.

Step 5: Treatment

At this stage, school personnel are no longer involved in the process. Parents must follow through with the referral to get their child the assistance that he or she needs. Unfortunately, in our study, only 49% of students completed the referral. This is consistent with all other research. Even when parents consent to having their children screened, the children screen positive for suicide or other mental health concerns, and the school personnel make a referral appointment, only about half of children get the care they need.

Ohio's Mental Health Check-Up Screening Process

The evidence from research on suicide prevention screening in schools has clear implications for this type of universal prevention. Most important, suicide screenings have the potential to identify at-risk youth who otherwise would go undetected and untreated. As many as a third of students at high risk for suicide attempts would not come to the attention of school personnel without comprehensive suicide screening programs. However, when students are identified as at risk through the screening process and this status is confirmed by follow-up face-to-face interviews with mental health professionals, only half receive the treatment they need. There is clearly much more work to be done in parent education and in reducing the stigma surrounding suicide and mental health.

CHAPTER SUMMARY

Schools have an important role to play in suicide prevention. Universal prevention models are based on a public health approach. They help limit stigma, increase help seeking, and promote strategies to reach out to those at risk. The three most commonly used universal approaches are suicide prevention education, gatekeeper training, and school-based mental health screening. Although the research on these types of programming is in its infancy, all three types of interventions have initial empirical support as methods to reduce suicide risk in schools.

EVIDENCE-BASED PROGRAMS FOR SCHOOL-BASED UNIVERSAL PREVENTION

Universal Suicide Prevention: Education Programs

SOS: *Signs of Suicide*

SOS is a two-day secondary school education program that includes screening and education. Students are screened for depression and suicide risk and referred for professional help as indicated. Students also view a video that teaches them to recognize signs of depression and suicide in others. They are taught that the appropriate response to these signs is to acknowledge them, let the person know you care, and tell a responsible adult (either with the person or on that person's behalf). Students also participate in guided classroom discussions about suicide

According to Suicide Prevention Resource Center Evidence-Based Practice Registry (www.sprc.org).

and depression. The intervention attempts to prevent suicide attempts, increase knowledge about suicide and depression, develop desirable attitudes toward suicide and depression, and increase help-seeking.

Web site: www.mentalhealthscreening.org/highschool/index.aspx
SPRC Classification: Promising
Target Age: 14–18
Gender: Male and female
Ethnicity/Race: Multiple
Level of Intervention: Universal

Lifelines

Lifelines is a comprehensive, school-wide suicide prevention program for middle and high school students. The goal of Lifelines is to promote a caring, competent school community in which help seeking is encouraged and modeled and suicidal behavior is recognized as an issue that cannot be kept secret. Lifelines seeks to increase the likelihood that school staff and students will know how to identify at-risk youth when they encounter them, provide an appropriate initial response, and obtain help as well as be inclined to take such action. Lifelines consists of four 45-minute or two 90-minute lessons that incorporate elements of the social development model and employ interactive teaching techniques, including role-play. Health teachers and/or guidance counselors teach the lessons within the regular school health curriculum. The Lifelines curriculum was developed specifically for students in grades 8 to 10 but can be used with students through grade 12.

Web site: www.hazelden.org/web/go/lifelines
SPRC Classification: Promising
Target Age: 12–17
Gender: Male and female
Ethnicity/Race: Multiple
Level of Intervention: Universal

(Continued)

(Continued)

Universal Suicide Prevention: Suicide Gatekeeper Training

Currently no suicide prevention gatekeeper training programs are included in the evidence-based registry for suicide prevention.

Universal Suicide Prevention: Suicide Screening

Columbia University TeenScreen

The Columbia University TeenScreen Program identifies middle school- and high school-age youth in need of mental health services due to risk for suicide and undetected mental illness. The program's main objective is to assist in the early identification of problems that might not otherwise come to the attention of professionals. TeenScreen can be implemented in schools, clinics, doctors' offices, juvenile justice settings, shelters, or any other youth-serving setting. Typically, all youth in the target age group(s) at a setting are invited to participate.

> Web site: www.teenscreen.org
> SPRC Classification: Best Practice
> Target Age: 13–17
> Gender: Male and female
> Ethnicity/Race: Multiple
> Level of Intervention: Universal

OTHER RESOURCES FOR SCHOOL-BASED UNIVERSAL PREVENTION PROGRAMMING

Universal Suicide Prevention: Education Programs

Youth Suicide Prevention School-Based Guide

This Web site provides free, accurate, user-friendly information for schools. The guide is not a program but a tool that provides a framework for schools to assess their existing or proposed suicide prevention efforts (through a series of checklists) and provides free resources and information that school administrators can use to enhance or add to their existing program. The guide provides information to schools to assist them in the development of a framework to work in partnership with community resources and families.

Web site: http://theguide.fmhi.usf.edu

Yellow Ribbon Suicide Prevention and Awareness Campaign

This universal education campaign is designed to promote awareness of suicide prevention and decrease stigma for seeking mental health services. Materials are incorporated into school curricula, and the central message of the campaign is "It is OK to ask 4 help!"® The curriculum has been taught to over 200,000 people in all 50 states. Yellow Ribbon also has a curriculum for parents. This program is unrated by SPRC at this time.

Web site: www.yellowribbon.org

Universal Suicide Prevention: Gatekeeper Training Programs

Question-Persuade-Refer

Question-Persuade-Refer (QPR), a 60- to 90-minute suicide gate-keeper training program, provides a skills-based curriculum to help gatekeepers learn to recognize the warning signs for suicide, offer hope to suicidal individuals, and refer suicidal individuals to appropriate resources. This program is unrated by SPRC at this time, although recent research supports improvements in gatekeepers' knowledge of suicide and confidence in their ability to intervene.

Web site: www.qprinstitute.com

ASIST

The ASIST workshop is for people who want to feel more comfortable, confident, and competent in helping to prevent the immediate risk of suicide. Over 750,000 caregivers have participated in this two-day,

(Continued)

(Continued)

highly interactive, practical, practice-oriented workshop. This program is unrated by SPRC at this time.

Web site: www.livingworks.net

WEB SITES WITH MORE INFORMATION ABOUT CHILD AND ADOLESCENT SUICIDE

School-Based Prevention Guide: http://theguide.fmhi.usf.edu
>A fantastic resource, with free checklists, programs, and resources for schools.

American Association of Suicidology: www.suicidology.org
>For up-to-date information, professional conferences, and suicide research.

Suicide Prevention Resource Center: www.sprc.org
>For resources, magnets, posters, fact sheets, and other information.

American Foundation for Suicide Prevention: www.afsp.org
>Research, education about suicide and mood disorders, policy promotion.

www.Notmykid.org (sponsored by the American Association of Suicidology)
>Information for parents, resources for families.

National Institute of Mental Health (NIMH): www.nimh.nih.org
>Research, professional information.

Suicide Prevention Advocacy Network: www.spanusa.org
>National hotline, public policy.

Substance Abuse/Mental Health: www.samhsa.org
>Grant opportunities, best practice guidelines, research dissemination.

NATIONAL SUICIDE PREVENTION ORGANIZATIONS

National Suicide Hotline: 1-800-273-TALK (8255)
American Association of Suicidology (AAS)

A nonprofit organization dedicated to the understanding and prevention of suicide.

Web site: www.suicidology.org

The American Foundation for Suicide Prevention (AFSP)

Dedicated to advancing our knowledge of suicide and our ability to prevent it.

Web site: www.afsp.org

The Jason Foundation

An organization dedicated to teen suicide awareness and prevention.

Web site: www.jasonfoundation.com

The Jed Foundation

A nonprofit public charity committed to reducing the young adult suicide rate and improving mental health support provided to college students nationwide.

Web site: www.jedfoundation.org

Life Savers Training

A peer-support crisis prevention program aimed at training young adults to be caring listeners in their interactions with their peers. It involves a team approach to helping teenagers cope healthfully with the challenges of drugs and alcohol, peer and family relationships, sexual issues, violence, academic problems, death and grieving, aggression, anxiety, and suicide.

Web site: http://thelifesavers.net

The Link's National Resource Center for Suicide Prevention

Programs of The Link include counseling and psychotherapy, children in crisis and grief, suicide prevention and aftercare, community education, training, and supervision.

Web site: www.thelink.org

Living Works Education

Dedicated to enhancing suicide intervention skills at the community level through training products such as ASIST, suicideTALK, safeTALK, and suicideCARE.

Web site: www.livingworks.net

(Continued)

(Continued)

National Center for Injury Prevention and Control (NCIPC)

A branch of the Centers for Disease Control and Prevention working to reduce morbidity, disability, mortality, and costs associated with injuries.

Web site: www.cdc.gov/injury/index.html

National Center for Suicide Prevention Training (NCSPT)

Provides educational resources to help public officials, service providers, and community-based coalitions develop effective suicide prevention programs and policies.

Web site: http://training.sprc.org

National Organization for People of Color Against Suicide

(NOPCAS) A 501(c)(3) organization founded whose goals are to bring suicide and depression awareness to minority communities.

Web site: http://nopcas.com

National Suicide Prevention Lifeline:1-800-273-TALK (8255)

Twenty-four-hour, toll-free suicide prevention service available to anyone in suicidal crisis

Web site: www.suicidepreventionlifeline.org

Preventing Suicide Network

A national suicide prevention Web site developed by iTelehealth, Inc., with a grant from the National Institute of Mental Health. Its mission is to leverage the power of technology to assist persons in informing themselves and others regarding preventing suicide.

Web site: www.preventingsuicide.com

QPR Institute

A multidisciplinary training organization whose primary goal is to provide suicide prevention educational services and materials to professionals and the general public.

Web site: www.qprinstitute.com

Samaritans

The coalition whose primary purpose is to befriend people who are depressed, in crisis, and suicidal.

Web site: www.samaritansnyc.org

Stop a Suicide Today!

Developed by Harvard psychiatrist Douglas Jacobs, MD, Stop a Suicide, Today! teaches people how to recognize the signs of suicide in family members, friends, and coworkers, and empowers them to make a difference in the lives of their loved ones.

Web site: www.stopasuicide.org

Suicide Awareness/Voices of Education (SA/VE)

Dedicated to educating about suicide and speaking for suicide survivors.

Web site: www.save.org

The Suicide Support Forum

A safe place for discussion of suicide-related issues, and also a place for those whose lives have been affected by suicide to share their stories.

Web site: www.suicidegrief.com

Suicide Prevention Resource Center (SPRC)

A national resource center that provides technical assistance, training, and information in order to strengthen suicide prevention networks and advance the National Strategy for Suicide Prevention.

Web site: www.sprc.org

The Suicide Reference Library

A centralized location that offers materials for use by anyone who is involved in suicide education, awareness, support, and prevention activities.

Web site: www.suicidereferencelibrary.com

Yellow Ribbon Suicide Prevention Program

A community-based youth suicide prevention program.

Web site: www.yellowribbon.org

3

Working With Suicidal Students in Schools

Assessment and Intervention

Students who are at risk for suicide need special attention in schools. These students can be challenging to manage within the school setting, and they can represent a significant drain on school resources and staff time. Some school personnel are uncomfortable working with this population. Others believe it is not the role of the school to intervene. But the reality is that at any moment in any given school building in the United States, about 20% of students are seriously thinking about suicide or have made a suicide attempt. Whether any of us want the responsibility of managing this difficult population to fall to our already overburdened and underfunded schools or not, we do not have a choice. These students are in the building, and they need our help.

Even those who recognize the importance of the task of managing suicidal students in the schools can feel a bit overwhelmed by the magnitude of the need and the seriousness of the responsibility. Suicidal individuals need intensive and extensive care. Comprehensive suicide risk assessments require advanced clinical skills and experience, and the ongoing management of highly suicidal individuals can be quite challenging. Clearly, there are inherent limitations to the amount and type of mental health services that schools can provide to suicidal students. For example, most schools do not have adequate numbers of trained mental health professionals available in the building. Although the American School Counselor Association (ASCA) recommends a student to school counselor ratio of 250:1, the national average is actually 460:1, with great fluctuations based on location (National Center for Education Statistics, 2009). There are even fewer school psychologists available to assist these students. The National Association of School Psychologists (NASP) recommends a student-to-school psychologist ratio of 1,000:1, but the national average is actually more than 1,600 K–12 students for each school psychologist (NASP, 2006). Other mental and behavioral health care professionals, such as school nurses or school social workers, often are not available to students at all. Fewer than 50% of public schools have a full-time registered nurse on staff, and even fewer schools meet the standard of 1 school social worker for every 800 students that was recommended in the No Child Left Behind legislation (NCLB, 2001). Although there are many school teachers who are available and willing to intervene with suicidal students, most have insufficient training and experience in mental health and crisis intervention to work with students at high suicide risk. As a result, many schools are left with few staff resources to help manage the segment of their population that requires this additional level of support and care.

In spite of these challenges, however, schools offer youth unparalleled access to resources to help prevent suicide. With more than 52 million young people attending over 110,000 schools, and more than 6 million adults employed in schools, about one-fifth of the U.S. population can be reached within K–12 schools (President's New Freedom Commission on Mental Health, 2003). Schools can reduce or remove many of the barriers to traditional mental health care, such as transportation, child care, and ability to pay/lack of insurance (Weist, 1999). Additionally, the school setting reduces the number of no-shows to appointments, which is typically a problem for community behavioral health care providers. If students are unavailable for appointments, typically their time slots can be filled easily with another student needing care. Perhaps most important, however, there is evidence that schools can reduce stigma associated with mental illness and help seeking and can promote a healthy approach to wellness and support (Stephan, Weist, Kataoka, Adelsheim, & Mills, 2007).

In the last chapter, we discussed a model for school-based suicide prevention and intervention that was divided into three levels: universal, selective, and indicated. Recall that universal approaches to prevention are directed to all students, staff, teachers, and parents, and include training and education as well as suicide and mental health screening. Universal interventions were the focus of that chapter. In this chapter, we move to selective and indicated suicide prevention and intervention. *Selective interventions* are targeted to subpopulations that are characterized by certain risk factor(s). Students in transition periods, students with poor coping skills, and students who have been exposed to a suicide are examples of targeted populations. These individuals are at elevated risk for suicide and must be sought out for additional support and care. *Indicated interventions* are targeted to specific individuals who have been identified as at risk for suicide through some screening procedure. These are specific people (not just groups of people, as is the case with selective interventions) who require specific clinical care. Clearly, students who require selective or indicated interventions represent a significant challenge and responsibility within the school setting.

SELECTIVE INTERVENTIONS

Also called targeted interventions, selective interventions provide services for targeted groups of students. In general, these services are intended to address existing risk factors or build protective factors in groups of students who may have behavioral and/or mental health problems but are not at immediate risk for suicide. Although these subgroups will by definition have been exposed to universal prevention programs in the school, the information contained in those universal approaches may not be of sufficient amount or focus to affect specific vulnerable populations, such as disenfranchised or depressed students. Thus, selective interventions provide additional information, training, and support to these identified subgroups.

Many selective intervention strategies in schools are related to increasing students' social and emotional competence, which has been linked to improvements in academic achievement (Franklin, Harris, and Allen-Meares, 2006). Although selective intervention programs are intended to help *prevent* suicide, they really can be thought of as early *intervention* strategies. That is, groups of students are given additional assistance at more intense levels than is typically part of a school's suicide prevention services. The goal is to move them from a place of elevated risk back to within the behaviors and boundaries of the typical or average population within the school.

Selective interventions require an understanding of what groups might be at elevated risk and a mechanism to determine which students fall into these high-risk groups. Because we know that suicidal behaviors are associated with these higher-risk groups, selective prevention strategies focus specifically on seeking out these youth and proactively offering them additional services and care. In general, these strategies are expected to impact the 25% to 30% of youth who are at high risk for the development of suicide or suicidal behaviors.

Some students identified through this approach may already be known to school personnel, particularly if school staff and parents are educated to identify troubled students before they make overt suicide attempts or statements. School suicide prevention gatekeeper training (discussed in the previous chapter) can help identify youth who could benefit from participation in selective intervention programming. Additionally, teachers can be asked to identify students who are displaying problematic behaviors in the classroom. Specific behaviors that have been linked to suicide risk (e.g., impulsivity, hopelessness, withdrawal) may serve as the foundation for these referrals.

In our work in schools, we recognize that many of the positive interventions that are intended to promote mental health that school counselors, school psychologists, school social workers, and school nurses provide are all forms of selective intervention. Students with learning disabilities; victims of physical or sexual abuse; substance abusers; lesbian, gay, bisexual, and transgender students; students who have had problems with anger management; and students with poor social skills are examples of the types of students who may benefit from selective interventions, and programs for these students may have the potential to decrease suicide risk. For example, when elementary-age children with no friends are singled out to join a psychoeducational group to teach them social skills, this can provide the kind of protective factors that ultimately can help buffer against suicide risk. When middle-school special education students who exhibit problems with aggression and anger are put on a behavioral management plan to limit their angry outbursts and to get their needs met in more appropriate ways, this can be a form of selective intervention. When high school males who are isolated and withdrawn are given wallet cards with the local suicide hotline number, this also is a form of selective intervention. In other words, whenever a student is identified as being part of a group at high risk for mental health problems and an effort is made to intervene, this is selective intervention.

Using this broad definition for selective intervention for suicide risk means that many of the programs and activities in schools can be included under this umbrella term. However, the inclusion of so many programs and interventions makes assessment of their effectiveness, particularly as they relate to suicide risk, impossible to determine. Nevertheless, it is still important for school personnel to employ strategies that measure the effectiveness of these programs to reduce behavioral problems, improve functioning, and lower stigma for help seeking, all of which are correlated with reduced risk for suicide.

INDICATED INTERVENTIONS

Indicated interventions are targeted to specific students who have been identified as at risk for suicide either through universal screening programs or through detection by a school staff member, a peer, or a parent. The goal of the programs is to reduce the incidence of suicidal behaviors among students who already display risk factors or warning signs associated with suicide.

Indicated interventions require individuals in the schools to be trained to screen students for risk through a basic suicide assessment and, once students are identified as at risk, to provide the indicated programs or interventions. Typically, these interventions include some community mental health or school-linked services, and they always include involvement of a parent or guardian. School personnel trained in behavioral health (e.g., school counselors, school psychologists, school nurses, or school social workers) can provide some of the necessary interventions, but they must be specifically trained in suicide risk assessment and management of suicidal students in schools in order to assist these students appropriately. Some of the basic skills necessary when working with potentially suicidal students include consultation, counseling (crisis counseling and ongoing), risk assessment, and referral.

COLLABORATION, CORROBORATION, AND CONSULTATION

When working with suicidal students, the school staff member (counselor, psychologist, social worker, or nurse) must be prepared to *collaborate, corroborate, and consult* (Granello, in press a). "Collaboration" means working together with other school personnel, parents, community resources, peers, family members, and anyone else who can provide assistance in helping the suicidal youth. The key is that counselors recognize that keeping someone safe is a responsibility that works best when shared and when information flows freely among all who can help. It is important to note that concerns about student safety override issues of confidentiality. In fact, "harm to self" is one of the main exceptions to confidentiality in the helping professions. Of course, we do *not* mean that when a counselor faces a potentially suicidal student, the counselor makes general announcements to teachers and other staff. Rather, it is important to consult with those members of the school who can have a direct impact on student safety, who have specific information that is needed to help keep the student safe, or the student identifies as a person that he or she would feel comfortable using as a resource in the school. In our work in schools, we have found that counselors and other school personnel struggle to find this balance. Beginning school professionals will find that this is an important area to seek supervision and guidance from more experienced school staff.

Collaboration includes notification of parents. Parents of minors must be notified when their children are determined to be at risk for suicide. Sometimes young people who tell us they are suicidal will ask us not to tell anyone. That request *cannot* be honored. When the welfare of our students is at stake, we must involve the parents quickly so that the school and the parents can act together to help the student.

Parental notification is critical to suicide prevention in schools. Parents need to be informed and actively involved in all decisions regarding their child's welfare. Even if a child is judged to be at low risk for suicidal behavior, schools typically ask parents to sign a document indicating that all relevant information has been provided to them so they can continue to monitor the student for suicide risk. Additionally, parents often have information critical to making an appropriate assessment of risk, including mental health history, family dynamics, recent traumatic events, and previous suicidal behaviors (NASP, n.d.).

Sometimes parents do not believe the school staff when they tell them their child is at risk for suicide. They may refuse to come and get them from school or be adamant in their demands that the school withdraw their involvement. We have seen this occur, and we believe it is often caused by a defensive response that parents take when they believe the school is somehow pointing out their inadequacies or accusing them of "bad parenting." Telephone conversations can quickly escalate to angry confrontations by both sides, which is never productive. The more that school staff can help parents to recognize that *we are all on the same side in our desire to protect the student*, the better off we will be. If we can frame the problem in this way—"Clearly, we all want what is best for [the student]. We are a team here, and we need to use the skills and expertise of everyone involved. We really need your expertise on our team, because you know your child better than anyone"—we might take the edge off some of the defensiveness. If parents still adamantly refuse to seek assistance for a suicidal student, then, depending on level of risk, it may be necessary to move forward in spite of the parents' objections. Although some school professionals worry about liability issues in such circumstances, it is clear that liability problems are much more serious if the young person is allowed to leave the school premises unmonitored and with no provision for follow-up assistance. School personnel are encouraged to confer with legal counsel to fully understand liability issues and to ensure that best practices are followed in these circumstances (Capuzzi, 1994).

Corroboration is another essential skill for school personnel working with potentially suicidal youth. For example, a student may be identified as at risk because a peer comes forward and shares a story with a counselor, or a teacher comes to talk with a counselor because she is worried about a student. It is important, when possible, to corroborate the story with the student, parents, or others in the school who may have specific information to share. The more information available to the counselor, the better the risk assessment will be.

Consultation involves seeking assistance and input from others. School personnel who are asked to work with suicidal students typically recognize that doing so requires advanced clinical skills that can feel stressful and overwhelming. Consulting with other professionals, talking through the steps taken, and seeking supervision are all important components of managing suicidal students in the school setting. School personnel with limited experience in suicide assessment and intervention should never rely on their own clinical judgment but should seek consultation with others (Granello, in press b). Even mental health professionals with many years of experience often seek consultations in suicide risk assessment and management of suicidal clients. There is no shame in asking for assistance when working with this very difficult population.

COUNSELING

Once a student has been identified as someone at risk for suicide, he or she will need some specific interventions from school personnel. Students at imminent risk for suicide will need crisis counseling, while those who present with an ongoing, lower-level risk will require ongoing supportive counseling to help them manage.

The goals of immediate interventions with students at high risk are based on an expanded model of crisis intervention counseling (Granello, in press b; see Figure 3.1). In general, this model is intended to help counselors interact with students during times of high risk for suicide. *It does not replace assessment and intervention strategies by trained clinicians to determine appropriate levels of care.* Rather, these steps are designed to help school personnel manage their interactions with suicidal students in the school setting *in addition to* consultation with parents and community mental health professionals. These steps are intended only as a guide, and the needs of individual students may vary significantly. For example, specific developmental, multicultural, or cognitive limitations of clients may shape the implementation of these strategies.

Step 1: Assess Lethality

The first and most important step in working with suicidal students is accurate assessment. Although this assessment may occur slowly, over the course of the entire discussion, with more information becoming apparent as the student tells his or her story, a general understanding of level of lethality will be important information to guide the entire process. School personnel must

---

Step 1: Assess lethality
Step 2: Establish rapport
Step 3: Listen to the story
Step 4: Manage the feeling
Step 5: Explore alternatives
Step 6: Use behavioral strategies
Step 7: Follow up

Figure 3.1 Crisis Counseling with Potentially Suicidal Students
Source: From "The Process of Suicide Risk Assessment: Twelve Core Principles," by D. H. Granello, 2010, *Journal of Counseling and Development.*

take steps to ensure the immediate safety of their students. If they believe a student to be in a suicide emergency (i.e., the student will take the first opportunity to kill him- or herself), it is important to never leave the student alone, not even for a moment to go down the hall or make a phone call. Clearly, at this point, the parents should be called, and the student must be transported to a hospital for a full suicide risk assessment. Schools should have in place ahead of time the steps that will be taken if a highly suicidal student attempts to leave the school premises.

Step 2: Establish Rapport

Research consistently demonstrates that one of the most important factors in assessing suicide risk and determining prognosis for success of suicide interventions is the quality of a therapeutic relationship with a counselor or other helping professional (Bongar, 2002). Suicidal adolescents state that this relationship is one of the most, if not the most, helpful aspects of their treatment. Basic counseling skills and the Rogerian core conditions of warmth, empathy, congruence, and unconditional positive regard help convey a genuine, caring, and nonjudgmental therapeutic stance (Chiles & Strosahl, 2005).

It is important to normalize the topic of suicide without normalizing the behaviors. The reality is that suicidal thoughts are quite common among young people. However, because these thoughts are processed with other teens and seldom spoken of in front of adults, young people do not have much accurate information or understanding to help them make sense of their thinking. As a result, they can think they are the only ones who feel this way, or they must be "going crazy" to have thoughts like these. A calm, caring adult who helps them process the feelings and understand that just because they have these thoughts does not mean they have to engage in the behaviors can be very helpful.

Any interactions with suicidal students should be based on an approach that conveys calm and reassures the student that it is okay to talk about suicidal thoughts and behaviors. We can help students feel comfortable talking with us by saying things such as "It's okay. I know this is hard to talk about. Take your time. Use whatever words are most comfortable for you to describe what you are thinking and feeling." Even if we feel anxious about our own skills and overwhelmed by their story, a calm approach and matter-of-fact tone reassures students that we are able to help. In a time of crisis, having a strong, confident adult to lean on can be reassuring.

Whenever possible, acknowledge the willingness of students to talk about their problems. *In a genuine way*, acknowledge whatever steps they have taken toward help seeking. It is very hard for students—for anyone—to admit to another that they are feeling suicidal. It is, in fact, one of the most difficult conversations anyone can have. Recognizing the courage that it takes to reach out (or to be willing to have the conversation once someone else has reached out) can be powerful. It may be appropriate to say something like "I am so very glad you are willing to talk with me about these feelings. I very much recognize the courage that it takes to say these things out loud" or "You won't be alone in this. Now that you have reached out, we will get you the help you need." This support must be genuine; students can tell when praise or emotional support rings hollow.

In our work with graduate students in counseling, we are careful to teach some very specific skills that help convey this calm. We teach our graduate students to speak in short declarative sentences and downspeak. People in crisis cannot follow long or complex sentences. They need simple sentences that are easy to follow, even when they are distraught and distracted. Downspeak, where the pitch of the voice goes down at the end of sentences, results in declarative statements, whereas upspeak, the pattern that implies a question through a raised tone at the end of sentences, implies uncertainty and tentativeness. Many of our graduate students, particularly females, find themselves naturally in a pattern where their voice goes up at the end of sentences, and this can make anxious clients even more distressed. Listen to your own speech pattern or that of your peers to see if you can spot these differences. Downspeak, short sentences, and a slow pace communicate safety, control, and calm.

Finally, as you work to establish rapport with suicidal students, be sure to manage your own countertransference. Remember, suicidal students can present to others as angry and unlikable. They are hurting, and they often lash out. Suicidal students can make us feel fearful, anxious, angry, and defensive. None of those feelings is particularly helpful in our work with students. Finding ways to manage those feelings so you can be completely present for your students is essential.

Step 3: Listen to the Story

Students often tell us that every time they have tried to talk with an adult about their suicidal thoughts, they have been shut down. Well-meaning adults often minimize their stories. They are told "That's ridiculous" or "Don't talk like that" or "[The boy- or girlfriend] is not worth it." Other common responses to a declaration of suicidal intent include silence or changing the subject. As a result, although about 80% of young people tell someone they are suicidal in the weeks prior to their deaths, most never have a chance to fully tell their stories or fully process their emotions.

The telling of the story is, in itself, therapeutic. This is a foundation of the counseling process. Talking with someone else *who actually listens* is the first step in moving forward. It is, of course, not sufficient, and no one suggests responding to suicidal students solely with a person-centered approach that involves listening only. But it is the cornerstone of developing rapport and helping the student feel heard. We might say, "The reason I'm asking is because I want to help. I want to listen. Tell me what's on your mind."

One of the most important things we can do is to give students time and space to tell their stories. In schools, this is sometimes challenging. There is a press to move quickly and not spend too much time with any one student. Nevertheless, when it comes to suicidal students, we must give them our full attention as they tell their stories. In our work, we find that suicidal students often try to rush through their stories because they do not believe that we will fully listen to them. We say things like "It's okay. You don't have to rush through your story. I will listen. Take your time. Take a deep breath and tell me what you want me to hear." We even take a few deep breaths ourselves to model this. Then we settle down, make eye contact, and listen.

School personnel must take every suicide threat or behavior seriously. They must take care not to discount students' stories or their perceptions of the seriousness of the situation. In all cases, students who threaten suicide must have a suicide risk assessment. We remind school personnel that during a suicide crisis, when a student is threatening suicide and emotions are running high, it is not the time to tell the student that you believe he or she is just seeking attention. If the suicide threat is minimized or dismissed, all students learned is that *next time*, they must escalate in their threats or behaviors to get their needs met. When school personnel tell us, "But they're just threatening suicide to get our attention!" our response is "How sad that they have learned that this is the only means they have to get an adult to take them seriously." Do a suicide risk assessment. Then, *when students are not in crisis and not threatening suicide*, teach them other, more appropriate ways to get your attention. And (this is the hard part), when they do those appropriate things to get our attention, we have to follow through and give them the attention they have earned. We know this is hard. Not long ago, we worked with an elementary-age girl who threatened to kill herself every time she got upset. Of course, it was not long before all of the adults in her life started to ignore that threat. Her behaviors started to escalate, and she threw herself down a flight of stairs. We helped the parents and the school staff recognize that she needed other ways to get their attention or she would continue to escalate. They worked with her *when she was not in crisis* and taught her what she needed to tell them so they would understand when she started to feel angry and out of control. They decided on some key message words that she could say, and they agreed to respond appropriately when she asked appropriately for their time. It was an important first step in reducing her suicidal threats and behaviors.

Step 4: Manage the Feelings

Most people who are suicidal do not want to die. They simply want the pain to end. They feel a tremendous amount of psychological pain, and they cannot imagine living with that pain another day. Because of the ambiguity that is frequently part of the crisis (i.e., not wanting to die but wanting the pain to end), it is not unusual for many different emotions to occur simultaneously, and suicidal individuals often feel overwhelmed by their emotions. Helping students to express their emotions is an important part of the healing process. Giving them space to cry, to express their anger, or to be scared teaches them that emotions are part of the human condition, and we do not have to cover them up. It is important to note that the goal is *not* emotional escalation, and we do not want to fuel the flames to encourage emotional expression. However, statements such as "I know it feels overwhelming—this is a safe place for you to talk about these things" can be particularly helpful.

Step 5: Explore Alternatives

Suicidal individuals have difficulty with problem-solving skills and typically have diminished capacity to generate alternatives. The developmental limitations of young people, who often have difficulty with problem solving anyway, compound the dangers during times of suicide risk. People who are suicidal often fail to recognize the reasons they have for living or the potential alternatives to their current situation. If possible, fortify reasons for living. Because suicidal individuals may be ambivalent, it means that there are at least some reasons why they would want to stay alive.

Importantly, exploring alternatives is *not the same thing* as providing advice or answers, which is generally seen as minimizing or demeaning to those in crisis. Rather, developing a framework where the student works with the school staff member to develop a problem-solving strategy can be productive. Effective problem solving includes: (a) problem identification, (b) identification of alternative solutions or strategies, (c) evaluation of the likely outcome of the alternative strategies, (d) selection of a specific problem-solving technique and formulation of a plan, and (e) implementation of the strategy and evaluation of its effectiveness (Chiles & Strosahl, 2005).

Exploring alternatives is critical, but it is also critical that this not be done too early in the process. In other words, if students are asked to move too quickly to this stage, before a relationship is fully established, before they have a chance to tell their stories or express emotions, they may feel minimized and rushed and not ready yet to engage in problem solving. Timing is important.

To help students move from a problem-focus, which keeps them stuck in their suicidal thoughts, to a more positive mind-set where they can help generate alternatives, we offer the following two specific strategies.

Help Students Uncover a "Plan B"

When students talk about killing themselves, challenging them about whether suicide is a "good" idea can be extremely counterproductive. In fact, almost any attempts to explore alternatives with suicidal students can result in comments that actually defend suicide. For example, if we were to tell a student "I wish you wouldn't kill yourself," the student would be almost *forced* to say "But here are the reasons why I should." If we say, "Let's see if we can think of some alternatives," the student will inevitably say, "I've thought of everything, there is no answer except suicide." In other words, the dynamics of conversation highlight the potential that once one person takes a stance on one side of the issue (e.g., against suicide), the other person is almost forced to take the other side (e.g., in favor of suicide). This moves a person who was uncertain and ambivalent about suicide to a position of defending suicide as the only logical choice. In our work with suicidal individuals, we have hit upon a simple linguistic strategy that can be used to help generate alternatives. In this strategy, we say: "I understand that suicide is an option that is open to you. I do not agree that this is the best possible outcome of this crisis. However, I understand that of all the options available to you, suicide is one. Therefore, let's leave suicide on the table and call it Plan A. It's on the table. Now let's try to come up with a Plan B or Plan C." If the student begins to defend suicide, we say, "I agree. It's an option. It's already on the table as Plan A. Now we're working on Plan B." The point is when students no longer have to defend suicide, they are free to work *with the counselor* to develop other alternatives. A simple linguistic shift moves the counselor and student from opposite sides of the problem to working collaboratively on the same side, and suicide becomes the "other." Obviously, this strategy requires some finesse and depends greatly on the student's developmental level and abstract reasoning ability. Nevertheless, when used appropriately, we have found it to be very helpful (Granello, in press b).

Make Hope Tangible

Often, the core of suicidality is hopelessness. Finding ways to restore hope is a critical component of all interventions with suicidal students. The key is to work to restore hope without appearing to minimize the crisis. Suicidal young people can perceive adults who present as too hopeful as inauthentic, unempathetic, or glib. In fact, statements such as "You have so much to live for" or "[The boy- or girlfriend] is not worth it" can inadvertently place students in a position of *defending* their decisions to die by suicide. Rather, messages that help instill hope might be: "I understand that you are feeling hopeless right now. I have to tell you that from where I sit, I do not believe the situation is hopeless," or "I am hopeful that there is a way out other than suicide. I believe that if we work through this together, we'll figure it out," or "I'm willing to stay with you as we work through the problem together." These words convey a sense of calm and optimism without minimizing the students' problems.

In our work, we use a strategy in which we become the "holder of hope." For instance, we might say, "I understand that you don't have hope right now. That's okay. I want you to know that I have enough hope for both of us. In fact, I will become your 'holder of hope.' When you are ready, you let me know, and I will give your hope back to you." This strategy does not force a student to pretend to feel hopeful. Paradoxically, the relief of not having to pretend actually can increase hope. In the heart of a crisis, abstractions are difficult for students to understand. Making an abstraction like hope into something concrete and tangible can be particularly useful. Using hand motions to "reach out and grab" hope and to "put it in the drawer for safe-keeping" can be quietly reassuring for students. In fact, in our work, it is not uncommon for students to return at a later date and carry through the analogy by stating "I am ready to get my hope back now." When this happens, we "reach back into the drawer" to return the hope to the students, a symbolic gesture that can have great significance for them (Granello, in press b).

Step 6: Use Behavioral Strategies

Consider the use of a short-term positive action plan. In this strategy, students and school personnel (and others, as appropriate) work to develop a concrete, detailed plan that helps the student move in a more positive direction. The goal in this action plan is to create small steps that can have a great impact on the student's quality of life rather than trying to make major changes or solve all the student's problems. It is critical that the steps on the plan be doable for the student, lest the inability to complete the action plan become one more failure in his or her life. When working with school-age youth, these plans may be developed with the assistance of an off-site clinical mental health professional. In this instance, the role of the school personnel is to be a resource and support mechanism for the student's implementation of the positive action plan.

Consider a safety plan instead of a no-suicide contract (Chiles & Strosahl, 2005). Many school professionals have been taught to use a no-suicide contract that elicit promises from students that they will not kill themselves during a predetermined period of time. Although they are in widespread use and there is no evidence that they cause harm, there is *no evidence* that no-suicide contracts actually reduce suicide attempts, and these contracts *do not guarantee student safety*. Recently, there have been concerns that these contracts actually can increase school liability with potentially suicidal clients. Safety plans, however, are put in place to help students know what to do when they have suicidal ideation or an increase in suicidal risk. They provide students with a concrete set of strategies to use when they start thinking about suicide. Most safety plans include a step-by-step individualized process that student and mental health professional develop together.

A safety plan is *essential* for all potentially suicidal persons who are being seen outside of inpatient hospitals. Just as with a short-term positive action plan, the role of the school in a student's safety plan can be determined by the student and the student's off-site counselor.

Step 7: Follow-Up

Within the school setting, follow-up care is quite different from therapeutic settings in the community. School personnel will want to maintain contact with the student and parents as the child or adolescent goes for more intensive mental health care. Referrals to appropriate agencies or assistance are important, and the school should follow up to ensure that these referral appointments are kept. If a young person has to be removed from the school environment because of a suicidal crisis, readjustment to the school is a critical component of care that will be discussed later in this chapter. Finally, as with all crisis situations, there is a great opportunity for school personnel to assess the intervention strategies employed to make any necessary modifications or alterations for the future.

SUICIDE RISK ASSESSMENT

Suicide risk assessment is a complex set of skills that requires knowledge, training, and experience. In general, the determination of suicide risk is based on a comprehensive assessment of individual risk factors and warning signs as well as a careful appraisal of protective factors that can work to mitigate the risk. School professionals who engage in suicide risk assessment often do so as a first step, recognizing that a clinician specifically trained in conducting comprehensive risk assessments will need to do a more complete screening than is typically done in schools. The school has an important role to play in the identification of students at risk for suicide and in initial assessment for suicide risk. Because school personnel often know students well and have the benefit of a longer-term understanding of the individuals at risk, their risk assessments can provide useful context for mental health providers who conduct more comprehensive risk assessment. School personnel may notice changes in behavior or mood that trigger the need for an individual interview to assess risk. However, the school is *not* the place for comprehensive clinical risk assessments. The inherent limitations of the school environment (e.g., the setting, lack of after-hours emergency care, the number of students who require assistance, the time limitations of the staff, and the lack of training in comprehensive suicide risk assessment) make comprehensive suicide risk unmanageable for schools. Rather than being the final judge of suicide risk for a student, the school ideally should be just one layer (albeit an important one) in an inclusive assessment of suicide risk.

The foundation to an appropriate suicide risk assessment in schools is *recognizing that a student may be at risk* and *reaching out to conduct an individualized assessment*. In the school setting, there are some important steps to take to assess individual suicide risk and determine whether more detailed risk assessment is necessary. These strategies can be divided into two major types: (1) informal (unstructured) interviews and checklists and (2) formal (structured) assessments.

Risk Assessment Interviews

All school personnel are encouraged to use, at a minimum, an informal or unstructured interview for suicide risk assessment. The first and most important component of a risk assessment is to *ask the suicide question directly*. In our work with school personnel, we are surprised to learn that many never ask about suicide, even if they think a student might be at risk. Not long ago, we did a training of school staff regarding appropriate ways to reach out and talk with students who may be at risk about suicide. After 90 minutes of training, we called up several staff members for a role-play. About 5 minutes in, when the person portraying a school staff member still had not asked about suicide to the person portraying the at-risk student, we stopped the role-play and asked: "When are you going to ask about suicide?" The school staff person responded, "Oh, I would *never* ask about suicide in *real life!*" After all the training, the person still had not made the connection about the importance of asking the suicide question. Unfortunately, that response is all too common. The most important thing to do to assess suicide risk is to *ask the suicide question*, and yet research shows again and again that very few people reach out and ask another if they are thinking about suicide. It may be because they are fearful that talking about suicide will "put the idea in someone's head." That is a myth. Solid research shows that talking about suicide in appropriate ways actually *decreases* risk. It may be because they are worried what they will do if a student says yes. We understand that it can be frightening, but it does not excuse inaction. We know that most young people who are thinking about suicide *tell someone in the weeks prior to their death that they are thinking of suicide.* Sadly, the most common response they receive from others when they make that disclosure is silence. This is unacceptable.

Ask the Question

Use the word "suicide." Ask it in several ways. It is not about memorizing the "right way" to ask a specific question but about allowing students to feel safe talking with you about the struggles they are having. For example, it may be appropriate to say something like "Sometimes when people are in so much pain, they think about suicide. Have you thought about suicide?" It may also help to frame the question not just as a yes/no but in ways that allow students to talk about the complexity of their feelings. "Can you talk with me about any thoughts you are having about living versus dying?" Some people ask: "Are you thinking of hurting yourself?" We have encountered several people, however, who answered no to that question even though they were suicidal. Their logic was that they intended to find a way to kill themselves that was painless and would not hurt. The point is, ask the question in several different ways, have the conversation, use the word "suicide," and open the topic up for discussion. Perhaps the only questions that we absolutely *do not* recommend are ones like these: "You're not thinking of killing yourself, are you?" or "You were just kidding about suicide, right?" Clearly, those types of questions do not open up lines of communication.

Areas to Assess

In general, the determination of suicide risk is based on a comprehensive assessment of individual risk factors and warning signs as well as a careful appraisal of protective factors. The following general areas are those that should be included in any suicide risk assessment.

Suicide Plan

Understanding a student's suicide plan, if he or she has one, can help better assess risk. For example, we have had students say to us, when asked about a suicide plan, "I don't know. I would probably take some pills or something, or maybe jump into traffic." We also have had students say something like "I get home at 3:30, my parents don't get home until 6. I will call my mom to tell her I got home safe from school, otherwise she will check up on me. I will get my dad's gun. He keeps it locked up, but I know where the key is. I know how to load the bullets too. I will go into my bedroom, lock the door behind me, and shoot myself in the mouth." Clearly, the second scenario represents a student at higher imminent risk. In general, when assessing a suicide plan, we consider five issues:

1. Details of the plan (the more details, the higher the risk)
2. Intent (in general, students who fully intend to die are at higher risk than those who are more ambivalent)
3. Means (more lethal means relates to higher risk)
4. Access to means (easier access equals higher risk)
5. Proximity of help (the less likely that someone will intervene, the higher the risk)

Remember that many suicidal people will withhold some information, and it is best to assume that they have done more (made more preparations, had more intense thoughts) than they are admitting. It is always better to err on the side of caution.

History of Suicidal Thoughts or Behaviors

A previous suicide attempt is the best predictor of a future attempt. However, only about 40% of individuals who die by suicide have a previous attempt. In other words, although it is the best predictor, it is not relevant for more than half of the suicide deaths. It is important to assess previous attempts but also important to remember that lack of a previous attempt does not mean a student is not at risk. It is also important to assess suicidal behaviors within the family, as there is evidence that young people can model behaviors from other members in the family. They might think: "This is how we handle stressful situations in my family."

We ask students to tell us about their suicidal thoughts. Are they frequent? Becoming more frequent? When did they first notice these thoughts? What led up to the thoughts (e.g., interpersonal or intrapsychic antecedents)? How close have they come to acting on the thoughts in the past? How likely are they to act on them in the future?

Mental State/Stability of Mood

More than 90% of individuals who die by suicide have some psychiatric disorder, most commonly depression or bipolar disorder. However, most people with depression or bipolar disorder are not suicidal. Clearly, then, assessing psychiatric problems is important but not sufficient. Other mood states to assess include hopelessness, impulsivity, agitation, stress, worthlessness, and self-hate. It is also important to note whether the student is currently receiving any behavioral health care for mental health concerns.

Psychological Pain

Edwin S. Shneidman, the "father of suicidology," coined the term "psychache" to describe the extreme psychological pain of the suicidal person (2005). The basic formula for a suicidal crisis is "emotional or physical pain that [the person believes] is intolerable, inescapable, and interminable" (Chiles & Strosahl, 2005, p. 63). Remember, our assessment of the student's situation does not matter. It is the student's perception regarding this pain that is important, and a risk assessment attempts to understand to what levels the student will go (including death) to avoid the pain. When assessing this psychache, we must understand and acknowledge the emotional desperation and unbearable emotions that the student feels. Anything that the student might perceive as diminishing or disconfirming of this pain can lead to escalation. If the pain is not acknowledged, a student might think, "You don't understand how bad I really feel. Let me show you."

Warning Signs, Triggering Conditions, and Risk Factors

In a previous chapter, we discussed warning signs (e.g., withdrawal, verbal threats, talking about death, impulsivity, giving away prized possessions, seeking means, refusing help), and a good suicide risk assessment will collect this information. Triggering conditions (e.g., social embarrassment, bullying or victimization, conflict, substance abuse, changes in mood or behaviors, difficult and unavoidable transitions or circumstances) also can provide insight into the mind of the suicidal person. Finally, risk factors (e.g., gender, race, cognitive or emotional risk factors) are important to assess, although all risk factors are based on overall population risk and can be misleading when applied to an individual case.

Protective Factors

Suicide risk assessment also includes protective factors. What are the things within the environment that are helping to keep students safe? Do they have the support of a caring family or friends? Are they currently receiving treatment, or if they have received treatment in the past, can their individual therapist be contacted for ongoing interventions (with parental involvement, of course). What resources can they identify that can help if they are in crisis? What are the strengths the students can identify? Finally, all suicide risk assessment should include an assessment of reasons for living. Simply asking "What helps keep you alive?" can yield a lot of insight into the mind of the suicidal person and give important clues regarding level of risk.

Using an Acronym to Guide Assessment Interviews

Sometimes acronyms can help guide the risk assessment, reminding the interviewer of some of the major areas to cover. These should be used with caution, however, as they are simply reminders of areas to assess and not assessment checklists. For those who wish to use this approach, the American Association of Suicidology recommends IS PATH WARM? as a helpful mnemonic. Each letter corresponds to an important risk factor for suicide (see Figure 3.2 on the next page). Although other acronyms exist to help with suicide assessment, IS PATH WARM? is the agreed-on standard.

Specifically, these warning signs are linked to:

- **I**deation about suicide, including talking about or writing about suicide or death
- **S**ubstance (alcohol or drug) use, particularly increases in use
- **P**urposelessness, no reason for living; no sense of meaning in life
- **A**nxiety, agitation, inability to sleep (or sleeping all the time), unable to relax, extreme perturbation
- **T**rapped, no way out of the current situation, no other choices between living in extreme psychological pain or death
- **H**opelessness and helplessness, including negative view of self, others, and the future
- **W**ithdrawal from friends, family, and society or activities that used to bring pleasure
- **A**nger, rage, uncontrolled fury, seeking revenge
- **R**eckless behaviors, engaging in risky activities, seemingly without thinking
- **M**ood changes that are dramatic and erratic

Suicide Assessment Checklists

Many checklists are available to guide questioning around suicide risk. However, just as with the "IS PATH WARM?" acronym, these checklists are intended only as a guide for the assessment interview, not as a definitive suicide risk assessment. They are useful to the degree to which they help us remember

I   Ideation
S   Substance Abuse

P   Purposelessness
A   Anxiety
T   Trapped
H   Hopelessness

W   Withdrawal
A   Anger
R   Recklessness
M   Mood Change

Figure 3.2 IS PATH WARM?
Source: American Association of Suicidology, "Warning Signs for Suicide," 2006, www.suicidology.org/web/guest/stats-and-tools/warning-signs.

the important areas to cover. Sometimes we talk with school personnel who worry that during the middle of talking to a potentially suicidal student, they might forget some of the major areas to cover. They are concerned that their own anxieties will get in the way. In these instances, a checklist might be useful, but only to help guide the process. Two cautions are necessary.

1. If students perceive you are just reading questions off of a standard checklist, it may have negative consequences for rapport. Be careful about stilted or canned approaches to a suicide risk assessment interview.
2. Some suicide risk checklists include "objective" scoring systems that yield a number at the end that is then linked to a predetermined level of suicide risk. These scoring systems are *extremely dangerous* and can encourage inappropriate use. We recommend removing all scoring from any checklist that is used and having the questions and/or topics covered as *general guidelines only*.

Typical questions on a suicide assessment checklist include (but are not limited to):

- Does the student have frequent suicidal thoughts?
- Are these thoughts intrusive and/or out of the student's control?

- Has the student had a suicide attempt in the past?
- Does the student have a detailed plan?
- Does the student have access to the means to complete the plan?
- Has the student made any arrangements to complete the plan?
- Does the student fantasize about death or the afterlife?
- Does the student believe it is likely he or she will act on these suicidal thoughts?
- Has the student spoken to anyone else about the suicidal thoughts?
- Is the student in severe psychological distress?
- Does the student feel hopeless?
- Is the student demonstrating changes in mood?
- Is the student demonstrating changes in behavior?
- Is the student actively using substances?
- Does the student have any recent, severe stressors?
- Is there a history of family violence?
- Is the student isolated and/or withdrawn?
- Does the student have a strong support system?
- Does the student have a trusted adult to talk with about suicidal thoughts?
- Can the student identify any reasons for living?
- Does the student have cognitive rigidity/poor problem solving?
- Does the student display poor impulse control?

Using a checklist may help a school staff member to cover the major areas that should be included and can serve as a springboard for further discussion and exploration of important topics.

Formal (Standardized) Assessments

Dozens of published standardized suicide risk assessments exist, as do hundreds of unpublished questionnaires and assessments available for use. There is, however, great variability in their quality, and some published instruments have very low reliability and validity. Standardized assessments can be useful in providing adjunctive information that helps provide a clearer picture of the situation, but other than suicide screening instruments that are used in universal approaches to suicide prevention (such as those included in Chapter 2), they are seldom used in schools.

REFERRALS

Too often, the burden of student mental health falls to school systems. But in the case of management of suicidal students, the school cannot function without community resources and referral agencies. Research has found that one of the most essential components of a comprehensive school-based suicide prevention program is established relationships and links between the school and community resources (Lazear, Roggenbaum, & Blase, 2003). Because schools are not equipped to handle ongoing counseling of suicidal students, these referrals are essential. The key is having these resources and relationships already in place so that students are managed within the school and community in a seamless system of care.

Once students have been identified as potential suicide risks and given an initial assessment by a school staff member, students requiring more intense interventions will require a referral, through the parents or guardians, to a community mental health resource. Kalafat and Underwood (1989) provide some suggestions for school staff wishing to make a mental health referral in the community. These include:

- **Make sure you have a full understanding of the student and his or her problems.** Inappropriate or poor referrals waste time and money and may lead students to believe that adults do not truly understand them, making them less likely to follow through with mental health assistance in the future.
- **Give students an opportunity to talk about their reluctance or apprehension to see mental health professionals in the community.** This provides the school staff with an opportunity to allay concerns or find other ways to make the idea of completing the referral more amenable to the student.
- **Involve parents in the referral process.** Use a referral that matches the family's and student's background (e.g., culture, language, religious affiliation, payment system, transportation options).
- **Limit the number of referrals to one or two.** Too much information can overwhelm students and their families.
- **Provide the family with as much information as possible about the referral.** Contact name, telephone number, directions, information about cost, and insurance coverage all help remove some of the mystique and make it easier for the student to get help.

- **Follow up with both the referral agency and the family.** The agency may not be able to release information about whether the student attended the appointment unless release forms have been signed. Encouraging parents to sign these forms can help keep lines of communication among the family, the school, and the community agency open.

After a school notifies a parent of a child's risk for suicide and provides referral information, the responsibility falls on the parent to seek mental health assistance for the child. Parents must:

- **Continue to take all threats seriously.** Follow-through is important even after the child calms down or informs the parent that he or she "didn't mean it."
- **Access school supports.** If parents are uncomfortable following through on referrals, they can give the school staff permission to contact the referral agency, provide referral information, and follow up on the visit. The school also can assist in providing transportation to get the parent and child to the referral agency, if possible.
- **Maintain communication with the school.** After such an intervention, the school also will provide follow-up supports. Open communication between parents and the school will be crucial to ensuring that the school is the safest, most comfortable place for the at-risk student (NASP, n.d.).

SUICIDAL STUDENTS AND SCHOOL READJUSTMENT

One of the more challenging areas in which schools are asked to work with suicidal students is when they return to school after a suicide attempt, psychiatric hospitalization, or other mental health crisis that required a prolonged absence from school. In spite of everyone's best efforts to keep this information confidential, other students in the school typically know all the details of the crisis (and all too often fill in any missing details with rumors and gossip). As a result, the affected student often returns to school to face taunts, ridicule, social isolation, or, in some cases, awe and unwelcome interest from peers. All this occurs at a time when the student is extremely emotionally vulnerable and at risk for another period of crisis.

Unfortunately, there is not much research available to guide the development of a successful school reintegration plan. Nevertheless, research and information from reintegration after other types of prolonged school absences, such as those caused by medical illness or traumatic brain injury, can help inform the basis of school readjustment.

Readjustment to school is a complex, many-phased process that requires individualized planning for each student. In general, studies have demonstrated that it benefits the student when schools, families, and appropriate community agencies or hospitals all work together to facilitate the student's return to school, to make the student's transition back to school as seemless as possible (Kaffenberger, 2006). A proactive approach to managing the most common barriers to the reintegration process is appropriate.

Common Barriers to Positive Reintegration

Lack of Communication

Lack of communication among schools, families, and community-based clinicians and hospitals represents a significant barrier to a smooth transition back to the school. During the time of crisis, families often are so focused on their child that they limit contact with others. They may delay getting in touch with the school, mistakenly believing that academics are no longer a priority for the student. They may be embarrassed by the suicide attempt, unwilling to talk with a school secretary or other staff member, and uncertain about how to access appropriate school personnel for these difficult conversations. Without information, school personnel are uncertain of how to proceed or how to best help the child and the family.

Parents must sign releases of information to open lines of communication among the family, the school, and the treating clinicians. Without these releases, school personnel have limited access to important information that can assist with the transition. Specific staff members can be included on these releases to help assuage parents' fears that information about their child will become "public" among the school staff.

Lack of Information and Training

A second potential barrier is the lack of information or training of school personnel on school policies, legal and ethical expectations, and appropriate transition guidelines. In our work in schools, we generally find school personnel who want to do the "right thing" to help the student who is reentering the school. However, we also have found instances when school staff members have contributed to the rumors and gossip, made inappropriate comments or disclosures to other students, or made the returning student feel uncomfortable by seeking him or her out for unwelcome discussions or questions.

Teachers often wonder how to communicate with students when they return to school or how to address the inappropriate behavior of classmates who tease or make improper comments to the student. In all cases, teachers and other school staff members must take care to maintain the confidentiality of the student involved and to protect him or her from teasing or bullying. We have found that education and training, outside of the context of any particular student and not during a time of transition, is most useful.

Unhelpful or Unsupportive School Policies

Sometimes policies and procedures are written in the wake of a particular event and never reviewed. We have encountered schools with written policies regarding suicide risk that have been handed down and no longer reflect current research or trends. We strongly encourage school personnel to read through the existing policies to see if changes or modifications are necessary.

Guidelines for School Reintegration

After a suicide attempt, students are particularly vulnerable as they transition back to school. Research shows that the first three months to one year after the attempt represents a time of heightened risk for future attempts. Appropriate planning for school reintegration can help lessen the risk for future attempts. The following guidelines are intended for general planning purposes only and are based on several state models for school reintegration (e.g., Maine, Wisconsin). However, it is important to remember that all reintegration policies must be flexible enough to allow for individualized approaches that meet the needs of the specific student.

1. **Contact the parents as soon as possible after learning of the crisis.** Offer to meet with the parents in person, even before the student is ready to return to school. Offer any resources or suggestions that may help the family. Offer to collect academic assignments to give to the

parents so the child does not fall behind in classes. Begin planning for the student's return to school. Keep lines of communication open while the student is away from school to help ease the transition.

2. **Consider whether your school will require approval of a mental health professional before the student can return to school.** Not all schools require this, and it is controversial. Some believe it helps protect the other students and ensures that the school is not asked to monitor a student who is at a level of risk that exceeds its ability to manage. Others believe that this requirement stigmatizes the student and places another barrier to school reentry. Nevertheless, the time to decide whether this will be part of the school's reentry policy is *before* the student crisis occurs.

3. **Assign a designated person to serve as a liaison among the school, the parents, and the treating clinician(s).** This person should be included on all releases of information to ensure a smooth communication process. The school counselor might serve as the liaison, but it is important to allow the student to have significant input into the choice of this person. If the student does not feel comfortable talking with the liaison, even the best procedures and protocols will be ineffective. The liaison can be a teacher, administrator, or trusted staff member, and the liaison should:

   a. Review and file written documents as part of the student's confidential health record.

   b. Serve as case manager for the student. Understand what precipitated the suicide attempt, and be alert to what might precipitate another attempt. Be familiar with the practical aspects of the case, such as medications and full versus partial study load recommendations.

   c. Help the student through reintegration procedures, monitor the reentry, and serve as a contact for other staff members who need to be alert to reoccurring warning signs.

   d. Serve as a link with the parent/guardian. With the written permission of the parent/guardian, serve as the school liaison with any external medical or mental health services providers supporting the student.

   e. Prior to the student's return, schedule meetings with appropriate staff members to discuss possible arrangements for services and to create an individualized reentry plan. It may be appropriate for the liaison to meet with the family upon the student's discharge from the hospital.

4. **Notify classroom teachers on the student's overall progress and whether the student is on a full or partial study load.** They do not need clinical information or a detailed history, but they may need certain information to make accommodations and modifications when necessary. Discuss the case among school personnel directly involved in supporting the student only regarding his or her treatment and support needs. Discussion of the student among other staff members should be strictly on a need-to-know basis, or what the staff person needs to know in order to work with the student.

5. **Talk with the student to understand his or her needs upon returning to school.** Students want different levels of support, and individual differences (within the limits of safety) should be respected. Students may request sessions with the school counselor as they transition back to school.

6. **Check in with the student each day.** In our work with schools, we insist that the liaison and the student have at least a brief check-in (just a minute or two is fine) each day. That helps keep the lines of communication open and reminds the student that she or he has an advocate in the school building.

7. **Work with family to understand the needs of siblings.** Siblings of the student who is readjusting to school may need extra support and care during this time of family crisis. Often families with a suicidal child have difficulty attending to the emotional needs of the other children, and they may need extra attention from school staff.

8. **Monitor student as long as necessary.** If there are changes in the student's functioning, mood, or behaviors, notify the parents immediately. School personnel may wish to engage in a tapering-off approach (e.g., contact with the liaison every day for one month, three times a week for one month, and once a week for one month) to help with a gradual and safe transition back to regular functioning.

When working with students who are reintegrating into the school, we have found that one of the biggest problems is *student fears that others will tease them.* In other words, even more than the reactions of classmates, the student's *perceptions* of those possible reactions is what feels overwhelming. Again and again we see and hear of students who are afraid to reenter school because they are afraid of feeling trapped. They wonder, *What if I get anxious and cannot leave the classroom? What if other students are teasing me, and I have nowhere to go to escape?* Of course, "feeling trapped" is, in and of itself, a significant risk factor for suicide. In their clinical treatment outside of school, these students work with their counselors and doctors to help them gain control over their emotions, to learn to recognize when their thoughts and feelings are escalating out of control, and to safely remove themselves from dangerous situations. Then, when they return to school, they are forced into an environment that does not support these positive approaches to self-care.

To help students face their fears and to reinforce positive self-care approaches, we offer two suggestions to school personnel working with students who are reintegrating after a suicide crisis.

Consider Teaching Mindfulness Skills

Mindfulness is gaining attention as an important psychological skill that allows people to stay immersed in stressful situations without becoming overwhelmed. Relaxation techniques and meditation can be important parts of mindfulness. Teaching suicidal individuals to focus on their experiences without judging them or equating these experiences to facts has been shown to help reduce cognitive distortions and feelings of anxiety (Williams, Duggan, Crane, & Fennell, 2006). Mindfulness skills can help give students a sense of control over their world.

Consider Giving Students a Sense of Control

One day, when working with a returning suicidal student, one of us (Dr. D. Granello) brought in a "Get out of jail free!" card from our Monopoly set at home. I had been thinking about her return to school and knew she was particularly nervous, so I considered her to be at high risk for another attempt. When I saw her the next morning, I handed her the card. I told her, "If you ever feel stressed and overwhelmed, and you just can't stay where you are for another moment, you can use this card and come down here to the office. No questions asked." She was incredulous. She asked, "You mean *anytime?*" "Yes," I said. "Anytime." I explained to her that I trusted her with her own mental health. She had been through a lot, and she knew, better than any of us, what she needed.

What began as a simple strategy for one student has become one more tool in the arsenal many of our school counselors use to help their reintegrating students. You see, I did not want her to have to explain to a teacher that she needed a break. I did not want her to have to raise her hand and ask permission to take care of herself. When I gave her the card, I showed her I trusted her and that I thought she was responsible.

Of course, I had to clear it with the administrators and inform all the teachers before I gave the card to her. Several teachers expressed concern. What if, for example, she used the card to get out of a test? What if she skipped an important class? I knew those were potential risks, but the reality was that this was a student at high risk for death. Given that, skipping a class or a test did not seem too serious.

That student, however, taught me an important lesson that I still remember. She did not misuse the card. She carried it with her every day, until it started to crumble and turn to dust. I had to take another card out of the Monopoly set to give to her. This time I had it laminated. In all the months she carried it, she used the card only once. She flashed it to a teacher and came down to the office. I offered her a seat and told her I could talk or she could just sit quietly. She sat for a moment and said, "I'm ready to go back to class now." She did not need anything. She just wanted to test the system. It worked, she was satisfied, and she never used it again. But she carried the card with her every day, as her own version of a security blanket. She knew that if she needed to, she could escape. Just *knowing* that was all she needed.

The point is that if we want students to take responsibility for their own mental health, then we have to help them. Clearly, this intervention is not appropriate for everyone, and certainly there are students who would misuse the privilege. The "pass" does not allow them to go home, or to nap, or do something fun; just to remove themselves from a stressful situation to a quiet place where they can regroup and prepare to reenter the classroom. At least for some students, it is an important strategy for reintegration into school.

CHAPTER SUMMARY

Students who are at risk for suicide need special attention in the schools. Selective interventions target students who have certain risk factors that require remediation and support. Most of these interventions focus on the development of positive social and emotional skills. Indicated interventions are for those students who have been identified as at risk for suicide. A prompt and accurate assessment is necessary to determine whether community-based clinical interventions are needed. Working with students in suicidal crises within the school requires a specialized set of clinical skills, with advance training, supervision, and experience. Students who return to school after a suicide crisis require special assistance to help with their reintegration. Together, school personnel, parents, students, and community-based clinical supports can provide an integrated and seamless approach to working with suicidal students in the schools.

4

Working With Students who Engage in Nonsuicidal Self-Inflicted Injury

Sarah is a 13-year-girl old currently enrolled in middle school. She is quiet, achieves average grades, and is not a discipline problem. At present she is living with her grandmother, as her mother is in residential treatment for substance dependency. Her mother and father are divorced, and Sarah has not seen her father in many years. She was recently observed by a teacher in the lunchroom pulling up her sweatshirt sleeves to show her forearms to another girl in her class. The teacher noticed that there were numerous cuts on Sarah's arms, several of which appeared to be recently inflicted. Concerned, the teacher sent Sarah to the school nurse, who bandaged the cuts and asked someone to have a more in-depth conversation with her. As you talk with Sarah, you discuss her behavior and try to assess her motives for self-injury. Is she suicidal? How long has she done this to herself? What is going on here: Is she depressed, anxious, does she have a personality disorder? She states that she is not suicidal, although she has thought about it in the past, but that she needs to cut in order to feel better. "It takes my mind off everything that builds up inside of me," she states.

In our work with teachers, counselors, administrators, and other school professionals throughout the United States, we are increasingly confronted with stories like Sarah's. Nationally, school personnel report that they are more concerned about the frequency of self-injurious behavior among children and adolescents. Teachers and high school counselors report that they have strong negative emotional reactions to self-injurious youth that makes working with these students particularly difficult. Many want more information and practice guidelines to help them work with Nonsuicidal Self-inflicted Injury (NSSI) behavior in students (Heath, Toste, & Beettam, 2006). In our work presenting suicide trainings around the country and internationally, we are increasingly being asked about the relationship of NSSI behavior to suicide. Research demonstrates that NSSI is a complex behavior with biological, psychological, and social variables that are related to its origin and severity. There are no easy answers to working with these students, and each case must be assessed in its unique context. Fortunately, however, the research on NSSI is improving steadily, and there is at least a baseline of information that can help school professionals work with students with NSSI behaviors in their schools. Thus, the focus of this chapter is on the etiology, assessment, referral, and treatment of NSSI behavior in the school setting.

About 4% of the U.S. population engages in intentional self-harm, although there are clear differences in self-harming behaviors based on age. Rates are significantly higher among young people. One study found about 14% of university undergraduates engage in NSSI behaviors (Klonsky, 2007), while another study of 18- to 20-year-olds found that 14% of participants had self-harmed at some point in their lives and 7% were currently self-harming (Young, Van Beinum, Sweeting, & West, 2007). Rates as high as 25% have been reported among high school students (Brausch & Gutierrez, 2010), and there is some evidence that the prevalence of these behaviors is higher in high schools than in middle or elementary schools. It appears that most people who engage in self-injury begin these behaviors around age 14, with increasing severity into the mid-20s (Austin & Kortum, 2004). The point is that NSSI behaviors are very prevalent among young people, and anyone working in a school will need to understand that a significant proportion of the students will have past or current self-injurious behaviors.

Is Self-Injury Among Adolescents Increasing?

It is hard to answer this question from a research perspective. What is clear is that the number of NSSI cases being identified among adolescents in school settings is growing. However, it is impossible to say whether this is due to an actual increase in the prevalence of the behavior or just an artifact of increased awareness. Since 1980, and even more in recent times, there has been a sharp increase in the level of social consciousness of NSSI. There have been more and more portrayals of NSSI behavior on television, movies, and on the Internet. For example, a 2009 study found a significant increase in NSSI portrayals in the movies from only 3 in the entire period from 1966 to 1980 (15 years) to 25 in the period from 2001 to 2005 (only 5 years) (Nock, Prinstein, & Sterba, 2009). Further, there are now hundreds of Web sites on the topic and video material on YouTube that portray NSSI behavior to adolescents (Whitlock, Lader, & Conterio, 2007). Popular youth icons, such as Johnny Depp, Angelina Jolie, Marilyn Manson, and Princess Diana, have all publicly discussed their struggles with self-injuring behaviors. Clearly, this increase in awareness among both the adolescent population and school-based professionals leads to more cases being identified, even if the actual rate of these cases in the population is not increasing. Nevertheless, whether the actual rate of NSSI in the adolescent population is increasing or not may not matter, since the reality is that more and more youth with NSSI behavior are identified in schools, and schools must respond appropriately. The current levels of NSSI behavior being exhibited in the school setting are more than sufficient to warrant increased training for school staff so that they can identify, assess, refer, and work with youth who self-injure (Toste & Heath, 2009).

Definitions

The research on self-injury in youth is fraught with inconsistencies in both definition and methodology. A multitude of different terms have been used in the literature to define NSSI. Among the more commonly used terms are: parasuicide, deliberate self-harm, intentional self-harm, and self-cutting. The use of divergent terminology makes comparisons between research studies difficult because each of the terms define the phenomenon of self-injury in a slightly different way. For example, some terms consider the intent of the youth with regard to desire to die while others do not. Depending on their definition, researchers may include certain behaviors (such as suicide attempts) while not including other behaviors (such as overdoses without intent to die) in their counts for prevalence of self-injurious behaviors. Therefore, there can be significantly different estimates on the prevalence of the behavior. For our purposes in this chapter, we will use these definitions:

- Nonsuicidal self-injury (NSSI) is intentional, self-effected, low-lethality bodily harm of a socially unacceptable nature, performed to reduce psychological distress (Walsh, 2006).
- Suicide attempt is an attempt to harm oneself with high lethality, with the conscious intent to end psychological distress by death.

Differentiating NSSI and Suicide

Suicide is the third leading cause for adolescent death in the United States, and there is a high prevalence of suicidal thoughts and attempts in schools. Thus, there is a significant need for the assessment of suicidality among all adolescents, through universal screening (see Chapter 2 for more information). It must be understood, however, that at least some of the youth who engage in NSSI are not suicidal (Walsh, 2006). Research has shown that although NSSI is significantly correlated with suicidality in youth, there is no evidence that NSSI *causes* adolescent suicide (Muehlenkamp & Gutierrez, 2004).

The Relationship of NSSI and Intent to Die

Students typically engage in NSSI for the purposes of managing strong negative feelings, generating positive emotional states, or engaging or avoiding social contact (Nixon & Heath, 2009). Therefore, it is important to note that while suicide assessment needs to be part of working with any self-injuring adolescent, many self-injuring adolescents are not at imminent risk for a suicide attempt. To help differentiate between NSSI and suicide attempts, intent is the critical variable. In other words, students who engage in NSSI differ from those who have suicide attempts because *what they are trying to accomplish through their behaviors differs in intent.* Several other variables (listed in the table) may help differentiate between NSSI and suicidal behavior (Muehlenkamp & Kerr, 2009).

Differences between NSSI and Suicidal Behavior on Selected Variables

Variable	NSSI	Suicide
Intent	Emotional coping	Ending pain
Lethality	Usually low	Frequently high
Frequency	Chronic	Rare
Methods	Many	One or two
Cognitive	Interest in living	Hopelessness, helplessness
Emotional	Relief from negative affect	Continued distress and frustration

Each of these variables requires a bit of further explanation. First, *intent* must be understood. Students who engage in NSSI behaviors are trying to relieve negative emotions or generate positive emotions to feel better. Students who are suicidal look to suicide as a method to end their pain. The second variable, lethality, presents some difficulty as a distinguishing feature between NSSI and suicide. In general, NSSI methods such as superficial cutting, scratching, and burning are not life threatening, in contrast with the very dangerous methods of adolescent suicide, such as firearms or suffocation. Of course, we are well aware that many NSSI behaviors can cross the line and become life threatening, even unintentionally. We worked with a young woman who intended to cut herself on the arm to ameliorate emotional pain but ended up with deep lacerations that bled so much that she required a lengthy hospital stay and skin grafts to repair the damage. The nerves in her arm were lacerated, and she never recovered full function or feeling in her hand or arm. The point is, although lethality is often rather low with NSSI, permanent damage or death can occur. Frequency is a third method used to help distinguish NSSI behaviors from suicide. Generally, NSSI behaviors occur chronically. Some self-injurers engage in the behavior up to 100 times or more, whereas suicide attempts are rare by comparison. Method, the fourth distinguishing variable, also differs between the two groups. It is relatively common for NSSI youth to use many different methods to inflict self-injury whereas suicidal youth tend to select one specific method (such as poisoning) and repeat its use. Finally, the cognitive and emotional states connected to NSSI may be different from those in suicidal adolescents. Emotionally, NSSI serves to provide a relief from negative affect and reflects a cognitive state in which adolescents believe they are successfully coping with pain to make life livable. This is very different from the emotional state of a suicidal adolescent, which is characterized by such intense psychological pain and hopelessness that there is a desire to end the pain, not merely cope with it. Cognitively, suicidal adolescents may not believe that they can go on living, believing that they are helpless to face the future.

Many self-injurious youth readily meet criteria for co-occurring mental and emotional disorders. Although frequently not diagnosed in youth, personality disorders such as Borderline Personality Disorder (BPD) are highly related to NSSI (Muehlenkamp & Gutierrez, 2004). Interestingly, BPD is the only disorder in the *Diagnostic and Statistical Manual of Mental Disorders*, Fourth Edition, Text Revision that lists self-injury as a criterion for diagnosis. In fact, during the 1980s, when I (Dr. P. Granello) began to practice, the hallmark of a client with BPD was self-injury, and everyone thought that any client who had NSSI behaviors had to have BPD. That is no longer the case.

NSSI is now commonly seen in individuals with a wide variety of diagnoses. Some other diagnoses that are associated with NSSI include:

- Alcohol Abuse
- Anorexia Nervosa
- Antisocial Personality Disorder
- Anxiety Disorders
- Autism
- Bulimia Nervosa
- Depression
- Developmental Disabilities
- Dissociative Identity Disorder
- Lesch-Nyhan Syndrome
- Posttraumatic Stress Disorder

A further complication in understanding NSSI behaviors in students is the high level of comorbidity with suicide attempts and with other mental health diagnoses. Approximately 55% to 85% of self-injurers have made at least one previous suicide attempt (Jacobson & Gould, 2007). Among adolescents with both NSSI and past suicide attempts, there are higher levels of depression, impulsivity, and hopelessness than among adolescents with NSSI behaviors only (Dougherty et al., 2009). The point here is that if an adolescent has NSSI behaviors, it is particularly important to also check for past/current suicide attempts and ideation and for coexisting mental health disorders, which may compound the risk for suicide. This is a challenging and difficult population, and the complex mental health problems that many of these students exhibit require extra screening, assessment, and intervention.

Although it is clear that NSSI behaviors and suicide ideation or attempts often present together in the same student, the focus of this chapter is on the population of adolescents who use NSSI as a coping mechanism and are not at high risk for suicide. Students who are suicidal (whether they engage in NSSI behaviors or not) were covered in Chapter 3. Thus, the focus of this chapter is helping school professionals work with students who believe that their NSSI behaviors are helping them cope.

BASIC FACTS ABOUT NSSI

Despite the difficulties with consistent definitions and methodology in the current research on NSSI, a number of important findings concerning demographic patterns have emerged. Although the results of the research is not entirely consistent, it appears that these findings are gaining support:

- Currently 15% to 20% of high school students have engaged in NSSI at least once.
- Most youth begin to engage in NSSI between 13 to 15 years of age.
- Overall, there is no gender difference for the prevalence of NSSI (cutting, burning, self-hitting), although studies are mixed, with some finding higher rates among females than males.
- Females are more likely than males to cut. Males are more likely than females to self-hit with the intent to bruise.
- Caucasians are more likely to engage in NSSI behavior than African Americans.
- Youth who are gay, lesbian, or conflicted about their sexual orientation *may* be at increased risk for NSSI, but these reports are anecdotal only.
- There are no consistent differences for prevalence of NSSI based on school locations (urban, rural, suburban).

Common Methods for NSSI

These are the most common methods of NSSI employed by youth in the United States, presented in rough order of frequency (Walsh, 2006):

- Cutting, scratching, and carving
- Excoriation of wounds
- Self-hitting
- Self-burning
- Head banging
- Self-inflicted tattoos
- Other (e.g., self-biting, abrading, ingesting scrap, inserting objects, self-inflicted piercing, hair pulling)

It is interesting to note that these methods are not the same as those used by adolescent suicide attempters. Adolescent suicide attempters frequently use methods that are of higher lethality, such as firearms, suffocation, and poisoning (Granello & Granello, 2007). This difference seems to support the idea that NSSI youth do not have the intent to die. Thus, choice of method can be one indicator of how they can be differentiated from suicide attempters.

Risk and Protective Factors for NSSI

Risk factors are variables that have been shown to be related to a specific behavior, in this case NSSI. The presence of these variables may not be the direct cause of NSSI, but they do tell us that youth who have experienced or exhibit them are more likely to be at risk than those who do not. The current research on NSSI has indicated several significant risk factors (see Table 4.1). Among these are neglect, abuse, family violence, emotional deregulation, low self-esteem, exposure to peer NSSI models, and co-occurring psychological disorders. Conversely, protective factors are those variables that have been shown to lower risk of a specific behavior, again in this case that of NSSI. The protective factors for NSSI are, not surprisingly, the opposite of many of the risk factors. Encouraging active parental engagement in the treatment of youth who self-injure can produce positive results. Finding other positive adult role models and encouraging participation in other appropriate and healthy social outlets (club, sports) also may be useful. Importantly, teaching youth to express negative emotions is an essential skill—not only for NSSI but for many stress-related mental and physical health issues. Of course, appropriate referral and access to timely and competent mental health care are critical.

Youth who grow up in dysfunctional families characterized by neglect and abuse (emotional, verbal, physical, sexual) are at greater risk for NSSI (Jacobson & Gould, 2007). The impacts of abuse and neglect on development are not fully understood, but it is commonly believed that they are

Table 4.1 NSSI Risk Factors and Protective Factors

Risk Factors	Protective Factors
Neglect (emotional or physical)	Appropriate expression of negative emotions
Physical abuse	Parental support
Sexual abuse	Social network support
Emotional abuse	Access to timely and competent care for
Family violence	mental and emotional disorders
Intense negative emotions (anger, loneliness, fear)	
Comorbid psychological disorders	
Low self-esteem, self-derogation	
Exposure to peer NSSI models	

damaging in many different ways to children. Individuals who grow up in such settings may develop maladaptive emotional, cognitive, and social behaviors. Socially, these behaviors may be expressed as problems with developing appropriate attachments, forming meaningful relationships, or keeping appropriate boundaries in relationships. Emotionally, symptoms resulting from abuse may manifest as feeling intense negative feelings of anger or loneliness (Brown, 2009). Often these strong negative emotions are compounded by a lack of communication or social skills in how to appropriately express them to others. Cognitively, neglect and abuse can manifest in self-defeating patterns for perceiving the self, making self-attributions, or internalizing negative messages (e.g., "I am worthless and terrible"; "Nothing I do is right"). These internalized messages can have a perpetuating effect on maintaining discouragement and depression. Self-injurious youth are frequently highly self-critical and self-punishing (Klonsky & Muehlenkamp, 2007).

Part of the complexity in understanding NSSI behaviors, however, is the recognition that not all adolescents who self-injure fit this profile and that there is clearly a continuum of risk. Brausch and Gutierrez (2010) found that, in general, adolescents who self-injure have significantly lower risk factors than those who have suicide attempts. In their study, adolescents with NSSI behaviors had fewer depressive symptoms, higher self-esteem, and more parental support than those who had suicide attempts. They concluded that adolescents who had NSSI behaviors without a suicide attempt represented a discrete group that falls along a continuum of self-harmful behavior.

Motives for Expression of NSSI Behavior in Adolescents

School professionals may ask themselves, Why would a person ever want to hurt themselves? The "why" of self-injury is complex, and there may be biological, psychological, and social variables that combine to make an individual adopt the behavior (Askew & Byrne, 2009). Further, NSSI may serve multiple purposes for each individual, making it difficult to arrive at a specific single motive for engaging in the behavior. To add another layer of complexity, current thinking suggests that the reasons for NSSI for an individual may change over the life span. For adolescents, however, the number-one reason given for NSSI is to cope with intense negative feelings (Jacobson & Gould, 2007).

A useful model for understanding the motives behind NSSI is comprised of four components (Nixon & Heath, 2009):

1. Automatic-negative reinforcement
2. Automatic-positive reinforcement
3. Social-positive reinforcement
4. Social-negative reinforcement

The first component is *automatic-negative reinforcement* (A-NR). The term "automatic" as it is used here means intrapersonal or that which is experienced internally, within the youth. The model asserts that the use of NSSI by an adolescent may result in relief from or the removal of a negative cognitive or emotional state. Frequently, adolescents will say they self-injure to deal with stress or get frustration out. The A-NR addresses this desire to get rid of the negatives. The second component is *automatic-positive reinforcement* (A-PR). A-PR is described as the use of NSSI to generate some desired, or positive, internal state. Youth who act from an A-PR motive may say things like "I just wanted to feel something" or "I needed to feel real." The third component is *social-positive reinforcement* (S-PR). S-PR is a motive for NSSI when the youth is trying to communicate to others or access some resource. Statements made might include "I want you to know how I am feeling" or "I want my counselor to . . ." In other words, the young person uses the behaviors as a signal to others. Finally, the last component in the model is *social-negative reinforcement* (S-NR). S-NR is a motive when NSSI is used to escape from or control some interpersonal demand. Statements by youth using S-NR as a motive for NSSI may be something like "I can't face school again" or "I do it to get people to back off and leave me alone."

The utility of this model for understanding the causes of NSSI is that it can help guide the choice of therapeutic interventions for a particular student. In other words, once we understand what the young person is trying to accomplish with the NSSI behaviors, we have a better chance to intervene. For example, if the primary motivation of the youth's NSSI behavior is to modify an internal state and feel something positive, we can help him or her find other, more appropriate ways to understand and express emotions. If the primary goal is to keep others away, then we can help the young person learn to manage social relationships. Thus, understanding the causes of NSSI behaviors is the first step to developing appropriate interventions.

Other motives that have been identified in the research and literature include:

- Desire for peer recognition or inclusion
- Tension relief
- Desire to gain control
- Attempt to numb oneself
- Attraction to the feeling of "warm blood"
- Longing to replace emotional pain with physical pain
- Desire to show "battle scars"
- Self-punishment

In our work with people who self-injure, we have found that they often have difficulty expressing the specific motivation behind their behaviors. They sometimes just say "I have to do it" or "It feels like the right thing to do." While we always look for specific motivations to help us find appropriate interventions, it sometimes takes quite a bit of work before these individuals can come to understand what compels them to harm themselves.

PREVENTION OF NSSI BEHAVIOR IN SCHOOLS

Before we turn to intervention, it is important to talk about methods to prevent the development of NSSI behaviors in school populations. Clearly, the best intervention is to prevent the behaviors from occurring in the first place. As the saying goes, "An ounce of prevention is worth a pound of cure." Prevention programming is a powerful weapon in the arsenal of addressing NSSI in youth. Prevention efforts may be of particular importance in school settings because of the risk of contagion. Contagion, or copycat behavior, is a particular risk with youth NSSI, just as it is with suicide. School professionals already know that adolescents are looking to peers for guidance on what constitutes socially acceptable behavior and, perhaps even more important, for guidance on what behaviors are considered "not cool" or would lead to social ostracism. In today's world of instant text messaging, chat rooms, and social networking, youth are able to transmit correct or incorrect messages to each other and large audiences instantaneously. Ironically, school personnel are sometimes reluctant to engage adolescents on topics such as NSSI or suicide, erroneously thinking that discussion of the topics will somehow "put the idea in their heads." All too frequently, however, the reality is that by the time adults know about a youth who is using NSSI as a coping strategy, it is likely that many of that student's peers already know all the details. The unfortunate fact is that the topic of how to engage in NSSI is readily discussed on Internet chat sites and discussion boards catering to youth (Whitlock, Powers, & Eckenrode, 2006). Youth who are left to their own devices to understand NSSI behaviors will look to peers as role models. Some of these models will be self-injurers themselves and may seek to promote the behavior to their peers as an effective means of coping. Among adolescents, modeling by NSSI peers can lead to the spread, or contagion, of the behavior. Epidemics of NSSI have been seen among adolescent populations in high schools (Nixon & Heath, 2009). In our own work, we have seen NSSI behaviors travel through social groups of adolescent girls in high schools and colleges. Figure 4.1 presents strategies for minimizing NSSI contagion in schools.

Contagion is a real risk with NSSI behavior, as it is with suicide. There is virtually no research in this area. Some suggestions for strategies that may be helpful include:

- **Working with NSSI youth to limit their communications with peers about their behavior.** To the degree that the youth has a social conscious, he or she will understand how the behavior may be harmful to others. NSSI youth may use self-harm as a coping mechanism for themselves and yet not want others to be harmed.
- **Making sure teachers or other school staff do not comment on any individual's NSSI behavior in front of groups of students.** Train staff to intervene with students discreetly.
- **Refraining from group treatment or support group interventions for NSSI youth.** Adolescents with NSSI may be best treated or managed on an individual basis. Peer groups with NSSI clients may lead to one-upmanship and exacerbation.
- **Developing school policies on the use of Facebook or other social media.** This is a controversial area, particularly given the connection of social media to cyberbullying. Schools that implement policies limiting social media typically prohibit the distribution of images or information that may embarrass or be harmful to other students.

For more information on limiting contagion in schools, see Chapter 5.

Figure 4.1 Strategies for Minimizing NSSI Contagion in Schools

A public health approach to NSSI prevention in the schools can be used to provide accurate education and to reduce self-injurious behaviors among students. Currently, there is very limited research on the outcomes of prevention programming for NSSI, so the information to be presented is derived from application of prevention strategies for other maladaptive coping strategies (e.g., substance abuse, smoking) that have been used in school settings.

Just as with the public health approach to suicide prevention in schools that was discussed in Chapter 2, an active prevention approach for NSSI requires the development of "universal" programs for the entire student body as well as "selective" or "targeted" programs for high-risk groups. Additionally, school counselors and other health professionals can provide training and information to help teachers and other staff gain an understanding of how they can be better prepared to help a self-injurious youth.

Universal Prevention Strategies

Universal prevention programs are directed to the entire school population and may focus on developing healthy coping and increasing wellness skills. Currently no specific universal prevention programs are available for NSSI. Rather, universal approaches should be aimed at keeping the school climate one that is perceived as a safe, nonjudgmental environment where students can talk to adults. An open and caring environment can have preventive effects for NSSI and other at-risk behaviors (Nixon & Heath, 2009). School staff should be trained to respond to difficult topics, such as NSSI, by using active listening skills and remaining emotionally neutral (see "Teacher Training" later in the chapter).

Programs in health education where NSSI is contextualized as one of many maladaptive methods that adolescents may use to cope with intense emotions or stress may be useful. Education about harmful coping behaviors, such as alcohol abuse, drug use, NSSI, social withdrawal, and sexually risky behaviors, and their potential harmful long-term consequences, is essential (Toste & Heath, 2009). These programs should be aimed at increasing students' awareness that while maladaptive coping strategies may provide short-term relief, ultimately they do not solve the underlying problems and can compound existing problems. Further, classroom guidance or group programming should seek to arm all students with healthy coping skills, such as emotional regulation skills (mindfulness meditation), relaxation skills (breathing and imagery), emotional communication skills (affect vocabulary), and problem-solving skills (negotiation, problem-solving models). Prevention education programming that stresses intellectual, emotional, and physical wellness can be incorporated into almost any classroom curriculum.

Signs of Self-Injury (SOSI) is a universal education approach for reducing self-injury in high schools. It is similar to the universal suicide prevention program Signs of Suicide (SOS), and uses a similar premise. SOSI is designed to increase knowledge of NSSI behaviors, including warning signs and risk factors, improve attitudes for help seeking and lower stigma, increase help-seeking behaviors among youth who engage in NSSI, and lower NSSI behaviors among students. There are modules for staff and faculty as well as a student module that uses video vignettes to teach students how to reach out to others. The SOSI program uses the acronym ACT (Acknowledge the signs, Demonstrate Care and a desire to help, and Tell a trusted adult). The program is based on two important findings:

1. Although some adults may know of NSSI behaviors in young people, peers are far more likely to know about these behaviors in students.
2. There is strong evidence that young people are very uncomfortable confronting their peers about NSSI behaviors and are very likely to avoid the topic of help seeking.

SOSI is intended to give adolescents the knowledge, skills, and confidence to reach out to peers who self-injure. Initial findings of the SOSI program are promising, with both staff and students demonstrating increased knowledge and intention to reach out to others in distress. Importantly, the program did not produce any iatrogenic effects among the students. In other words, participating in the universal education program did not increase self-injurious behaviors among students (Muehlenkamp, Walsh, & McDade, 2010). This is particularly important, as, historically, there has been fear that education campaigns could have the opposite effect and actually teach self-injurious behaviors to students. Clearly, more research is needed, and the SOSI program is not yet considered a best practice model. At present, however, it is the only universal education approach available for schools that has any empirical support.

Selective Prevention Strategies

Another avenue for providing prevention services in school is to define a specific at-risk target group of students for provision of prevention services.

Students who are identified by staff as at risk because they are evidencing behaviors that are related to NSSI (e.g., eating disorders, emotional dysregulation, depression, anxiety, alcohol or drug abuse) can be screened and recommended to attend groups or individual sessions to strengthen their wellness skills.

It is also possible to deploy in school mental health screening programs, such as Signs of Suicide and or TeenScreen. Information about both programs now in use in hundreds of locations nationally may be found in the best practices registry of the Suicide Prevention Resource Center (www.sprc.org/featured_resources/bpr/index.asp). These screens reliably identify students at risk for mental health problems, including NSSI, so that preventive services (or referral for mental health care) can be offered. More information about these programs is included in Chapter 2.

Teacher Training

It is very important that teachers and other school staff learn how to cope effectively with a youth who is self-injurious. While it is true that teachers are not expected to provide counseling services in schools, they should be trained as "gatekeepers." Gatekeepers are individuals who know how to recognize NSSI, are willing to engage the youth, and know how to facilitate a referral to a school counselor or mental health professional in the school.

Teachers and school staff should know that it is appropriate to engage with an NSSI youth and should be trained to take a nonjudgmental approach. Although NSSI behavior can be disturbing, as professionals, we need to approach the student's behavior calmly and with a caring attitude. Teachers need to listen to the student and understand how he or she is using the behavior as a method of coping with emotional pain the student may be feeling inside. It is important to encourage and support the student and assist with follow-through to appropriate services within the school or community. Teachers need to know that it is not their role to stop NSSI but rather to help identify and refer students whom they suspect of NSSI to the designated school professional (school counselor, school nurse, school administrator). Teachers are an extremely important link in this chain. They spend the most time with students, and they can serve a vital role in sharing information with school counselors concerning student interactions with peers; clues or warning signs presented in the schoolwork, such as artwork or writing; and other behavioral observations.

Just as important as it is to know what to do, it is important to help teachers and others in the school know what *not to do* with a youth exhibiting NSSI behaviors. It is important not to shame or guilt the student or publicly discuss the NSSI in front of the class or peers. Further, school staff and teachers should avoid colluding with a student regarding NSSI behavior or making deals with a student to get him or her to stop. These types of negotiations are sometimes tempting, but they are *always* inappropriate. Students may plead with teachers to keep their NSSI behavior secret, but this request *cannot* be fulfilled. Finally, punishment or other negative consequences are not appropriate responses if a student self-injures.

As with all prevention and treatment programs, the time to develop a policy regarding how to handle any potentially harmful situation, including NSSI, is *before* the situation presents itself. School staff and administrators should have conversations about school policies regarding students with NSSI behaviors. As you read this, stop and think about your own school for a moment. If possible, talk with colleagues and school administrators about the current policies, training, and intervention approaches concerning NSSI in your school. Is there a need to develop some prevention programming and training? Chances are that work needs to be done in this area. Most schools have very limited written policies and procedures for working with these students. In fact, in a national study of school counselors, only 23% said their schools had an identified policy or plan for working with students who self-injure (Roberts-Dobie & Donatelle, 2007). A proactive approach to developing a school-wide policy and procedure for working with these students will benefit everyone at the school.

ASSESSMENT, REFERRAL, AND INTERVENTIONS WITH SELF-INJURIOUS YOUTH

School professionals all over the country, no matter the location, type of school, or age of the student body, will be confronted with youth who self-injure. The prevalence of these students in schools across the country highlights the need for all school professionals to have the skills for the appropriate initial assessment and referral. Yet many of our best professionals in school mental health feel inadequately prepared to work with self-injurious youth.

A 2007 study of school counselors found that 81% had worked with youth who engage in NSSI, but only 6% rated themselves as "highly knowledgeable" about working with this population (Roberts-Dobie & Donatelle, 2007).

Warning Signs for Self-Injury

Although there are many methods for self-injury and many different ways in which warning signs might manifest within students, some physical and emotional cues might indicate the need for an individual assessment. For example, physical indicators include inappropriate clothing for the weather (e.g., long-sleeve shirts to cover arms even in summer); bloodstains on clothing, unexplained scars or bruises, and secretive behavior (e.g., spending lots of time in the bathroom or other isolated areas). Emotional indicators can include such things as inability to cope with strong emotions, anger, rage, anxiety, fear, or depression, isolation and withdrawal, or self-loathing.

Assessment and Referral

The primary responsibility of the school-based professional is to assess and appropriately refer a youth who has been identified as engaging in NSSI behavior. Teachers, staff, and even other students can alert appropriate school personnel of a youth who may be at risk for self-injuring behaviors. Once a youth has been identified, he or she will need to be properly assessed. NSSI assessment should include gathering some basic information about:

- Medical history
- Substance use
- Identification of possible comorbid mental health diagnoses
- Evaluation of risk and preventive factors
- Evaluation of family and other social supports (Walsh, 2006)

Further, a behavioral analysis should be conducted specifically regarding the NSSI behavior, including:

- Antecedents (stressors, situations, thoughts, emotions) that lead to self-harm
- Current level of NSSI behavior (frequency, intensity, duration, methods used)
- Consequences of the behavior, such as emotional relief or social attention (Peterson, Freedenthal, Sheldon, & Andersen, 2008)

Finally, a suicide assessment should be conducted. If the suicide risk is high, then the student's legal guardians/parents will have to be informed and the student should be referred to the appropriate mental health resources in the community. (Remember to document these consultations and referrals.) Even if the suicide risk is low, however, parents will need to be engaged, particularly if the behaviors are dangerous. Schools and parents must work together to promote the best interests of the child. All interactions with parents on this topic should be documented. In general, parents and their children need psychoeducation about NSSI so that they can make informed choices about pursuing treatment. Referrals to mental health providers in the community or to school-based services may be helpful at this point. Parents need to be given information and recommendations for getting help for the student both in school and in the community.

Barent Walsh (2006), in his outstanding book entitled *Treating Self-Injury: A Practical Guide*, provides a very useful protocol for managing NSSI referrals in a school-based environment. This protocol is presented next with some adaptations.

School-Based Protocol for Assessment and Referral of NSSI Youth

1. Any staff member will contact the designated point person (e.g., school counselor) immediately when a student evidences:
   - Suicidal behaviors: talk, threats, "joking," notes, poetry, other writings, artwork, or other communications that have suicidal themes.
   - Self-injury or self-mutilation, such as wrist, arm, or body cutting; self-scratching; self-burning; self-hitting; picking of wounds; crude self-inflicted tattoos; disfiguring hair pulling and removal; or excessive accident proneness.
   - Eating-disordered behavior, such as self-induced vomiting, sustained fasting, marked ongoing weight loss or gain, use of diet pills or laxatives.
   - Disclosures regarding risk-taking behaviors, including:
     i. Physical risks (e.g., walking in high-speed traffic, walking on an elevated railroad bridge, straddling the edge of a high roof).
     ii. Situational risks (e.g., getting into a car with strangers, walking in a dangerous area of a city alone late at night).

      iii. Sexual risks: having many sexual partners, having unprotected sex.

      iv. Substance use behavior that exceeds "normal" adolescent experimentation, suggestive of abuse or addiction (e.g., students who get high before school or who drink or smoke marijuana multiple times per week).

- Discontinuation of or hoarding prescribed medications without their doctor's knowledge.
- Behaviors that suggest serious emotional distress: uncontrollable crying, explosive anger, frequent fights, extreme reactions to minor events, serious isolation, or extremely poor hygiene.

2. The school point person will then investigate and assess the referral by discreetly and confidentially making contact with the student.

Three possible outcomes may be determined from this assessment:

1. **Minor incident.** Document the referral and encourage the student to contact the school counselor if she or he needs help or becomes distressed in the future. Feedback to the referring staff member on the outcome and recommendations of the assessment should be provided in a timely manner.

2. **Significant incident.** Document the referral and recommend further intervention. Make sure to ask for any required releases of information that may be needed to help facilitate referrals for the student. Student's parents should be informed about the situation and offered an opportunity for further education about NSSI. Parents should be encouraged to pursue a psychiatric consult and outpatient mental health assessment and treatment for the student or the family. The development of a safety plan and the availability of enhanced academic and counseling assistance for the student within the school setting should be discussed with the student and parent.

    For students with a significant incident of NSSI, it is strongly suggested that the school counselor or other school personnel follow up within a short period of time to make sure that the recommendations have been pursued by the family. If the parents have not acted on behalf of the student, they should be asked about any barriers (transportation, financial, stigma) that may be preventing them from doing so. It may be necessary to help them with these in order to achieve the desired compliance. In some cases it may be necessary to file a neglect report with the state child protection agency if the parents will not take action to address the mental health needs of the child.

3. **Emergency situation.** Work as a team with the school counselor or other school staff to immediately arrange for psychiatric and/or medical evaluation of the student at the appropriate health care facility (emergency room, crisis center, psychiatric unit). Imminent suicide risk or severe mutilation (e.g., cutting on neck or in a fashion requiring immediate medical attention) requires immediate medical intervention. Document all information concerning the referral, assessment, and recommendations for care.

Developing and implementing a protocol such as this one can help provide consistency and guidance to school staff in referring and assessing NSSI and other high-risk behavior cases.

Intervention Within the School

The high association of NSSI with so many psychiatric disorders underscores the importance of school and community partnership. School personnel working with students who exhibit NSSI behaviors must know how to make appropriate referrals to community mental health providers. School counselors and others who work with self-injuring youth need to develop a clinical understanding of the common co-occurring disorders in order to help encourage these students to comply with treatment.

Although there is no agreed-on single therapeutic approach for working with youth who engage in NSSI behaviors, dialectical behavior therapy (DBT) has received attention in the research and literature as an appropriate response (Peterson, Freedenthal, Sheldon, & Andersen, 2008). DBT emphasizes problem solving, emotion regulation, and functional assessment and analysis of the behavior, all of which have direct application to NSSI behaviors. Additionally, cognitive behavioral therapy (CBT) techniques may be useful. Cognitive restructuring and working to reduce all-or-nothing thinking are linked to the reduction of NSSI behaviors. No pharmacological approaches have been demonstrated to help decrease NSSI behaviors, although some youth may be given medication to help treat an underlying comorbid disorder. Finally, strong therapeutic relationships have been shown to be particularly important (Kress & Hoffman, 2008; Muehlenkamp, 2006). Youth who self-injure often feel alienated and misunderstood. When they share their self-injuring thoughts and behaviors with others, they can experience further rejection or ridicule. A strong relationship with a caring adult is the cornerstone of treatment. The ability to accept the person, regardless of the behaviors, is essential.

While it is beyond the scope of this chapter to provide detailed information regarding DBT or CBT, the next strategies are offered to school personnel as a starting place for working with youth who engage in NSSI behaviors.

- **Relationship building**. Therapeutic alliance has been shown to be a very important variable in helping at-risk youth and has curative properties in and of itself. A strong and accepting relationship will probably not be sufficient to eliminate NSSI behaviors, but it is necessary to help create a climate of trust where youth feel free to discuss their concerns. Even school staff members who do not engage directly in counseling with self-injuring youth can employ some of the basics of person-centered therapy, such as warmth, empathy, and unconditional positive regard, in their interactions with these students. It is important not to minimize the feelings that lead to these self-destructive behaviors or to be judgmental or directive. A slow approach that focuses on building an alliance and providing hope is much more productive.

- **Communication skill building**. For at least some students, NSSI behaviors are a way to communicate to others. Teaching these youth other, healthier ways to express their needs is important. When we work with middle and high school students, we often see how difficult it is for many to recognize their own feelings and to find ways to express them. Traditionally, feelings identification has been thought of as a skill for elementary-age children. But our work with older youth, particularly those who self-injure, has taught us that many adolescents have not yet mastered this skill and need assistance. It is not enough to tell a student "Tell others when you are angry or sad" if the student cannot identify those emotions when they are felt.

- **Affective expression**. Once students have identified their feelings, they need appropriate ways to express those feelings to others. Teaching affective vocabulary and language skills can be useful. Individualized efforts to help youth find healthy methods for expressing emotional pain, such as through dance, art, or journaling, is another approach that has had some success.

- **Behavioral intervention**. Once students have identified their feelings and expressed them to others, they will need ways to help them cope with the negative emotions. Appropriate behavioral techniques, such as relaxation, meditation, or exercise, are useful. Instruction in self-soothing techniques may be helpful as well. Finally, young people need to learn to develop tolerance for negative emotions. The goal is not to get rid of all disturbing thoughts or feelings but to teach them to "make room for them and do what needs to be done to get on with life" (Chiles & Strosahl, 2005, p. 117).

- **Cognitive intervention**. Instruction and practice in general problem solving and negotiation skills are appropriate. Methods that help youth with NSSI behaviors identify and replace self-defeating and negative thoughts concerning their ability to tolerate psychological pain can help. Common distortions in thinking by youth who self-injure include:

  Self-injury is appropriate.
  My body is disgusting and deserving of self-punishment.
  If I don't self-injure, I will kill myself.
  I can't control my actions.

  Clearly, these distortions (and others) represent important avenues for therapeutic interventions.

- **Safety plans**. Youth who engage in NSSI behaviors need a safety plan to help them know what to do if they start to feel overwhelmed by the desire to self-injure. Safety plans can be developed by school personnel in their work with these youth, but more often such plans are created by students in their work with mental health professionals in the community. In these instances, school professionals can be thought of as another resource for students to use when they are feeling unsafe. The safety plan should specify healthy strategies for coping with intrusive thoughts or intense emotions. The plan can include activities for the student to engage in, appropriate suggestions for communication, and how to contact help when needed.

LEGAL AND ETHICAL CONSIDERATIONS

School personnel who work with NSSI youth need to keep in mind five ethical and legal considerations.

1. School policies regarding the referral and management of NSSI youth in the school must be in compliance with state laws and other school policies already in place regarding the management of high-risk behaviors (Nixon & Heath, 2009).

2. NSSI management policies need to be shared with all school staff members who may identify or refer a youth for NSSI behavior. Just as with suicide prevention education, it is wise to train *all* school staff members, including bus drivers and janitorial and kitchen personnel. Many times self-injuring youth will talk to or confide in these staff members about their risky behaviors rather than seeking out the school counselor or nurse.

3. The role of confidentiality must be considered. School personnel need to assess the risk level of an NSSI student in the context of their need to inform parents and, when necessary, medical personnel. Significant self-harm is a situation when confidentiality does not apply. School personnel must take whatever steps are necessary to keep the child safe. If ever in doubt concerning the safety or suicide risk of a youth, we must err on the side of caution and get others involved.

4. School personnel must recognize the limits of the services that can be provided in the context of a school environment. Youth who engage in serious self-injury probably cannot be treated within the confines of the school. School personnel must be knowledgeable about the procedures for referral to mental health providers in the community and have appropriate referral sources available for students and their families.

5. School personnel who work with NSSI youth are reminded to document all contacts, phone calls, assessments, consultations, referrals, and reporting (to authorities and to parents) regarding NSSI behaviors. Because of the volatility of these situations, lawsuits may arise, and there may be a need to provide proof that appropriate steps were taken. Although the health and welfare of the students are of foremost concern, school personnel need to protect themselves as well.

CHAPTER SUMMARY

Many students who self-injure do not have concerns about these behaviors and have no desire to stop them. Although school personnel and other adults often find the behaviors upsetting and frustrating, the lack of interest in quitting can be even more challenging than the behaviors themselves. Perhaps this attitude helps explain why mental health professionals report that NSSI is one of the most frustrating client behaviors they encounter (Kress & Hoffman, 2008). It is important to remember that for adolescents who engage in NSSI, the behavior (no matter how self-defeating) is a coping strategy. We all know how hard it is to give up a behavior that "works" (or is reinforcing) in the short term, even if there are long-term consequences or the copying strategy has gotten out of control. Anyone who has tried to give up smoking, lose weight, eat healthier, or use relaxation strategies to reduce stress knows how challenging this can be.

Finally, it is important to remember:

- NSSI is complex and has biological, psychological, and environmental causality.
- NSSI has not been demonstrated to lead to suicide. However, there are correlations between NSSI and suicide attempts, and it is important to assess suicide risk in all NSSI youth.
- The time to develop prevention and management policies concerning NSSI and suicide is *before* the school is faced with a student suicide or an epidemic of NSSI.
- Teachers and all school staff will benefit from training on how to manage students with NSSI behaviors.
- Youth who express NSSI behavior need to be responded to with calm and empathy.

Self-injuring behavior is something that no one likes to discuss. Working with students who self-injure can be unnerving, and it is natural to react with anger, disgust, or pity. With education and training, however, school personnel can provide more appropriate responses to these students. Perhaps, if more of us begin to address the problem of NSSI with our "eyes wide open" and a willingness to engage, we can begin to teach and counsel youth in ways that will allow them to find more healthy ways to express mental and emotional pain.

5

After a Suicide

Postvention in the School Environment

Schools play a pivotal role in the aftermath of a suicide by a student, staff, or faculty member. In the days following a death, schools can become either a hotbed of rumor and speculation that can increase suicide risk or a place of safety where students can turn to trusted sources of information and support. In our own experiences as counselors and consultants to schools (Drs. D. and P. Granello), we have seen both of these responses. We have seen schools grow into stronger and more caring environments after a suicide. Unfortunately, We have also witnessed the tragic results of inappropriate responses and copycat suicides. The key difference is whether a school has in place, and follows, a suicide postvention strategy.

The delivery of crisis response services in the aftermath of a youth suicide is referred to as suicide postvention. "Suicide postvention" is defined as "the provision of crisis intervention, support and assistance for those affected by a completed suicide" (American Association of Suicidology, 1998, p. 1). A comprehensive suicide postvention strategy that is developed *before the school is in the aftermath of a suicide* allows school staff to immediately implement guidelines that promote a healthy and safe environment. During the time of crisis, there is no scrambling around to determine what to do. Rather, each member of the staff follows predetermined protocols that are intentionally designed to limit risk.

Unfortunately, many of the best postvention strategies are somewhat counterintuitive. That is, if left to our own devices and without the benefit of existing resources or research, many of us might implement strategies that could actually increase risk among students. Although none of us would ever raise risk intentionally, that is what could easily happen if we were left to make decisions on our own, particularly in the moment of crisis and chaos that occurs after a suicide. This is one of the major reasons why advance planning and preparation is essential.

Not long ago, we were called to assist in a postvention response at a school. (Please note that all identifying information, including information about the school, has been altered.)

We received a call by a frantic vice principal at a religiously affiliated school after a second student died by suicide within a 2-month period. Previously, there had been no recorded incidents of student suicide in the school's more than 100-year history. Nevertheless, a Caucasian male sophomore died by suicide in early autumn, and a second Caucasian male sophomore took his own life less than 2 months later. Both boys used the same method of death (a very specific method of hanging at a location on the school's campus), giving all indications of a copycat suicide. The school was uncertain of how to respond to the second suicide. The school staff, faculty, and students were terrified that it would happen again. The administration felt guilty, wondering if they had inadvertently "caused" the second suicide. The students were angry, lashing out at their teachers for the "uncaring atmosphere" that was making students kill themselves. The freshmen were worried that there was something about their sophomore year that made students kill themselves. Rumors were rampant, text messaging was out of control, and by the time we arrived on campus the next day, an atmosphere of uncertainty and panic threatened to overtake the entire school.

As we listened to the administrators talk about their responses to the student deaths, it was clear that they did not have a postvention plan in place. After the death of the first student, the school went into grieving. As a religiously affiliated school, the administrators fell back on their faith to guide them. They held prayer vigils and candle-lightings. They canceled classes so everyone could attend a school-wide memorial service in the school's chapel. They flew the flag at half staff. Students also participated in developing mourning rituals. They made special pins for them all to wear to remember the deceased student, and they put up a large banner of remembrance where all students could write their memories of the classmate they had lost. On the surface, it would be easy to think that these responses were appropriate, even admirable. After all, the administration was sending a clear message to students that the school is a caring environment that mourns the death of one of its students and relies on faith to help them get through.

When the second student died by suicide weeks later, the administrators put a hold on all postvention activities and started searching the Internet to learn what they should do. They quickly learned that their responses to the first death may have inadvertently contributed to the death of the second student. But when they responded differently to the second death, the students became angry. They accused administrators of "being unfair." The first student who died was a popular athlete while the second student was unpopular and a bit of a "loner." They said the school was "playing favorites" and demanded another memorial service and prayer vigil. It was into this environment that we stepped onto campus to assist.

This case illustrates the critical role that postvention planning can play. As you will read in the pages to come, many of the school's responses may indeed have contributed to the death of the second student. It is certainly unfair to "blame" the school—the student made an unfortunate and sad choice, and others are not responsible for that decision. It is certainly possible that he would have made the choice to die by suicide regardless of the school's response to the first suicide. However, there are things schools can do to *minimize* the risk of contagion, and it is certainly possible that a different response by the school could have led to a different outcome.

FOUR MAJOR GOALS IN ANY POSTVENTION RESPONSE

Comprehensive suicide postvention plans outline specific actions that should be implemented in response to a suicide. These plans provide structure during difficult and potentially chaotic times. When schools develop a comprehensive suicide postvention strategy, four major goals should guide the process. Ultimately, a postvention strategy should (1) reduce the risk of suicide contagion, (2) provide the support needed to help survivors cope with a suicide death and express their grief, (3) address the social stigma associated with suicide, and (4) disseminate factual information (Weekley & Brock, 2004). Throughout the process, school personnel must help students and staff members stay focused on learning and maintaining a healthy school environment.

Goal 1: Reduce the Risk of Suicide Contagion

Suicide contagion occurs when suicidal behavior is imitated. Also called cluster suicides, this type of suicide risk is relatively rare. However, when it does occur, it is most common in schools, among elderly persons, and in close-knit communities, such as within police precincts or military units. It is difficult to say what motivates suicide contagion, but guilt, overidentification with the deceased person, and modeling are all thought to play a role. Among teenagers, cluster suicides account for between 1% and 5% of all suicide deaths, resulting in 100 to 200 cluster suicides among teenagers each year (Zenere, 2009). There is evidence that the rate of cluster suicides among teenagers is increasing in the United States.

Clearly, a single exposure to the suicidal behavior of another person does not *in and of itself* result in imitative behavior. In other words, a student with no risk factors for suicide or preexisting mental health problems is unlikely to become suicidal after the death of a classmate. Rather, it is the combination of that exposure and a predisposed psychological vulnerability that can result in increased risk for suicide contagion.

Certain groups of students may be at increased risk for suicide contagion. These include: victims of bullying, team members of the deceased, classmates who shared common schedules or activities, romantic interests, close friends, or others who perceive that they had something in common with the deceased student. Young people may overidentify with the deceased student if they believe they have similar life circumstances or experiences. In schools, this phenomenon has been observed following the suicide of a perceived leader, a popular student, or an athlete.

To reduce the potential of contagion, schools should (and should not) employ some specific strategies.

Never Glamorize, Romanticize, or Glorify the Student or the Death

Locker memorials, flags at half staff, planting a tree, and armbands or specialized pins can inadvertently increase risk. Certain groups of students are psychologically vulnerable or feel isolated or lonely, and may now see suicide as a way to gain "popularity" or "acceptance" within the school. Images that students have from the media or popular fiction can make suicide seem romantic or sensational, and witnessing these mourning rituals firsthand can play into those images. Although students who are survivors of a suicide by a classmate may initially be angry or upset that they are not allowed to set up a locker memorial, they typically understand the rationale for refraining from such activities when it is explained to them. Finally, just as it is important not to glamorize the student who died, however, neither should he or she be vilified. Instead, a message of "a good person who made a bad choice" is appropriate.

Do Not Announce the Student Death Over the Intercom or Other Public Address System

It is best if the death is announced in small groups, such as in a homeroom class, where faculty can follow predetermined protocols for announcing the death. In this way, teachers and staff can watch for extreme reactions from individual students, which may be indicative of increased risk.

Do Not Hold In-School Memorials or Cancel Classes or School

Again, the goal is to reduce the possibility that members of the school community overidentify with the deceased student. In one high school nearby, the funeral service for a student who died by suicide was held in the school auditorium. The following year on the anniversary of the funeral, there was a copycat suicide. Within the last two years, there have been three more student suicides at the school.

Never Discuss Suicide as a "Way to End Pain"

Suicide does not end pain. Suicide *causes* pain for everyone who is left behind. Suicide survivors are left with the burden and sadness of the suicide death for the rest of their lives. It is natural for adults to try to explain a suicide death to a young person by saying something like "He was in such pain, he just couldn't go on. He killed himself as a way to end the pain." But that message can inadvertently teach young people that suicide is a way to make their pain go away.

Minimize Discussion of the Details of the Suicide Death

Students can ask a lot of questions, and it is easy to get caught up in the details of the death. Too many details can encourage contagion. Students learn from hearing the story of the student death, and copycat suicides are the result of modeling the behaviors.

Thus, in an effort to minimize contagion, a postvention protocol takes care to implement strategies that allow students to grieve without increasing suicide risk for a segment of the school population. From this perspective, then, it is easy to see how many (well-intentioned) errors were made at the school with the two student suicides. School officials had a school assembly and campus memorial service, canceling classes to encourage attendance. These events may have allowed the second student, who was unpopular and isolated, to begin to believe that the way to gain attention and acceptance at the school was through his own death. The first student who died was a popular athlete, which may have contributed to the inappropriate modeling by the second student. It is possible that the second student sat at those events and imagined what they might say about him or how his classmates might grieve his death. Additionally, the school allowed specific details of the student death to be discussed at length, and the copycat suicide used the same, unique method of death. Next, students were allowed to set up memorials to the first student, with a special banner and pins. Again, for a segment of the student body, including perhaps the second student who died, this became an appealing way to gain popularity or fame within the school. Although it is clear that none of these activities *caused* the death of the second student, it is possible that they inadvertently contributed to an atmosphere that made suicide more appealing for that student.

When we met with student leaders at the school after the second death, many were angry because they were not allowed to wear armbands or have special memorial pins for the second student. By this time, school officials had investigated appropriate postvention responses and learned that these types of memorials can unintentionally glamorize the student death. Students, however, thought the administration was being "unfair." They accused the school officials of "liking the first student better" or "trying to keep the students quiet" so parents of future students would not think poorly of the school. When we met with groups of students, we explained to them why these types of memorials, although well intentioned, could increase risk for their psychologically vulnerable classmates. Although most students understood and backed away from their original stance, one young woman got very angry. She challenged, "Are you telling me that because of the 5% of the students here who are psychologically unhealthy and might take it the wrong way, the 95% of us who are healthy can't have the memorials and services we want to have?" Our answer, "Yes. That is *exactly* what we are saying." The reality is that those of us who are relatively healthy psychologically *do have a responsibility* to help protect and assist those of us who are not. It is a tough life lesson but an important one. No one, not even this young woman, really *wants* to contribute to someone else's emotional pain. When she stopped and thought about whether her right to wear a special pin or hang up a sign was really worth the possibility of losing another classmate to suicide, of course she backed away.

If a comprehensive suicide postvention plan had been in place before the first student suicide, none of this would have happened. The administration would have had a consistent response to both student suicides (and it is possible that the second suicide may not have occurred), and students would have been given factual information and education about why the postvention choices were made.

Goal 2: Provide Support

Of course, at least part of the reason that the students were angry and upset after the second student suicide had very little to do with the administration or the school and everything to do with the fact that they were feeling scared, guilty, angry, sad, and overwhelmed in general. At least some of the students were looking for a person (or group) to lash out against in order to help make some sense of their mixed feelings. The idea that anger is displaced (e.g., expressed against another person or object rather than the true object of our feelings) is commonplace. We need only look at the child who is angry at a parent and kicks the dog or a person who is angry at his boss and punches his hand through a wall to see evidence of how this affects our lives. In this instance, the students felt many feelings, including anger toward the students who died by suicide. It is difficult to be angry at someone and sad because he or she is gone at the same time, and it may have been easier (or safer) to be angry at the administration instead. Of course, school officials made some choices that caused the students to be angry, but at least some of the wrath they were experiencing had very little to do with these choices and very much to do with the chaotic and uncomfortable emotions the students were experiencing. A postvention response that helped students process their complicated emotions in appropriate ways would have helped them navigate this difficult grieving process.

Suicide bereavement differs from other types of grief. Most suicide survivors (those who are left behind after a suicide) report feeling guilty and angry (at the person who died, at themselves, at others whom they perceive did not offer help, at God, or at the world in general). In fact, compared to individuals who lost loved ones to homicide, accidents, or illness, suicide survivors:

- Have more intense grief reactions than any of the other survivor groups.
- Are more likely to assume responsibility for the person's death, believing they should have done something to prevent it.
- Are more likely to engage in self-destructive behavior.
- Have higher levels of shame and perceived rejection (Bailley, Kral, & Dunham, 1999; Silverman, Range, & Overholser, 1994–95).

In schools, classmates who knew that the student was at risk for suicide, knew about the suicide plans but kept them a secret, or who became the "self-appointed therapist" to the suicidal student are at increased risk for suicide themselves. This is particularly problematic because research demonstrates that the majority of young people who know a peer is suicidal do not take appropriate steps to intervene. In fact, although 85% of teenagers who die by suicide tell someone they plan to kill themselves, and 90% demonstrate clear warning signs, only 25% of teenagers say that they would tell an adult if they knew a peer was suicidal (Helms, 2003). As a result, after a suicide, there may be many members of the student body who are grieving intensely and who are at increased risk for suicide. These individuals need extra support and assistance to work through the grieving process.

Postvention strategies must include several different mechanisms for emotional support. Students who need immediate assistance must be given easy access to counseling and care, and ongoing help must be available (either at the school or through identified off-campus providers).

Goal 3: Address Social Stigma

Suicide is surrounded by stigma and taboo. As difficult as it is to talk about mental health in general, discussions about suicide are even more challenging. One of the dangers of the stigma surrounding suicide is that it contributes to the development of suicide myths. One of the most damaging suicide myths is the belief that talking about suicide leads to more suicidal behaviors. In reality, talking about suicide *in appropriate ways* can be an important component of suicide prevention. A study of more than 2,000 teenagers found depressed teenagers were no more likely to consider suicide after it was brought up in class. In fact, depressed teenagers who had attempted suicide in the past reported that they were *less likely* to be suicidal or upset after the discussion (Gould et al., 2005). Giving young people the skills, information, *and permission* to talk about mental health, mental illness, and suicide prevention is critical. Appropriate postvention approaches help reduce the stigma surrounding suicide and give survivors the skills and support they need to talk about suicide and the impact it had on their lives.

Goal 4: Provide Information

After a suicide, rumors, gossip, and stories can race through a school and spiral out of control. In today's world of text messaging and social media, the speed at which news (and rumor) travels through the student body is nearly instantaneous. Therefore, suicide postvention strategies must provide accurate, thoughtful, and developmentally appropriate information to students about suicide and suicide prevention. In general, the aftermath of a suicide is not the time for school-based suicide prevention education. However, all messaging and information given during the postvention period can help provide accurate education about suicide prevention. Information can be disseminated in small classroom settings, in information sent home to parents, and through ongoing suicide prevention education that resumes after the immediate aftermath of the suicide. Large assembly-type education sessions have not been demonstrated to be effective, and if they occur after a student suicide, they may inadvertently serve to sensationalize the death. It is important to understand that taking care not to glamorize or sensationalize suicide *does not mean that it should not be discussed*. Quite the contrary. After a suicide (frankly, even before a suicide), suicide is discussed by young people. They talk about it, text about it, search the Internet for information, and journal about it. If they are not given accurate and helpful information, they will fill in the void with anything they can find. Ideally, schools should have ongoing, developmentally appropriate suicide prevention education as part of the curriculum, and a postvention program cannot replace this. Nevertheless, after a suicide death, it is important to provide students with facts about suicide risk and mental health resources to counteract the rumors.

Suicide prevention education sessions in schools focus on two important messages: Get help for yourself if you need it, and tell an adult if you think a friend is suicidal (D. H. Granello & Granello, 2007). These are the same messages that should be highlighted in postvention information programming. It is important that students know the available resources (e.g., school counselor, school nurse) if they want to talk with someone about their concerns.

POSTVENTION PROTOCOL

The most critical aspect of a suicide postvention protocol is a *set of written procedures and guidelines* that are developed before a suicide occurs, are disseminated widely so everyone knows and understands their roles and responsibilities, and can be put into place at a moment's notice. A postvention team that has been well trained and is prepared to step up and implement the protocol is essential. The American Association of Suicidology (AAS, 1998) has developed a general protocol for postvention in schools, and resources at the end of this chapter can assist schools with developing such a protocol. The following steps are general guidelines only and are adapted from a variety of sources, including the AAS guidelines, the School-Based Youth Suicide Prevention Guide (2003), the Maine Youth Suicide Prevention Program (2009), and the work of Brock (2003) and Weekley and Brock (2004).

1. Contact the police, coroner's office, or local hospital to verify the death and get the facts.
   - It is essential that the suicide be officially confirmed before the postvention protocol is implemented. Often it is difficult to conclude a cause of death, and a determination of suicide must be made by a medical examiner or coroner. Even the most obvious cases of suicide should never be classified as such without official designation.
2. Inform the school superintendent and administrators of schools where siblings are enrolled.
3. Contact the family of the deceased student to express condolences.
4. Notify and activate the school's crisis response team.
   - Use a telephone tree or other approach that allows for *direct communication* with the crisis response team.
   - Be sure each member of the crisis response team follows individual specific crisis response duties (e.g., crisis response coordinator, media liaison, medical liaison, security liaison, liaison with the family) that have been preassigned to each team member.
   - Operationalize the plan for communicating the news to students and parents.

5. Schedule a time and place to notify faculty members and staff.
   - If possible, set up a meeting before the start of the school day.
   - Prepare school personnel for possible student reactions.
   - Remember support staff (e.g., kitchen staff, custodian, bus drivers, secretaries) and any substitute teachers.
   - Allow time for staff to ask questions and express feelings.
   - Clarify the prearranged steps that will be taken to support school personnel, students, parents (e.g., grief counseling, debriefing).
   - Remind staff of the possibility of suicide contagion. Reinforce the necessity of following the postvention guidelines in order to minimize the potential for contagion.
   - Ask staff members to identify any concerns they may have about individual students. Clarify how to monitor at-risk students.
6. Activate procedures for responding to the media.
   - Announce how the school will interact with media representatives.
   - Remind staff members not to talk with the press, spread rumors, or repeat stories. All inquiries must be directed to the designated media spokesperson.
   - Reinforce that specific media guidelines are in place to help minimize contagion.
7. Contact community support services, local mental health agency, other school counselors, and clergy to arrange for crisis intervention assistance, if previously arranged.
   - Be prepared to identify and refer students who are most likely to be at high risk because of their close physical and emotional contact with the deceased student. Consider siblings, students who may identify with the deceased student, team members, friends, romantic interests, and anyone who was considered to be at risk for suicide prior to the death (e.g., those with preexisting mental illness who lack coping skills or support systems).
8. Announce the death to students through a prearranged system.
   - Make the announcement in person, in small groups or classroom settings. If possible, all students should be given the same information at the same time (such as in their homerooms) by teachers or other adults they know and trust.
   - Teachers and others making the announcement should be provided with a written list of procedures for announcing the suicide

to students and for identifying students who may need additional support.

- The announcement should be honest and direct, including only the facts as they have been officially communicated. If the death has not yet been officially classified as a suicide, simply acknowledge that the cause is unknown.
- Allow time for initial reactions and discussion, but limit details of the death.
- Frame suicide as a poor choice, not as a way to end pain.
- Use words such as "suicide death" or "completed suicide" rather than "committed suicide" or "successful suicide."

9. For safety purposes, be very careful about allowing students to leave school unattended.
   - Students should be encouraged to stay in school and maintain a regular school routine.
   - Implement an enhanced system to carefully track student attendance, and allow students to leave school premises only with parental permission.
   - If the safety of a student is a concern and the parents cannot be reached, contact the police.

10. Provide written information for parents/guardians as soon as possible so they can be prepared and available to provide support to their children.
    - The notification should include information about how the school is responding to the crisis as well as resources and information on youth suicide prevention, local referrals, and specific person(s) at the school to contact with questions or for more information.
    - Consider parent meeting(s) to disseminate more information or to allow parents to ask questions about how to help their grieving children.

11. Have crisis team available in the deceased student's classes.
    - Follow the deceased student's schedule to observe reactions of students and to follow up, if necessary.

12. Establish support stations and counseling rooms and publicize their availability for students.
    - Be sure to document who attends and the time of their attendance. Follow up with these students, as needed.

13. Make sure administrators and staff are visible in hallways and during lunch to monitor students and provide a calming presence for the school.

14. Provide secretaries or others who answer the phone with a prepared script to field telephone calls or to answer inquiries from people who show up at the school.

15. Use a prearranged strategy to monitor and assist students who may be at increased risk for suicide.

    ■ Provide additional survivor support services and education about suicide bereavement.

    ■ Follow up with these students (and their families, as necessary) for as long as needed.

    ■ Make sure all students have access to suicide hotline numbers.

    ■ Provide extra support through special events (e.g., anniversaries, special events, transitions), which can be particularly difficult for students to manage after a suicide death.

    ■ Give special attention to students in peer groups, friends, teams, romantic partners, and others who may be at higher risk. They should be encouraged to talk about their reactions. Attention to these students during the postvention period may help limit future suicidal behavior.

16. Conduct daily debriefing with faculty and staff during the initial crisis and postvention periods.

17. Reschedule any immediate stressful academic exercises or tests, but try to stay with the general school schedule as much as possible.

    ■ Keep the school open, and follow regular school routines to the extent possible.

    ■ While the school must be attentive to those who are grieving, it is important to remember that not all students were equally affected by the death.

    ■ Convey the message that while we all grieve, life must go on.

18. Provide information about the funeral to students and parents.

    ■ Work with family and ask, if possible, if the funeral service can be held after school hours. If this is not possible, allow students to attend the funeral with parental permission and announce the policy regarding school absence for funeral attendance.

- Avoid use of the school as a site for the funeral. Not only can this glorify the student death, it can also increase the likelihood that some young people will forever identify the room in which the service is held with death.

19. Offer ongoing grief counseling for students and staff.
    - Provide opportunities to process the grief, recognizing that this may be the first time some students have encountered death.
    - Allow students to express their feelings, but take care not to give the death so much attention that it may make the idea of suicide attractive to other vulnerable students. This delicate balance will require a thoughtful and considered approach.

20. Follow up with students identified as at risk. Maintain follow-up as long as possible.
    - Use outside referral sources for students who need more care than the school can (or should) provide.

21. Carefully monitor memorial activities or events.
    - Appropriate commemorative activities must be carefully selected to minimize the possibility of glamorizing the suicide.
    - Instead of memorial activities, encourage donations to a charity or to community-based (as opposed to school-based) youth suicide prevention efforts, such as fielding a team for a suicide prevention walk. Although students and grieving families may insist that their deceased loved ones be honored, challenging the energy into constructive events that help the living is most productive.
    - Advance planning regarding memorializing student deaths is strongly recommended. Such planning guards against giving students who die by suicide more (or less) attention than students who die by other means. Examples of student memorials include dedication pages in student yearbooks and newspapers, where space provided and information contained within the dedication should be consistent. Many school yearbook publishers offer well-thought-out guidelines for dedication pages. Overall, with all student memorials, a fair and equitable policy eliminates the possibility that popular students or those who die by certain types of death will garner more attention. A policy developed in advance can help school personnel stay with school procedure, rather than being driven by the intensity of emotions during a time of crisis.

22. Follow prearranged protocol for emptying the student's locker and returning personal items to the family. Allow the family to determine whether they wish to do this in privacy or have the school return the items to them. If the family wishes to empty the locker, provide a quiet time and support to meet their wishes.

23. Determine how diplomas, athletic letters, or other awards will be given posthumously. Plan ahead and develop a school policy for how graduation and award ceremonies will be handled. If, for example, the school will award honorary diplomas, the criteria should be determined in advance to provide consistency and fairness to all students.

24. Get support for the crisis response team, allowing team members to debrief from the secondary trauma of the postvention period.

25. Document activities as dictated by school protocols.
    - Use learning and experiences to update the suicide postvention protocol for the future.

WORKING WITH THE MEDIA

Unfortunately, suicide can be a newsworthy event. This is even truer when the person who died was young. After a suicide, it is extremely likely that the suicide death will be reported, particularly in rural areas or small towns. However, research has demonstrated that how the media covers a suicide death has a significant influence on suicide contagion. Recognition of the role of the media began in the 1980s, after a suicide death by a man who jumped in front of a subway train in Vienna, Austria. Following the death, television reporters engaged in a series of dramatic and sensational stories of the suicide that culminated in a reenactment on the evening news. Over the following weeks and months, there were a series of copycat suicides on the same subway tracks. It became clear that the news reporting itself was increasing the risk for suicide. An alternative media campaign was put into place, and within 6 months, subway suicides and nonfatal attempts dropped by more than 80%. Importantly, *all suicide deaths*, not just subway deaths, decreased significantly (Etzersdorfer & Sonneck, 1998).

In the subsequent decades, we have learned much about the ways that the media can minimize (or encourage) the possibility of suicide contagion (American Foundation for Suicide Prevention [AFSP], American Association of Suicidology [AAS], & Annenberg Public Policy Center [APPC], n.d.).

In fact, implementation of recommendations for media coverage of suicide has been shown to decrease suicide rates. Further, research finds an increase in suicide by readers or viewers when:

- The number of stories about individual suicides increases.
- A particular death is reported at length or in many stories.
- The story of an individual death by suicide is placed on the front page or at the beginning of a broadcast.
- The headlines about specific suicide deaths are dramatic (such as a relatively recent example: "Boy, 10, Kills Himself Over Poor Grades").

The power of the media clearly can impact suicide and suicide prevention. Responsible handling of suicide by the media can help inform readers and viewers about the likely causes of suicide, its warning signs, trends in suicide rates, and recent treatment advances. Although media stories about individual deaths by suicide may be newsworthy and need to be covered, they also have the potential to do harm if proper protocol is not followed.

When the suicide of a young person occurs, schools are often the first place the media will go for information. Thus, it is essential that postvention protocols include working with the media and proper media guidelines for reporting a student death by suicide.

It is important to note that just as with the young woman who needed to have the rationale for the decision not to hold a memorial service following the second student suicide explained to her, it is clear that most journalists want to do the right thing and have no desire to encourage suicide contagion through their reporting. In fact, most people want to do the right thing, and it is the responsibility of everyone involved in suicide prevention to share education and prevention protocols with others, including the media.

A story from our own lives illustrate the point:

> Our house is in a suburban setting on the outskirts of a large midwestern city. Our backyard faces a small city park, and on the other side of the park, sits a middle and a high school. One afternoon, a man rode his bike into the park just before school was released, walked into the small woods, and shot himself. Students leaving the school building heard the gunshot, and several young people walking through the park on the way home from school found the body and called 911 on their cell phones. Within minutes, the park was filled

with police cars, fire trucks, and emergency personnel. Students were rounded up and put in the park shelter to wait to be interviewed by police. They were frightened and shocked by their experience. Before long, the streets of our otherwise quiet neighborhood were filled with satellite television trucks, newspaper reporters, and other members of the media. Everyone was excited to get the "scoop" about the poor young, white, suburban students, innocently walking home from school, who had such a terrifying encounter with death. Parents rushed into the park to be with the children, and before long, the scene was chaotic. We could witness all of this from the deck in our backyard, and we were angered by what we saw. The students were being interviewed one by one by the police and, once released from these official interviews, were surrounded by television cameras and microphones. Rather than sit fuming, we went upstairs to our home office and printed out several copies of the media guidelines for reporting on suicide, took them out to the park, and began distributing copies. We spoke with anyone who would listen about the harmful effects of sensationalizing this story. We spoke about the potential for suicide contagion and the potential to make the students who found the body into unwilling "celebrities" in their school. We reminded every reporter we spoke with that the possibility of an exciting story was certainly not worth the potential of another death. The reporters listened. They understood. Most took copies of the guidelines back to their newspaper offices and television studios. That evening, we surfed through all the evening news programs on the local television channels and heard nothing about the suicide. The next day, buried on a back page of the metro section of the newspaper, was a small story of an unidentified man who shot himself in a local park. There was no mention of the nearby schools or the students who found the body.

We learned a very, very valuable lesson that day. If we want responsible media reporting of suicide, it is our responsibility to educate members of the media. Most of the time, they listen because all of us recognize that suicide prevention is a shared responsibility, and we must all do our part.

The next guidelines can assist schools in their work with the media following a student suicide. These guidelines are based on those formulated by

AFSP, AAS, and APPC (1998) as well as the School-Based Youth Suicide Prevention Guide (2003).

In general, the school official appointed by the school to work with the media **should**:

- Have an established set of procedures in place *prior to the suicide* to interact with the media during the postvention time period.
- Write down key points before talking with reporters and have some basic information about the school ready to share with reporters.
- Express appropriate concerns for the deceased student's family members.
- Provide appropriate factual information (typically age and grade).
- Acknowledge the suicide (if it has been officially ruled a suicide by a medical examiner), but avoid discussion of details of the death (method, location).
- Encourage reporters to provide information that increases public awareness of risk factors and warning signs rather than focuses on the suicide.
- Provide information about local and school-based resources for suicide prevention and crisis intervention.
- Share with reporters information about media guidelines for reporting on suicide and discuss the dangers of suicide contagion.
- Encourage placement of the story on the inside pages of the newspaper or later in the television news broadcast rather than the headlines or lead story.
- Frame suicide and the deceased person as a "good person who made a bad choice." Acknowledge that suicide is complex and there are no simple reasons why people make this choice. Include positive aspects of the student's life to provide a more balanced picture and decrease peer overidentification with the student.

In general, the school official appointed by the school to work with the media **should not**:

- Present an overly simplistic explanation for the suicide. Suicide is never the result of a single factor or event.
- Sensationalize, romanticize, or glorify the suicide.
- Use a picture of the student who died by suicide.

- Use the word "suicide" in the headline of the article.
- Dramatize the impact of the suicide through descriptions or pictures of grieving friends, families, teachers, or classmates. This could encourage contagion.
- Allow peers or classmates on TV or in print media to tell stories of their own experiences with suicide or suicide attempts. This could lead to overidentification.
- Provide details or descriptions of the suicide.
- Describe suicide as a "way to end the pain."

A complete copy of the protocol "Reporting on Suicide: Recommendations for the Media" is available through the American Foundation for Suicide Prevention (www.sprc.org/library/at_a_glance.pdf).

Finally, school newspapers can provide a positive venue for sharing information about appropriate help seeking resources. Many school newspapers (and parent newsletters) provide information about student mental health as well as suicide risk factors and warning signs. In the weeks and months after a completed suicide, it is important to keep this information available for students. Newspaper articles need not refer directly to the suicide but can simply be "healthy reminders" of how to maintain optimal mental health and where to go to find assistance. For example, before exams, before the start of a break from school (e.g., winter holidays or summer vacation), student and parent newsletters can provide a story on "managing stress" that includes important resources. At our university, whenever there is a student suicide, the student newspaper makes no mention of the death but runs an "informational article" on help-seeking and mental health resources. In this way, students who are not aware of the death are not given information about it, but those who are aware (or who are feeling emotionally vulnerable for *any* reason) are reminded that there are those on campus who are willing and available to help. These types of articles and public service announcements should be an ongoing part of every school's media campaign.

CHAPTER SUMMARY

Suicide postvention is a critical component of school-based suicide prevention, yet it is often misguided and handled poorly. All too often, school personnel wait until a student dies by suicide and then scramble to try to make good choices. In this context, it is almost inevitable that mistakes will occur, and the consequences of those mistakes can be devastating. If you are working in a school right now, investigate the school's policies and procedures regarding suicide postvention, and if none are in place (or if they are outdated), update them now. It is one of the most important things you can do to help your school be a place that limits the potential for suicide contagion.

SUGGESTED RESOURCES FOR SCHOOL POSTVENTION PLANNING

American Association of Suicidology. School Suicide Postvention Guidelines
> This set of guidelines is available for purchase.
> Web site: www.suicidology.org

Maine Youth Suicide Prevention, Intervention, & Postvention Guidelines
> Developed in Maine, but suitable for other locations. These guidelines have been adopted by the Suicide Prevention Resource Center as a "Best Practice" in suicide prevention.
> Web site: www.main.gov/suicide/

School-Based Youth Suicide Prevention Guide
> This free, downloadable guide provides helpful worksheets and checklists for school-based suicide prevention, assessment, and postvention.
> Web site: http://theguide.fmhi.usf.edu/

Violence Assessment, Response, and Postvention

6

Utilizing Face-to-Face Clinical Interviews With Violent and Potentially Violent Students and Their Families

FACE-TO-FACE CLINICAL INTERVIEWS

It seems I (Dr. Juhnke) am "interviewed" nearly everywhere I go. When I walk into the newest, mega-super store, I am greeted by a 17-year-old "sales counselor" who "interviews" me to determine if I "should" acquire the store's deluxe discount card. According to this "expert," he can determine if my purchasing habits match an established buyer profile. Supposedly, if my profile is a match the deluxe discount card will save me hundreds of dollars. When I order printer cartridges from the company's customer service center somewhere in India, I am repeatedly "interviewed" by customer service representatives. Despite my continued protests, the operators claim they "must" interview me regarding my printing habits. This is supposedly done so they may "help" me determine if purchasing the company's "premium multiprinter cartridge pack" is best for me. Recently, a waitress "interviewed" me to determine if I was "a sophisticated enough wine connoisseur" to order the restaurant's overpriced specialty wine. Wanting merely to enjoy dinner without the need to be interviewed, I left.

My suspicion is that our students and their families experience similar "interviews." Often they are nothing more than casual, one-sided conversations conducted by persons who have an agenda to sell a product or service. Most of the time persons doing the interviews are minimally invested in our students' well-being. Frequently the interviewers are far less expert than they claim. The detrimental result is a prevalent generalization that interviews are little more than frivolous conservations conducted by uninvested nonexperts attempting to benefit by the student's pressing needs.

When it comes to conducting face-to-face clinical interviews with potentially violent students, this generalization is anything but true. School counselors and mental health professionals conducting face-to-face clinical interviews minimally have master's degrees. Their graduate degrees require coursework specifically relevant to their students' developmental stages and assessment. In other words, school counselors are experts. School counselors I know are highly invested in their students. Often their entire focus is to benefit the students they serve. Thus, this chapter provides the opportunity for us to better understand the differences between daily conversations and clinical interviews. Furthermore, the chapter describes how to conduct face-to-face clinical interviews and utilize the VIOLENT STUdent Scale in a manner intended to aid your clinical judgment and promote higher probability toward a positive clinical intervention.

Daily Conversation Compared to Face-to-Face Clinical Interviews

Regretfully, some people mistakenly perceive little difference between daily conversations and face-to-face clinical interviews. They view face-to-face clinical interviews as simple conversations. That, in fact, could not be further from the truth. Kadushin (1983) identified eight distinct differences between daily conversations and clinical interviews that is important for school counselors to understand. These differences include:

1. The individual clinical interview has a specific intent and purpose.
2. The counselor directs the clinical interview and selects the content to be explored.
3. There exists a nonreciprocal relationship between the counselor and the student in which the counselor questions the student and the student responds.
4. The counselor formally arranges the clinical interview meeting.

5. The clinical interaction mandates sustained attention to the clinical interview.
6. The counselor's behaviors are planned and organized.
7. In the majority of situations, the counselor accepts the student's request for a clinical interview.
8. Discussion regarding emotionally charged and traumatic experiences are not avoided; rather such situations are discussed in detail.

Thus, there exist striking and important differences between daily conversation and face-to-face clinical interviews. The most important difference is that clinical interviews are clinically and purposefully driven. In this chapter, the clinical purpose of face-to-face clinical interviews is to assess a student's immediate violence risk. Only when the violence assessment is skillfully conducted can effective intervention follow.

General Face-to-Face Clinical Interview Benefits

In addition to the clear differences between daily conversation and face-to-face clinical interviews just described, clinical interviews enrich the assessment process and potentially provide student benefits. For example, clinical interviews are far more accommodating to students than computer-generated assessment instruments. Clinical interviews allow school counselors the opportunity to seek further student input and clarification related to unclear responses, conflicting statements, or expressed statements and presenting emotions—all vitally important when assessing potentially violent students who are confused and uncertain regarding nonviolent options. Thus, if counselors are uncertain regarding student responses in the face-to-face clinical interview, counselors can restate questions or request clarification related to ideation of harm to others. Also, unlike computer-generated experiences, which promote little counselor-student interaction during the test-taking process, clinical interviews increase opportunities for student interaction and basic rapport building.

Moreover, highly anxious, emotional, or agitated students are better able to relate to counselors during interviews than when simply focusing on computer-generated test questions. Therefore, counselors can verbally direct students to relax or calm down when necessary. Counselors also can verbally address the needs of angry or irritated students, recommending short breaks to keep students engaged and focused on the clinical interview process.

Thus, angry students receive necessary support, which helps validate them and enhances the probability of successful data gathering.

Another clinical interview advantage is that counselors directly observe students within the face-to-face clinical interview. In other words, they have front-row seats, which allow them to view their students' important non-verbal reactions to various subjects and topics during interview conversations. Undoubtedly this is one of the most important benefits of face-to-face clinical interviews. For example, counselors can gain significant clinical impressions from students who avoid eye contact when queried regarding possible violent thoughts or who become agitated when asked about previously displayed violent behaviors. Such nonverbal reactions clearly warrant further investigation and inquiry to ensure that the best counseling treatment and support services are rendered.

Finally, during the course of the clinical interview, students have the freedom to openly express their concerns. This is particularly relevant for students of diversity. Here, clinical interviews present opportunities for nonmajority persons to provide a cultural context to their experiences and projected future behaviors. Hence, clinical interviews promote vital two-way communications between school counselors and students. Most important, students are encouraged to educate counselors of their presenting concerns within the students' culturally relevant context. In other words, students are not merely assessed by an external source—the school counselor. Instead, students actively contribute in the assessment process by teaching school counselors of the cultural context in which their concerns occur. Therefore, clinical interviews encourage students to mold counseling to their needs. Here, students learn that they codirect the counseling process and have the ability to change their violent thoughts and behaviors.

Clearly there exist many potential benefits to using face-to-face clinical interviews, and we wholeheartedly believe in their use with violent and potentially violent students. However, like any good counselor, we understand that few things in life are purely good or bad. The same is true for clinical interviews. There are some potential limitations to their use, and we would be foolish not to mention these. We believe the most likely limitation is potential error. As "live assessment instruments," counselors can be fallible. Counselors unintentionally may give certain cues, such as facial expressions, voice inflection, and eye contact. Such behaviors could inadvertently maneuver the student to answer in a particular manner. Additionally, counselors may misperceive or misinterpret student facial expressions, voice inflections, and other behaviors (e.g., looking away when questioned). Thus, counselors could erroneously misunderstand student behaviors as attempts to hide or disguise the truth. Also, some counselors may present as disinterested to interviewed students. This could result in students disengaging altogether from the interview process. However, we believe that these potential limitations are clearly outweighed by interview benefits. Most important, we believe the use of a semistructured question format within the face-to-face clinical interview process engages students and provides a balanced opportunity for feedback and discussion.

Our Face-to-Face Clinical Interview Experiences

We have found face-to-face clinical interviews an indispensable part of the assessment process with potentially violent students and their families. Clinical interviews often allow us to quickly secure vital information related to potential victims and the manner of intended harm against potential victims (e.g., shooting, fighting, driving a car into a crowd, etc.). Clinical interviews further ensure that students receive a thorough face-to-face clinical assessment. At the conclusion of that clinical assessment, a context is created in which to view student symptomatology identified by more traditional, broad spectrum assessments, such as the Minnesota Multiphasic Personality Inventory—Adolescent or the Millon Adolescent Clinical Inventory.

Here, for example, a more traditional assessment instrument might suggest the student responded in a manner consistent to others of the same age who are angry, hostile, depressed, and experiencing familial stressors. Responding in such a manner on a testing instrument is not the same as being angry, hostile, depressed, and experiencing familial stressors. Thus, the clinical interview is used as a means to both support and discard the broader generalizations generated via the testing instrument. More important, however, information generated by traditional testing instruments needs to be placed within the context of the information gathered during the student-counselor face-to-face clinical interview. In other words, the face-to-face clinical interview serves as the foundational lens to any assessment. All other assessment pieces are filtered through this foundational lens. Information that does not fit is discarded, whereas information that matches the information gathered via the face-to-face interview is used to supplement the school counselor's clinical judgment.

Concomitantly, face-to-face clinical interviews provide multisystemic contexts that aid counselors in understanding the violent behaviors and pressing needs in the context of the many systems in which students are immersed (e.g., family, school, neighborhood, gangs, etc.). Only by understanding such multisystemic contexts from a student's point of view can counselors fully comprehend the stressors experienced by students and the violent behaviors that are displayed or threatened. Equally important, we believe clinical interviews allow us to quickly engage potentially violent students and promote opportunities for them to interact within a therapeutically safe and inviting professional relationship.

In general, the potentially violent and violent students we have interviewed readily participate in clinical interviews, even when they have flatly refused to participate in more traditional psychological testing. Thus, when we believe students demonstrate a potential for violence, we typically begin by engaging them in general conversation. Once students perceive that we are invested in helping them resolve their pressing concern (which most often is the impetus for the violent thinking and threats), they generally become more comfortable and their overt anger within the assessment lessens. Only then do we ask if they would be willing to help us understand how the violent behavior will be helpful. After all, what child or adolescent does not want to tell others about perceived injustices or feelings of ill treatment? Once we respond to any potential student questions related to the proposed clinical interview process, we describe the purpose of the clinical interview and indicate how the information obtained will be used.

It is critical to indicate that the interview's purpose is to learn how the counselor can be helpful to students and to determine if students pose a significant threat or danger to themselves or others. Additionally, students need to be informed as to how information obtained will be used. Thus, you must tell students how the information gathered via the clinical interview will be used to: (a) ensure the students' safety as well as the safety of others; (b) learn whether further assessment is warranted; and (c) determine whether a secure or more structured environment, such as a hospital, foster care, or juvenile detention setting, is necessary. It is imperative to let both students and their parents know that if you perceive a threat of danger, you will be required to respond accordingly. Such responses may require: (a) breaking student-counselor confidentiality by informing student-identified victims (e.g., students, parents of students, teachers, administrators, etc.); (b) making required reports to agencies such as Child Protective Services; or (c) placing students in restrictive environments to ensure their or others' safety. If information derived from the clinical interview is to be used in any other manner, the intended use must be clearly described to both students and their parents. If the student is a minor, which is nearly always the case, we seek written permission from the parents (i.e., parents, guardians, etc.,) to conduct the interview. Such permission is always obtained prior to the interview process.

Should students or parents indicate an unwillingness to participate—a rarity given that most students and parents we encounter report either relief that someone "finally cares" or appreciation for demonstrating sincere and respectful interest in them—we typically indicate that nonparticipation virtually guarantees school expulsion for a very lengthy time and that students will be required to complete a battery of psychological tests and interviews before they are even considered potentially eligible to return. Nonparticipating students perceived at great risk for violent behaviors may be placed in more restrictive settings, where they will be monitored and assessed until sufficient information can be gathered to make an informed determination related to their violent risk potential.

The intent of the statements is not to threaten or intimidate. Rather, the statements merely reflect reality. When school administrators are faced with potentially violent students who refuse to participate in the assessment process and whose parents refuse to require the students to participate, the school must act to ensure its students' safety and to insulate the school district from potential liability risks. Thus, until it is determined that students identified as warranting a violence assessment are not an imminent violence risk, it is likely that they will be prohibited from returning to school. When presented with such information and the gravity of the situation, most students and their parents comply with the assessment process.

Empowering Students During the Interview

Often potentially violent and violent students feel disempowered and defensive. Therefore, we have found it important to explain to students that they control the clinical interview and may stop the interview at any time. Only rarely have students completely stopped a clinical interview. However, giving students both the permission and authority to stop the interview seems to dispel most of their concerns and reminds them that they control the assessment interview process.

Should students request that the interview be stopped, we typically respond to the request and later ask the reasons for the requested stoppage. For example, are the students becoming exhausted from the interviews, or do specific questions engender unpleasant memories? Often we ask those stopping the interviews if they wish to take a short break or if they would like to discuss another topic specific to the clinical interview. We find that it is important to stay with the students and attempt to engage them in nonclinical conversation if such conversations are not threatening or bothersome to the student. Here our intent is to continue to build rapport and continually engage students in general conversation. During this time we often ask questions related to persons perceived as being supportive to them (e.g., friends, teachers, family members, etc.) and enjoyed activities (e.g., sports, games, extracurricular activities, etc.). Once students again seem comfortable and able to proceed, we reinitiate the clinical interview. Should the students refuse or become too emotionally distraught to continue the clinical interview, counselors should note what questions prompted the request to discontinue. For example, were the questions related to a girlfriend or boyfriend? If so, attaining further information specific to this person and potential issues surrounding this area are important. Should students refuse to continue the interview or respond to queries related to the disconcerting subject area, clarifying data obtained via clinical interviews with family members or friends may be helpful.

Violence Question Core

Face-to-face clinical interviews have long been reported as demonstrating significant assessment utility and have been utilized within successful clinical practice (Vacc & Juhnke, 1997). Most frequently, clinical interviews focus on the specific behaviors, symptoms, or events being assessed within the student-counselor interview. Related to this book, clinical interview topics revolve around life-threatening behaviors, such as student-to-student violence. Thus, the question core, or central focus of clinical interviews related to this chapter, specifically focus on three core areas—frequency, strength, and duration—and an ancillary substance abuse-addictions area.

The first core area relates to the *frequency* of violent thoughts. In other words, how often does the student have thoughts of violence toward others? Are these violent thoughts infrequent (e.g., once a year), occasional (e.g., three or four times a year), or markedly frequent (e.g., two or more times per hour)? We ask such questions in a straightforward manner.

Counselor:	John you say you have had thoughts of stabbing Brian. It is 9 AM now. How many times have you thought about stabbing Brian today?
Student:	I don't know . . . probably 30 times.
Counselor:	So, you've had thoughts of stabbing Brian 30 times today?
Student:	Yes.
Counselor:	What time did you get up today?
Student:	About 7:30.
Counselor:	So between 7:30 and 9 AM today you have thought about stabbing Brian about 30 times?
Student:	Yep . . . maybe more.
Counselor:	How many more?
Student:	Maybe 35 or 40 times. I just keep thinking about stabbing that punk.
Counselor:	Did you have thoughts about stabbing Brian yesterday?
Student:	Yes. When I saw Brian stealing my backpack yesterday afternoon, I kept thinking to myself, "I am going to stab that punk."
Counselor:	Before that time, had you thought about stabbing Brian?
Student:	Nope. It all started yesterday after I saw him take my backpack off the bus.
Counselor:	How many times did you think about stabbing or hurting Brian yesterday after you got off the bus?
Student:	Lots of times. I just kept thinking about it and thinking about it. Maybe 100 times or more. I guess I kept thinking about it until I feel asleep. Then I thought about stabbing him first thing when I got up this morning. He might steal from others. But that is the last time he will steal from me.

In this vignette, we learn that the onset of the violent behavior ruminations began as a result of the belief that Brian had stolen this student's backpack. The student reports that he thought about stabbing Brian "100 times or more" last night. And today he has already thought about stabbing Brian on

30 or more occasions. This violent thought frequency is clearly noteworthy and warrants immediate intervention to ensure Brian's safety.

The second core question area relates to the *strength* of the violent thoughts. Is the strength of each violent thought nonchalantly considered (e.g., "I could punch Brian"). Or is the strength of the violent thought so powerful that the student concentrates and ruminates on the thoughts (e.g., "I hate Brian and must kill him"). At more extreme strength levels, students feel they "must" or "should" act on their violent thoughts. In particular, we are looking to ascertain the strength or intensity of the violent thoughts. Depending on the age and developmental level of the student, it is helpful to utilize questions related to strength in the form of a scaling question. Here, 0 represents a total lack of strength or intensity surrounding the violent thought. At the opposite end of the continuum, a 10 represents overwhelming strength that causes violent rumination. Consider the next vignette.

Counselor: Alex, on a scale of 0 to 10, where 0 indicates you just simply thought about stabbing Brian but had no intention of really stabbing him and forgot about stabbing him immediately after thinking of it, and 10 meaning that you not only thought about stabbing Brian but that you actually intended to stab Brian, what kind of score would you say matches your thoughts last night of stabbing Brian?

Student: Beats me . . . I guess I'd give myself a 9. If he would have been standing by me, I would have stabbed him. Each time I thought about stabbing him, I would think to myself, "Yes, I'm going to stab that punk," and I would think about how he would feel the pain.

Counselor: So, I'm hearing you say that it wasn't like "I'm thinking about stabbing Brian." Then thinking about other things for a while or thinking to yourself, "Okay, I'm over thinking about stabbing Brian now. I'm not really going to stab him. I'm going to think about something else now."

Student: Right. As soon as I would think about stabbing that punk, I would start thinking about when I would stab him and who would be there. When my mom called she asked me to make dinner for my kid sister. I had to stop thinking about stabbing Brian. But, as soon as I fed my sister, I began drawing pictures of what I was going to do to him. You know, it was something like a cartoon. Frame one, I would stalk him in the hall. Frame two, I would push him against his locker. Frame three, I would stab him in the neck. I couldn't stop thinking about it.

Here we note Alex's robust violent thought strength and intensity. Alex self-reports a significant intensity level (i.e., 9). He describes ruminating on his violent thinking, which even includes drawing cartoon pictures of the intended stabbing. Each cartoon frame reflects part of Alex's premeditated violence plan. Such intensity again reveals that an immediate intervention is needed.

The final core question area is *duration*. Although duration and strength of violent thinking may present initially as somewhat similar with some potential overlap, duration in particular is specific to the amount of time the student considers the violent act. In other words, when the student thinks about behaving in a violent manner, how much time does he or she commit to truly thinking about the violence? Is the thought merely fleeting and brief, or does the student dwell on the thought of perpetrating violence? Thus, we are seeking to determine if the violent thoughts are fleeting or sustained in duration. Sustained violent thoughts or ruminations typically result in elaborate schemes on how to carry out the violent behaviors. Well-delineated violence plans require sustained attention specific to the intended violent act. Such sustained attention requires time or duration. Next we utilize a vignette to query Alex related to the duration of his violent ruminations.

Counselor: When you initially thought about stabbing Brian, how long did you think about it?

Student: I couldn't stop thinking about it.

Counselor: What do you mean?

Student: It was like, "Man, I want to pulverize that punk and make him pay for stealing my backpack." You know I would just sit there and think about it.

Counselor: So, each time you thought about stabbing Brian, you would think about it for what? Maybe 30 seconds or a minute at the most?

Student: No. I would just sit there and think about it over and over again. I bet I sat there for at least 30 minutes just thinking about how mad I was at him and how I wanted to smash his punk head in for stealing my things.

Counselor: When you went to bed last night, did you think about stabbing Brian then?

Student: I couldn't even sleep. I kept thinking about what he had done to me and how I was going to make him pay for what he did to me. All night I kept thinking to myself, "You've got to quit thinking about breaking this guy apart because you've got to get some sleep."

The duration of Alex's violent thoughts was significant. Thus, based on his responses to the three violence core queries specific to frequency, strength, and duration, there is little doubt that Alex poses a clear and imminent danger to Brian.

An ancillary substance abuse–violence area has become increasingly important within recent years. Specifically, we have found a robust correlation among violence ideation and violent behaviors when students are under the influence. When we first began to assess potentially violent students, we primarily assessed for alcohol abuse. Certainly any student under the influence from any substance can become violent. However, we noted students abusing alcohol often had increased impulsivity, diminished self-control and boundary-setting abilities, an inability to use verbal skills effectively, increased combativeness, and tendencies toward argumentative and aggressive behaviors. Certainly not all students under the influence of alcohol become violent. However, a sizable portion of those under the influence of alcohol do act in violent ways. Therefore, students who abuse alcohol are at increased risk of violent behaviors.

We have expanded our substance abuse assessment with violent and potentially violent students to assess not only alcohol but also two other substance groups that seem particularly correlated with student violence. The first group is central nervous system (CNS) stimulants, typically cocaine and methamphetamines, which increase hyperactivity and restlessness. Some students report that while under the influence of CNS stimulants, their minds "race." This racing seems to increase the probability of them ruminating over perceived injustices and thoughts of violent behaviors toward others. Over time, this CNS stimulant substance abuse can result in paranoia, paranoid delusions, or hallucinations, all which can further contribute to violent behaviors.

A second substance group we assess is anabolic-androgenic steroids, more commonly known simply as steroids. Testosterone is one of the most widely known steroids that enhance muscle growth via individual cell protein synthesis. Aggression, violence, and "'roid rage" are correlated with the steroid use. Due to the potential incidence of violence among students who abuse steroids, such abuse should be investigated.

Extreme bravado is one overarching clinical presentation occasionally seen with potentially violent students who are abusing any of the three substances just discussed, but especially CNS stimulants and steroids. These students often "get in your face." They brim with a menacing presence and attempt to intimidate through their defiance. Frankly, when students present in such a manner, there exists only a paper-thin insulator between unsustainable safety and certain detonation. Whenever such extreme bravado is encountered and substance abuse is present, the student warrants a restricted environment with detoxification and addictions treatment.

Projective, Circular, and Directive Questioning With Violent and Potentially Violent Students

Next we describe three face-to-face clinical interview techniques that we have found exceptionally useful: projective, circular, and directive questioning. Each provides significant information regarding how violent and potentially violent students perceive significant others (e.g., parents, siblings, teachers, coaches, etc.). The techniques are easily implemented and take relatively little time to employ. Yet their potential benefits are great.

Remember, however, that student responses are frequently based on perceptions, not facts. In other words, even if the students' perceptions are completely inaccurate, their perceptions are their "reality." And their misperceived reality, no matter how inaccurate and falsely skewed, can significantly disrupt treatment. Thus, even floridly inaccurate perceptions must be taken into consideration when constructing treatment and building potentially helpful alliances with significant others. Indifference or failure to consider even faulty perceptions can result in flawed treatment planning and inappropriate treatment alliances that ultimately will hinder treatment progress.

Interestingly, attempting to correct inaccurate perceptions may not always work best. In fact, there are times when attempting to change such inaccurate perceptions actually may rob students of precious treatment time, resources, and energy. Some students may even disengage from the treatment process, because they perceive your attempts to challenge their misperceived "reality" as an alignment with those whom they distrust and dislike.

For example, we once counseled a 14-year-old student who perceived that his stepfather "hated" him. Certainly, it is within the realm of possibility that this stepfather had me completely fooled. However, everything we observed suggested the man was highly committed to helping his stepson reduce his substance abuse and comorbid violent behaviors.

After investing considerable time and energy confronting this student's misperceptions related to his stepfather, we realized that my efforts actually were impeding treatment. Therefore, instead of simply assuming we best knew whom this 14-year-old could trust, we utilized Projective Questioning (to be described next) to learn whom the student trusted and valued. Once we replaced the stepfather within treatment with persons the student self-identified as important to him, treatment quickly improved. If we would have continued attempting to clarify the stepfather's commitment to this student, we have little doubt that the stepson would have completely disengaged from treatment and perceived that we and the stepfather were working in unison to place him in detention.

Projective Questioning

Counselors using projective questioning typically ask students to use from one to five words to describe someone (e.g., parent, sibling, teacher), an experience (e.g., being mandated by the court to participate in a violence assessment), a violent behavior (e.g., fighting), or a calming behavior (e.g., breathing exercises). When counseling violent and potentially violent students, the primary intent of projective questioning is to gain increased understanding of the student's perceptions and to better understand how these perceptions can be used to promote effective treatment.

Therefore, a common projective questioning query would be:

Counselor: What four words would you use to describe your mother?

Here the intent is to learn how the student perceives his or her mother. Responses provide greater insight as to the degree the mother initially should be involved in treatment. For example, if the student responds by describing mother as "castrating," "hateful," "repulsive," and "domineering," the counselor may wish to utilize individual counseling initially without the mother's significant involvement. Conversely, should the student report mother as "supportive," "loving," "always there for me," and "kind," the mother's involvement during the initial sessions may be helpful. Thus, projective questioning can serve as a means for students to describe others within their immediate milieu and to indicate what can be done to address their most pressing needs.

Another projective questioning technique is to promote student insight and learn how the student experiences acts of violence.

> Counselor: What three words would you use to describe how you
> felt when you hit Kshawn?"

Should the student say "powerful," "in control," and "fulfilled," the counselor might respond by asking about other behaviors that engender similar feelings.

> Counselor: Based on your responses, it sounds as though when you
> punched Kshawn, you felt powerful and in control.
> Tell me about other times in your life when you are
> not violent when you feel powerful and in control.

The intent here is to help students identify nonviolent times when they experienced similar positive feelings. If a student responds by saying something like "I never feel powerful or in control," it provides opportunities to explore nonviolent empowering behaviors that could be practiced and utilized in the future.

Circular Questioning

Circular questioning is similar to projective questioning in that each solicits students' perceptions and beliefs. However, this time, students are asked to describe themselves as they believe others view them. Here the intent is not to learn students' perceptions of others but to learn how students believe others experience them. Circular questioning is invaluable within the clinical interview process, because it helps students identify and build on strengths they believe that others see in them. Furthermore, students can consider and address weaknesses that they perceive others believe they demonstrate.

Frequently, students are quick to dismiss others' compliments about them yet they often give unfavorable remarks and caustic statements considerable weight. Circular questioning allows noted strengths to be utilized and built on and unfavorable perceptions can be considered and dismissed, or needed improvements can be defined.

When initiating circular questioning, it is important to learn whom students consider most important. This can be accomplished by asking a simple question:

Counselor: Rosa, which three people mean the very most to you?

Once these persons are identified, circular questioning can be used to understand how students believe each of the three persons perceive them. Here circular questioning begins with the most important person and continues to the third most important person. Thus, counselors might state something similar to:

Counselor: Rosa, you said your father is the most important person in your life. If your father were sitting here right now, what would he indicate are your most positive attributes and skills?

This question is important. It encourages students to identify attributes and skills that they believe persons important to them would identify. Counselors can then begin building on these attributes and skills within the counseling process. For example, should Rosa state that her father would say she is intelligent, smart, and kind, the counselor might ask how she could use her positive attributes and skills in other ways that would bring about her desired life goals without the use of violence. The intent is to use perceived attributes and skills in order to replace the students' violent behaviors with nonviolent behaviors that engender feelings of success and accomplishment.

If students are unable to state positive attributes or skills that they believe others perceive in them, the dialog might be phrased like this:

Counselor: It sounds as though you may not know what attributes or skills this very important person sees in you, Rosa.

> Let's think about it in another way. What attributes
> or skills would you like your father to see in you?

Here the intent is to learn how students wish to be perceived by significant others. Once these attributes and skills are listed, counselors might continue by asking a question similar to the next one.

Counselor: Rosa, I'm wondering. What things would you need to begin doing so others who you really care about could begin noticing your many already existing favorable attributes and skills?

At this point, counselors can help students identify ways in which they can demonstrate such attributes and skills.

Finally, counselors can use circular questioning to encourage new behaviors by having students describe their perceptions of how their violent behaviors perceive them. Similar to an "empty chair technique" where clients assume the role of another individual, circular questioning allows the student to "become" their violent behavior and describe how the violent behavior experiences or perceives the student.

Counselor: Reggie, this is the second time this year that you have been suspended from school because of your violent behaviors. You say you want to go to college, become a lawyer, and make lots of money. But because you got into another fight on school property and threatened Vice Principal Harris, you are suspended from school and your grades are dropping. You have reported that your mother has cried because of your fighting and that your little brother cries because he doesn't want you to fight at school anymore. Given all of this, if fighting could talk, how would it describe you?

Should Reggie indicate that fighting would describe him as weak and stupid, the dialog might continue:

Counselor: How would you need to begin acting so that fighting would know you are strong and smart?

The intent is to have students identify new behaviors, which would serve as indicators that they are initiating nonviolent behaviors and committed to using nonviolence.

Directive Questioning

Directive questioning asks students about themselves, their violent behaviors, and their presenting concerns. In other words, instead of asking students how they believe others perceive them or how counselors could help students presenting with their violent behaviors, students directly respond to counselor-engendered questions. A typical dialog might be:

> Counselor: John, I've heard you say that you believe others perceive you as being violent, and you don't like that. According to you, you have said that some of the people who you were friends with no longer want to be with you because of your violent behaviors. Therefore, my question to you is this: Are you ready to exchange your previous violent behaviors for new nonviolent behaviors?

Such questions have particular merit in that they provide counselors with direct student self-reports and allow students to supply important information regarding their beliefs and concerns. Self-report is vital to any clinical interview, because it also allows counselors to gain an understanding of the students' commitment to counseling and willingness to participate in treatment.

Thus, using the prior example, if John stated, "No. I'm not willing to stop hitting people and getting in their face," the counselor might respond:

> Counselor: I guess I am a little confused, John. You told me that you lost some close friends because you were fighting. You specifically told me that Charlie no longer wants to be your friend because you broke his arm. Before that you stated that your mother called the police and had you removed from her home because you hit her in her face with your fist and threatened to kill her. Help me understand how it is helpful to you to continue your violent behaviors.

Here the counselor is using information from previous directive questioning to confront the student about his statement that he does not wish to change his violent behaviors. The intent here is to attempt to get John to understand that he was the one who reported that he wished to change his behaviors and to create potential cognitive dissonance related to past and current statements.

Conversely, should John have responded by saying, "You know what? I'm ready to exchange my previous violent behaviors for new, nonviolent behaviors," the counselor could again respond with directive questioning:

> Counselor: I'm glad to learn you want to give up your old way of acting for new and more effective ways of behaving. What is the first old, violent way of acting you are going to give up, and how are you going to interact in new ways that aren't violent?

Again, in this case the counselor is utilizing directive questioning to have John identify the behavior he is going to change. Concomitantly, directive questioning provides him the opportunity to identify a new behavior list. These listed nonviolent behaviors would become those from which he could first select when he perceives that he needs to become violent again.

The VIOLENT STUdent Scale in Face-to-Face Clinical Interviews

Thus far you have read much related to face-to-face clinical interviews. You have learned the differences between daily conversation and face-to-face clinical interviews, read about the potential benefits of general face-to-face clinical interviews, read about our clinical interview experiences and how to empower clients via clinical interviews, and learned how to utilize specific face-to-face clinical interview components. Here we focus on the violence question core and how to utilize projective, circular, and direct questioning techniques. Given all the information you have read, you may question whether a specific semistructured clinical interview is warranted. The answer is a resounding yes.

Even under the very best circumstances, face-to-face clinical interviews with violent or potentially violent students can be stressful. Students can present in a multitude of different ways. Often such sessions are convened in a rush, and the counselor has little if any advance warning that a violence assessment will need to be conducted that day. No counselors want to enter a violence assessment without having a clear understanding of the types of questions to be asked or exiting an interview without gathering at least the minimally required information to make a logical and informed decision regarding the student's immediate needs. Therefore, an organized and deliberate gathering of pertinent information specific to the student's past and present behaviors, feelings, perceptions, and beliefs ensures that key data are collected. A semistructured clinical interview provides the foundation questions necessary to confidently assess and respond to your students' pressing needs.

One final comment regarding legal counsel is warranted before describing the VIOLENT STUdent Scale in greater detail. Remember, *always* inform the school district's legal department of any situation where students are at potential risk for harm or injury. Proposed interventions should never occur prior to the district's legal department consultation and approval. In particular, the district's legal counsel must consider all legal factors regarding the case to ensure that the district, school, school counselor, students, and mental health team are thoroughly protected from risk of potential liability. As counselors, we sometimes fail to remember the potential liability risk that may be encountered. Any proposed clinical intervention or assessment should be conducted only after legal counsel authorization. Without such authorization, school counselors may be in jeopardy of legal ramifications that could result in emotional, professional, personal, and financial costs.

The VIOLENT STUdent Scale (see Figure 6.1) was created by Juhnke and published in 2000. Juhnke's intent was to create an atheoretical, semistructured violence assessment scale that school counselors can implement easily and quickly during a face-to-face clinical assessment. Proper use of the VIOLENT STUdent Scale ensures that, at a minimum, critical violence risk questions are asked. The scale generates both the suggested risk of a potentially violent student for immediate violent behaviors and general clinical intervention guidelines. The scale is based on 10 student violent risk factor clusters identified within the literature by the United States Departments of Education and Justice (Dwyer, Osher, & Warger, 1998) and by the Federal Bureau of Investigation's National Center for the Analysis for Violent Crime/ Critical Incident Response Group (Supervisory Special Agent Eugene A. Rugala, personal communication, August 31, 1998). These high-risk factor

Violent or aggressive history

Isolation or feelings of being isolated

Overt aggression toward or torturing of animals

Low school interest

Expressions of violence in drawing or writing

Noted by peers as being "different"

Threats of violence toward others

Social withdrawal

Teased or perceptions of being teased, harassed, or "picked on"

Use of firearms that is inappropriate or inappropriate access to firearms

Figure 6.1 VIOLENT STUdent Scale

clusters are presented next, with a brief summary suggesting the reason for their inclusion.

Violent or Aggressive History

Students with violent or aggressive histories are at greater risk of perpetrating violence or aggression toward others. Thus, they are identified within this scale as being at increased risk for potential violent or aggressive behaviors.

Isolation or Feelings of Being Isolated

The vast majority of students who isolate themselves from peers or who appear friendless typically are not violent. However, within the high-risk factor cluster suggesting increased potential for violence, isolation or feelings of being isolated can be associated with students who behave violently toward peers. For this reason, students who isolate themselves or report feelings of being isolated from others should be considered at greater risk.

Overt Aggression Toward or Torturing of Animals

There exists a high correlation between students who demonstrate aggression toward animals or those who torture animals with violence. Hence students who present with either of these factors should be considered at increased risk of violence.

Low School Interest

The genesis of this risk factor could come from any of a multitude of reasons that by themselves may not evoke violent behaviors. However, in combination with other possible violence-related risk factors noted within this scale, students presenting with low school interest may have an inability to perform as well as they desire and may feel frustrated by such inability. Additionally, these students may perceive themselves as belittled by those performing more favorably. Thus, when challenged to increase performance or when feeling harassed by those performing at higher levels, these students may become violent. For these reasons, this factor has been included.

Expressions of Violence in Drawing or Writing

Violent students often indicate their intentions before acting violently via drawings or writing. Such expressions of violence should be assessed immediately and should not be easily dismissed.

Noted by Peers as Being "Different"

On many occasions after student violence, peers and others will note that the perpetrating student was labeled as being "different" from peers or was associated with some group that was noted as being "different." Hence, students frequently labeled by peers as being "weird," "strange," "geeky," and the like may be at increased risk.

Threats of Violence Toward Others

Any threat of violence toward others should be assessed immediately and appropriate intervention action should be taken to ensure safety. Direct threats, such as "I'm going to kill him," as well as veiled threats, such as "You better enjoy yourself this morning, because your life may come to a quick end after third period today," clearly are inappropriate and warrant immediate assessment.

Social Withdrawal

Withdrawal from peers and familial supports can indicate the student is experiencing any of a number of concerns (e.g., depression, helplessness, etc.) that warrant further assessment and intervention. When combined with other risk factors, social withdrawal may signal potential violence toward others.

Teased or Perceptions of Being Teased, Harassed, or "Picked On"

Violent students often have hypersensitivity toward criticism. These students report perceptions of being teased, harassed, or picked on by those they were violent toward. Thus, when hypersensitive students present with other identified risk factors, the potential for violence increases.

Inappropriate Use of or Inappropriate Access to Firearms

Students inappropriately using firearms (e.g., shooting at buses, airplanes, people, etc.) or having inappropriate access to firearms clearly have the potential to act violently and do so with a high degree of lethality. When this risk factor is combined with other risk factors, it suggests even greater increased potential for violence.

VIOLENT STUdent Scoring and Intervention Guidelines

Each of the listed risk factors can receive a score between 0 (complete risk factor absence) and 10 (significant risk factor manifestation or presence) (see Table 6.1). Proposed intervention guidelines are based on the total number of points received. This number can range between 0 and 100. Remember, the intended purpose of this scale is to augment the school counselor's clinical judgment. In other words, the school counselor's clinical judgment supersedes the VIOLENT STUdent Scale scoring and intervention guidelines, and application of this scale to the general student population at large who are not perceived as violent would likely engender an unacceptable percentage of false positive responses. Therefore, the scale should be used only when a student is perceived as being at risk for violent behaviors. The corresponding general clinical guidelines represent a minimal standard of care logically determined in conjunction with the school counselor and other mental health professionals and after consultation with the school district's legal department. Should the school counselor, mental health team, and legal counsel determine that the scale's general intervention guidelines are too lax and fail to adequately ensure the restrictive standard of care deemed most appropriate for the presenting student, the intervention guidelines should be adjusted accordingly, and the student should be placed in a restrictive environment that best matches the immediate violence threat.

Table 6.1 VIOLENT STUdent Scale Scores and General Clinical Guidelines

Score (Points)	Clinical Guidelines
70+	Immediate removal from general school environment; structured living environment required.
40–69	Counseling with close follow-up required; collaborative meeting with parent(s) or guardians; formalized psychological testing warranted; evaluate and strongly consider structured living environment placement depending on student's: (a) willingness to participate in counseling, (b) cooperation in follow-up arrangements and sincere commitment to enter into a no-harm contract, and (c) family support.
10–39	Assess immediate danger to self and others; counseling and follow-up counseling offered and strongly encouraged; parental contacts established; additional psychological testing if perceived necessary; no-harm contract.
0–9	Consult with clinical supervisor and professional peers to determine whether: (a) the student was attempting to present self in an overly positive, nonviolent manner and is in need of more formalized psychological assessment and follow-up intervention; or (b) to provide the student with information on how to contact the counselor in case a future need arises.*

*Warning: Violence risk assessment is a complex process and cannot identify all persons who will behave violently. The VIOLENT STUdent Scale cannot identify all persons who will behave violently and should not be used as the sole instrument to assess violence risk or suggest intervention. The Scale and it's generally suggested actions should be used as merely one component of a structured, multicomponent, and thorough violence assessment process facilitated by an expert violence assessment, threat, or safety committee minimally comprised of multiple clinicians, clinical supervisors, legal counsel, and a client or student ombudsman or advocate.

Thus, students perceived at risk of behaving violently and having lower scores, between 0 and 9, may very well have suspect responses that may indicate that they are attempting to present in a favorable and nonviolent fashion. Such scores suggest that students are indicating an absence of violent risk factors. The primary issue with such low scores is the incongruence between the counselor's initial concerns related to a student's violence risk, which originally led to the violence assessment, and the student's current score, which suggests little risk. Consulting with one's clinical supervisor and professional peers can help clarify whether original concerns were likely unfounded or whether such concerns suggest that the student's responses to the VIOLENT STUdent Scale questions are suspect.

Should the counselor's original concerns seem unfounded, the student should be provided information specifically indicating how to contact counselors in the future should he or she perceive feelings of anger or intent to harm others. Two follow-up meetings with the student to reassess risk for harm to self and others as well as current situation are warranted. The first follow-up should occur within 24 hours of the first assessment. The second should occur between 48 and 72 hours of the first follow-up meeting. The school counselor should document these meetings and the outcomes of those assessments. Should the student's responses appear suspect, additional assessment is clearly warranted, and depending on the outcome of such additional assessment, appropriate interventions should be conducted to ensure the safety of the student and others.

Additionally, it should be noted that the presence of certain risk factors, even by themselves, warrant immediate investigation and intervention. For example, any student making violent threats toward others should minimally participate in further formal psychological testing, counseling with case management, and parental conferencing until the school counselor and the consulting mental health team all believe the student is not an imminent risk of danger to self or others. Although these steps will not prevent all forms of violence, they are a means to provide a reasonable safety standard.

Students perceived at risk for violence with scores between 10 and 39 should be assessed regarding immediate danger to harm an identified person or persons. Participation in follow-up counseling should be strongly encouraged as a means to address any presenting concerns, parental contacts should be established, and additional psychological testing should be encouraged if believed necessary. Follow-up visits to the school counselor can be used to monitor the student's immediate condition and ensure that appropriate services are made available, should a change in the student's condition warrant more intense interventions. Giving students a business-size card with the local 24-hour crisis telephone number printed on it can provide them with the means to obtain help should they need it. A no-harm contract may also be useful. Here students promise the school counselor and trusted family members that they will call the 24-hour crisis hotline should they feel overwhelmed, "angry enough" to hurt someone, or "intent" on harming someone.

Those perceived at risk and receiving scores between 40 and 69 points are required to participate in counseling with close follow-up services. School counselors are obligated to contact parents or guardians whenever a child is considered a danger to self or others. A thorough risk assessment should occur anytime a student indicates intent to harm others. Intent may become manifest in a number of ways. A student may make a verbal statement (e.g., I'm going to kill Shannon tonight with my dad's gun) or may indicate homicidal intent in written work (e.g., journals, assignments, etc.). Artwork depicting the student demonstrating violent behaviors (e.g., dousing and igniting a fellow student with gasoline) deserves further investigation and warrants contacting parents or guardians. Thus, even students with these moderate scores should be evaluated and strongly considered for placement in more structured environments (e.g., foster care, group homes, or psychiatric hospitals specializing in the treatment of violent children) where the opportunities to harm others are reduced and effective treatment for potentially violent behaviors can occur.

Certainly students with these scores warrant more formal psychological testing and likely a more structured home environment. The requirement for increased structure within the current living environment or a more restricted environment, such as a psychiatric hospital, depends on a number of factors, including the school counselor's confidence in the follow-up arrangements and the student's and parents' willingness to comply with comprehensive treatment recommendations (e.g., individual counseling, family counseling, substance abuse counseling, etc.). Should the student and the student's family fully support the comprehensive treatment recommendations and a more structured living environment is deemed unnecessary at the time, a school interdisciplinary team should be mobilized to develop an academic and socialization support network. Child protective services should also be notified if neglect or abuse is suspected.

Scores of 70 or greater suggest significant environmental turmoil and emotional stressors. These students are at significant risk of violence toward peers and are likely unable to function adequately without direct intervention.

Those whose scores are at the extreme end of this risk continuum warrant immediate removal from the general school environment and placement in a structured living environment (e.g., specialized foster care, inpatient psychiatric hospital, etc.) to ensure safety to peers and self. Of course, such a placement requires parental support. Should the student be deemed an immediate danger to self or others and the parents are unwilling to appropriately support evaluation for a more structured living and learning environment, child protective services should be notified. In many cases child protective services can intervene to ensure that the child is placed in a safe environment until the immediate danger to self or others disappears.

Clearly one should recognize that the presence of any single 10-point factor does not mean a student will behave violently. However, a cluster of high-risk factors suggests increased risk. Additionally, high scores with single factors such as low school interest or isolation may not by themselves suggest potential violence risk but may suggest a student's need of more general counseling services. Last, it should be noted that students identified as imminent future victims or targets of violence and their parents or guardians should be notified regarding such specific and intended threats. One should discuss with one's clinical supervisor and with legal counsel the need for student and parental contact as well as the best method in which this contact should be made (e.g., telephone call, registered letter, etc.).

Undoubtedly, the VIOLENT STUdent Scale will not identify every violent student. No assessment scale will. The intent of the scale, however, is to augment the school counselor's clinical judgment and to provide a general template for the face-to-face clinical assessment, which also includes the violence question core and traditional psychological testing. The next part of the face-to-face clinical interview should include direct input from family members and persons who know the student well.

Face-to-Face Clinical Family Interviews

Face-to-face structured clinical interviews can also help the counselor better understand students' familial supports. Specifically, family clinical interviews provide a nonthreatening opportunity to interact with students' families. Such interaction can reduce family members' possible defensiveness, encourage students to see their family systems as more helpful and less caustic, and actually serve as part of the counseling intervention itself. Thus, direct, nonthreatening questions can be used to gain additional information about the student's violent ideation and behaviors. In addition, family members may be able to provide their thoughts or observations related to precipitating events or behaviors that seem to occur frequently prior to the student's violent behaviors or verbal threats.

Counselor:	You say that you have heard Ricky threaten to kill his younger brothers and sisters. What kinds of things do you see happening or hear being said just before you hear such threats?
Mother:	Well, he usually says those things because his younger brothers are goofing around and won't help him get dinner ready.
Counselor:	So, Ricky, what things are you thinking or saying to yourself when your brothers are goofing around and not helping you get dinner ready?
Ricky:	I'm thinking, "Mom, why am I always the one who has to get dinner ready for them?" It is unfair. I've got a lot more homework to do, and my homework is harder than theirs. Why can't they make dinner on nights before my tests? How am I going to get to college if I can't study? They should be making dinner, not me. It's not fair.
Counselor:	So when you were at school and threatened to kill Marco, were you saying or thinking to yourself that something wasn't fair?
Ricky:	Exactly. I was saying to myself "It is not fair that Marco is rich. He never has to work at home or baby-sit his brothers and sisters. He always has time to do his schoolwork, and when he doesn't understand his homework his parents get him a tutor. It is not fair."

In this sequence, Mother provides direct observations of behaviors occurring immediately prior to Ricky's threats to his younger siblings. The counselor asks Ricky about potential precipitating self-talk that engendered his threats at home. Then the counselor queries Ricky about having the same "It's not fair" self-talk prior to his threats toward Marco. Once such precipitating violence self-talk can be identified, counselor and student can establish effective ways to disrupt or dilute the self-talk and change the violent behaviors associated with the self-talk.

Clinical interview can also be used in a manner to engender change. A sample counselor statement during a family interview with a potentially violent student and his parents is presented next.

> Counselor: Ricky indicates that he is the oldest son in this family and suggests that at times he enjoys participating in a parental role with his younger brothers and sisters. Yet there seems to be times when Ricky finds some family responsibilities overwhelming, and he becomes angry. Certainly there are times when all of us have responsibilities that we don't find enjoyable. However, I am wondering, should Ricky feel overwhelmed or angry, would you be willing to hear his concerns and talk with him?

This statement begins by summarizing Ricky's perceptions and beliefs, "At times he enjoys participating in a parental role" and follows by explaining that everyone, at one time or another, has duties they don't find enjoyable. These statements are noncondemning to the parents and remind Ricky that all responsibilities are not enjoyable. Also, the statements imply that the parenting role is the parents' responsibility, not Ricky's. Thus, Ricky can be a parenting helper, but he cannot be a parent and should not be expected to behave like one.

Next the statement utilizes a concluding question and asks Ricky's parents if they would be willing to listen to his concerns and talk with him, should he feel overwhelmed or angry. Again, this question is made in a noncondemning manner. Few parents whom we have counseled have indicated they would be unwilling to listen to their child's concerns or feelings. As a matter of fact, most parents with whom we interact truly love their children and desire opportunities to engage them in conversation. Therefore, if Ricky's parents indicated they would be willing to listen to his concerns and feelings, we would ask them how he should present these concerns to them. For example:

> Counselor: Roberto and Marie, I hear you say that you would be very willing to listen to Ricky should he have any concerns or should he feel overwhelmed or angry. Should Ricky ever have those feelings in the future,

> how would you want him to indicate such concerns
> or feelings?

Here the intent is to have Ricky better understand that his parents want to hear his concerns and learn how he can present his concerns or feelings to his parents in a nonthreatening, nonviolent manner. The intent is also to have the parents become more aware of how Ricky may present his concerns or feelings and to encourage their listening commitment.

On rare occasions, we have had parents indicate that they are unwilling to listen to their sons' or daughters' concerns or feelings. Typically, these parents present as rather immature and angry, and they frequently indicate their children have relatively few responsibilities in comparison to the many significant demands they place on the parents. Consider this dialog.

Mother: No, I am not willing to hear Ricky's concerns or talk with him when he feels overwhelmed or angry. He has no "real" concerns, and he shouldn't feel angry. Ricky lives a life of Nintendo, Coca-Cola, HBO, and loud music. I work two jobs, and he doesn't lift a finger around the house. Ricky throws a fit whenever I ask for just a little help. I go to work at 7 AM, get out at 3:30 PM, and race to my second job where I wait tables and endure rude people from 4:30 until 8 at night. Ricky sleeps until 9 AM, usually is tardy for his first class, refuses to take care of his three younger siblings, and refuses to grow up.

Here, the counselor might respond by validating the mother.

Counselor: It sounds as though you're working very hard and feeling unappreciated. What is it that you are really asking Ricky?

The intent of this question is to open previously closed communication between Ricky and his mother and continue to assess the family's needs. Here is a likely response.

Mother: What is it that I really want from Ricky? I want him to be a man, to quit whining, and to help with household and parenting duties.

The dialog might continue in the manner shown.

Counselor:	Ricky, what do you hear your mom asking you to do?
Ricky:	She just wants me to be her slave and work like a dog around the house.
Counselor:	Maybe I am wrong, but I don't hear her asking you to be a slave or to work like a dog. Mom, are you asking Ricky to be a slave or work like a dog?
Mother:	No, I just want some help around the house.
Counselor:	Help me understand exactly what you want Ricky to do.

Thus, the counselor would attempt to have the mother indicate in realistic, concrete, behavioral terms the specific charges she wishes Ricky to complete. The counselor could help mother and Ricky establish a token economy. Here, based on Ricky's completion of identified tasks and corresponding time requirements (e.g., each night by 5 PM), he would receive meaningful privileges, such as watching HBO movies that the parents believe are appropriate.

The intent of these vignettes is to demonstrate how clinical interviews serve a number of important purposes. Clinical interviews assess the specific needs of Ricky and his mother and provide vital information regarding family dynamics. Furthermore, the counselor can use an assessment process to reduce family members' defensiveness while encouraging students to perceive their family members' behaviors in a more favorable manner. In other words, if Mother assigns chores to Ricky, Mother's intent is not to unjustly assign chores to punish Ricky. Mother's assigned chores are instead viewed as helpful to the functioning of the family system. Finally, the assessment process actually can serve as part of the clinical intervention itself or can provide a segue into an intervention such as a token economy.

Family Interview Contraindications

Not all families are sufficiently functional or invested to participate in family interviews with violent or potentially violent students. We use two factors in deciding whether to initiate family interviews. First we talk with the students being assessed. Specifically, we discuss the potential utility of inviting parents into the face-to-face clinical interview and describe how parents have been helpful in the past.

> Counselor: Ricky, some of the students we have previously inter-
> viewed have found it helpful to invite their parents to
> participate in the interviews. Often parents can pro-
> vide their thoughts about their sons or daughters and
> describe what types of things are going on at home.
> This frequently is helpful. At other times some stu-
> dents are frustrated over things at home. They want
> change. Having Mom or parents here allows students
> the opportunity to voice the ideas and suggestions
> they have for change. I think it would be helpful to
> have your parents here. What are your thoughts about
> asking your parents to participate?

As demonstrated, we *ask* for Ricky's thoughts about inviting parental
participation rather than *tell* him that he will allow parents to participate.
Asking whether he wishes parental involvement empowers the young man.
Concomitantly, as professional counselors who are not part of the criminal
justice system, we are unable to require parental involvement within the
assessment. In other words, we cannot force parents to participate in a family interview nor can we force students to request that parents be included
in a face-to-face family clinical interview. Instead, we present the potential
benefits of involving the mother or parents.

Some students quickly accept this parental involvement invitation.
Others do not. We believe that during this initial violence assessment,
the decision as to whether to invite parents is up to the student. At the
same time, potential consequences of inviting or not inviting parents is
the student's. The reality is this: The school administration will contact the
parents if a student has acted violently or is perceived at imminent risk.
Administrators have no choice. Violent or imminently violent students
will not be allowed to return to the school milieu without significant parental involvement. Students who readily accept parental involvement often
perceive parental support or anticipate that participation in the interview
process will allow them to change family dynamics in a manner perceived
as beneficial to the student. Here for example, a student who agrees to participate in the interview process may believe he will stay out of juvenile
detention if he participates. When students agree to the family interview,
we obtain releases of confidential information from the student and parents

and invite the parents to engage actively in the face-to-face family clinical assessment.

When students deny a desire for parental involvement and refuse to provide a release, we frequently find significant family dysfunction. Sometimes this dysfunction is engendered by the student's psychopathology (e.g., substance abuse, Conduct Disorder, Oppositional Defiant Disorder, etc.). At other times, the dysfunction results from chaos within the family system itself. Often family chaos is present due to a parent's addiction or personality disorder, such as Antisocial or Borderline Personality Disorder. Therefore, parental involvement in the face-to-face clinical interview may be contraindicated should it become apparent that the student will be in danger of harm if the parent(s) is involved or if extreme parental psychopathology is evident. Should we suspect the students' parents likely present with addiction issues or florid personality disorders, based on student or teacher report, our primary assessment will focus on the student with limited or no parental input. Despite the perceived psychopathology, parents are encouraged to engage in treatment either for themselves or their children.

Conduct Disorder, Oppositional Defiant Disorder, and Intermittent Explosive Disorder

Jacobson and Gottman (1998) rocked the domestic violence and treatment communities when they classified domestic violence perpetrators into two broad but separately important groups: pit bulls and cobras. Both groups are pathological and potentially dangerous to their partners. Jacobson and Gottman classified the overwhelming majority of their batterer research group as pit bulls. These men were insecure and needy and dependent on their partners. Metaphorically, like a pit bull that intimidates by barking, growling, and showing its teeth, these men intimidated their partners. They overtly threatened their partners and ruled by clear and evident acts of intimidation with the unmistakable threat of violence.

In contrast, cobras comprised a significantly smaller batterer group. Although the cobras are significantly fewer in number, according to Jacobson and Gottman (1998), they are far more dangerous. Most cobras met the criteria for Antisocial Personality Disorder. Thus, metaphorically, unlike noisy, snarling pit bulls that are readily seen and therefore potentially avoided, cobras are stealthy and covert. Their deadly bites come with little advance warning. According to Jacobson and Gottman, this group of batterers presented significantly greater lethality risk.

Although the metaphor is far too simplistic to address all the potential types of violent students school counselors may encounter, it does establish an important point. There exists a subgroup of potentially violent students who will not overtly present as a clear and present danger to others until they strike. This group will likely not be fully identified as an imminent danger via the VIOLENT STUdent Scale or even during an initial face-to-face clinical interview. As a matter of fact, members of this violent subgroup often understand how to deceive others and hide their true violent intentions. Many within this deceptive and potentially violent subgroup will fulfill either Conduct Disorder or Oppositional Defiant Disorder criteria. Clearly it is beyond the scope of this chapter to conduct an in-depth examination of these or other disorders that may be related to violent students. However, because of this potentially violent student subgroup, general descriptions of Conduct Disorder, Oppositional Defiant Disorder, and Intermittent Explosive Disorder are warranted.

Conduct Disorder

Jacobson and Gottman (1998) noted that the vast majority of cobras could be classified as having Antisocial Personality Disorder. However, students under the age of majority cannot be diagnosed with formal personality disorders (American Psychiatric Association [APA], 2000). Thus, anti-social elementary, middle, and most high school students are ineligible for this diagnosis due to their age. Yet there exist two disorders that often are later associated with an adult diagnosis of Antisocial Personality Disorder: Conduct Disorder and Oppositional Defiant Disorder.

In the case of Conduct Disorder, the most predominant characteristic is a pattern of persistent behaviors in which students deny others' rights (e.g., the student initiates physical fights in an effort to get what he or she wants) or ignore major age-appropriate social norms (e.g., the student breaks into cars to steal electronics) (APA, 2000). In particular, a Conduct Disorder diagnosis includes four main categories: (1) aggressive behaviors that threaten or harm other people or animals, (2) behaviors that cause damage to property, (3) lying and stealing, and (4) full violation of societal rules or norms.

Students who fulfill Conduct Disorder criteria will likely have a checkered history revolving around the four categories just mentioned. Often they will be identified by both peers and teachers as threatening or intimidating. In our experience, entry-level school counselors sometimes fail to recognize Conduct Disordered students, because graduate assessment courses often focus on "hellions" vis-à-vis "Machiavellians." Hellions are far easier to identify. They have clinical presentations that scream "I'm a badass. Don't mess with me." Even their dress often reflects "intimidation" or "meanness." Metaphorically, they are the pit bulls described by Jacobson and Gottman.

Conversely, Machiavellians initially present as budding professionals or politicians: intelligent, able, and invested. These are the cobras. They often dress well with expensive fashions and present in respectful and politically correct ways. However, do not be fooled. Machiavellians are just as shrewd, cunning, and scheming as their hellion counterparts. They fulfill the same Conduct Disorder criteria but do so in a manner that is often more difficult to identify initially. As a matter of fact, at first the Machiavellians are so liked by teachers and counselors that less experienced professionals are fooled into believing that whatever claims made about them are unjustified and inaccurate. I know. I have been there.

Some time ago, Kevin, a 10-year-old student was referred to me (Dr. Juhnke). His grandmother, Dorothy, initiated contact. Tearfully, she reported how the boy's parents had "temporarily" sent Kevin to live with her. Dorothy reported that Kevin's parents were going through a difficult divorce. According to Dorothy, the divorce had "gotten way too ugly" for Kevin to stay. She asked that I assess Kevin to determine how he was coping with the move and his parents' divorce. I really liked Dorothy. She reminded me of the way grandparents "should be"—invested in their grandchildren, caring, nurturing, compassionate toward her daughter who was caught in an awful divorce, and totally committed to the complete well-being of her young grandson. The only two things missing from our initial meeting were the American flag and Lee Greenwood's rendition of "God Bless the USA." I felt very positive about the referral and commended Dorothy for her interest in ensuring Kevin's healthy transition.

At our first joint session, Dorothy and Kevin were exceedingly polite. When Dorothy introduced me to Kevin in the waiting room, he immediately stood. He shook my hand with a firm grip and said something like, "I am pleased to meet you, Dr. Juhnke. I like the paintings on the wall. Did you paint them yourself?" Kevin was well groomed, engaging, intelligent, and articulate and strikingly different from most of my 10-year-old clients.

He was like a candidate running for office without the tie. I questioned Kevin and found him to be making a successful transition with no remarkable concerns or worries. He sat straight, began or ended most sentences with the word "sir," and made direct eye contact throughout the session. At the session's conclusion, Dorothy and I met. She appeared relieved when I provided my clinical opinion that Kevin was adjusting well to the transition. However, when I reported no remarkable reason to meet again, she became visibly anxious. She immediately stated that I "needed" to meet monthly with Kevin "just to make sure" things were well.

When I stated my confusion and asked why Dorothy wanted monthly sessions, she reported Kevin had "accidentally" shot his friend with a BB gun. The incident had reportedly occurred in the backyard of his parents' home in another state. Dorothy said that the incident had been "completely blown out of proportion." Reportedly the victim's parents contacted the police. This resulted in the assignment of a juvenile probation officer, who required monthly updates about Kevin to stop his detention. According to Dorothy, this was little more than a formality, and the victim had sustained no injuries.

I then invited Kevin to join grandmother and me back in the treatment room. Given the boy's clinical presentation, I couldn't conceive of this articulate and respectful student harming someone else. When I asked Kevin about the incident, he provided a detailed and benign story of erecting a target in the backyard with a neighborhood friend. According to Kevin, the boys took turns shooting the target until boredom set in. Then they began shooting soda cans. Unfortunately, one BB ricocheted off a can and struck his playmate in the face. The boy was unscathed except for a small red mark to his cheek. Given the details and my clinical impressions of Dorothy and Kevin, I simply *knew* they were telling the truth. Perhaps it would be more accurate to say that I *wanted* to believe that Kevin was innocent. Little did I suspect that the saintly presenting grandmother most likely fulfilled adult Antisocial Personality Disorder criteria and the grandson was the Machiavellian-type Conducted Disordered student that I would later describe to my future counseling students during psychopathology courses.

The next morning I left a message for Kevin's juvenile probation officer. When the officer returned my call, he divulged a significantly different story of a very violent boy with a checkered legal history. As a matter of fact, the story was so strikingly different that I requested the officer describe Kevin's physical appearance to ensure that we were discussing the same person. There was no doubt. I had been duped.

I have three reasons for sharing this rather embarrassing story of my inaccurate initial assessment of Kevin. First, we must be aware that many Machiavellian-type students who present with Conduct Disorder can be excellent at deception. Specific to this chapter's discussion on violence assessment, some rather antisocial students will deny any intent to harm others. Instead, they masterfully weave a relatively believable tale. Second, this story reminds us that we must verify the veracity of information and stories provided by potentially violent students who may fulfill Conduct Disorder criteria. Third, we must always consult with professional colleagues. In my case, I failed to adequately consult. Had I not spoken with Kevin's probation officer, I might have written a glowing report and failed to ascertain the truth about the boy for a long period of time.

Oppositional Defiant Disorder

Oppositional Defiant Disorder is a second common disorder found with potentially violent students who later may be diagnosed with Antisocial Personality Disorder. Sometimes it can be challenging to determine whether the student being assessed for Oppositional Defiant Disorder is simply strong-willed or truly surpasses the minimal criteria threshold for the disorder. One of the chief distinguishing markers necessary to differentiate strong-willed students from Oppositional Defiant Disordered students is time. Oppositional Defiant Disordered students must present with a general pattern of negativistic, hostile, and defiant behaviors that have been ongoing for *at least six months* (APA, 2000). Four or more of these criteria must be present to fulfill the Oppositional Defiant Disorder. The student often:

1. Loses his or her temper
2. Argues with adults
3. Actively defies or refuses to comply with adults' requests or rules
4. Deliberately annoys people
5. Blames others for his or her mistakes or misbehavior
6. Is touchy or easily annoyed by others

7. Is angry and resentful
8. Is spiteful or vindictive

It is important to note that these criteria are met only if the behavior occurs more frequently than is typically encountered with students of comparable age and development levels.

Comorbid Conduct Disorder or Oppositional Defiant Disorder With Attention Deficit Disorder

The students we have counseled who have been diagnosed with Attention Deficit with Hyperactivity Disorder (ADHD) are typically not intentionally violent. Should they injure others, we have found that the injury was less than intended and frequently comes about due to their hyperactivity. For example, an ADHD student may "jump" onto others who are standing in line and accidentally cause injury. However, it is rarely the intent of the student to injure or harm others.

More frequently when students diagnosed with ADHD intentionally injure others, there exists a comorbid diagnosis of either Conduct Disorder or Oppositional Defiant Disorder. The prominent feature with ADHD is an inability to maintain age-appropriate attention and an inability to concentrate on the specific task at hand. Symptoms such as inattention include behaviors such as frequently:

- Failing to pay close attention to details and making careless mistakes in schoolwork, work, or other activities
- Having difficulty sustaining attention in tasks or play activities
- Not seeming to listen when directly spoken to
- Not following through on instructions and failing to finish schoolwork, chores, or duties in the workplace (not resulting from oppositional behaviors or an inability to understand instructions)
- Having difficulty organizing tasks and activities
- Avoiding, disliking, or demonstrating reluctance to engage in tasks that require sustained mental effort
- Losing books and items necessary for successful completion of tasks or activities
- Being distracted by extraneous stimuli
- Forgetting daily activities (APA, 2000)

Additionally, many students with ADHD demonstrate hyperactivity by often:

- Fidgeting with their hands or squirming in their seats
- Leaving their classroom seats at times when being seated is expected
- Running or climbing excessively in inappropriate situations
- Having difficulty playing quietly during leisure activities
- Being "on the go" or acting as if "driven by a motor"
- Talking excessively

Symptoms of impulsivity must be noted as well. Such symptoms would include frequently:

- Blurting out answers before questions have been completed
- Having difficulty waiting one's turn
- Interrupting or intruding upon others

Such symptoms must have persisted for at least six months (APA, 2000). Additionally, some symptoms need to have been present at or before age 7 and have been present in at least two separate settings (e.g., home and school). Also, the symptomatology should be creating significant impairment in social, academic, or occupational functioning or relationships.

Intermittent Explosive Disorder

Another subgroup of violent and potentially violent students who warrant special consideration is those who fulfill the *Diagnostic and Statistical Manual of Mental Disorders*, Fourth Edition, Text Revision (*DSM-IV-TR*) criteria for Intermittent Explosive Disorder. Frequently, these students will have histories of nonpremeditated aggressive acts. In other words, these students act aggressively in the spur of the moment. Often they report a sense or feeling of arousal or tension just prior to their aggressive outburst (APA, 2000). After the aggressive act, they may truly feel regret or remorse. At other times they may even report feelings of embarrassment related to their unexplained aggressive acts or experience feelings of bewilderment, not being able to articulate exactly what caused the aggressive outburst to occur. The *DSM-IV-TR* requires specific criteria as evidence of fulfilling this Intermittent Explosive Disorder (APA, 2000). These criteria include several episodes of impulsive behavior that result in serious damage to either persons or property, where the degree of aggressiveness is grossly disproportionate to the circumstances or provocation (APA, 2000).

CHAPTER SUMMARY

This chapter has addressed issues specific to face-to-face clinical interviews, including differences between face-to-face clinical interviews and general conversation and potential benefits and limitations of face-to-face clinical interviews. We also discussed the violence question core and types of questioning that can be used with violent and potentially violent students. In particular, you have learned basic information regarding the VIOLENT STUdent Scale and family interviews. Additionally, we described family face-to-face clinical interviews and identified times when such interviews may be contraindicated. Finally, we have provided a general overview of Conduct Disorder, Oppositional Defiant Disorder, and Intermittent Explosive Disorder and have discussed the implications of comorbid ADHD with either Conduct Disorder or Oppositional Defiant Disorder.

Two final points are important. You have worked hard to attain your graduate degree and your professional license. Do not risk losing your professional license. Unless you are an expert in school violence and law, you should *always* consult your school district's legal department and attain authorization prior to implementing any assessment or intervention specific to a student who may present suicide or violence risk. In a day and age when lawyers themselves hire other expert legal counsel to ensure that they are protected from potential liability risks, it is clear that one should always consult on any matter that has potential liability risks and carry adequate professional liability risk insurance. We strongly believe that the individual professional should purchase his or her own policy, even if one is "covered" under the agency's or institution's liability policy. Additionally, violence risk assessment is a complex process. One cannot identify all students who will behave violently. Thus, it is imperative that a structured, multi-component, and thorough violence assessment process facilitated by an experienced violence assessment committee minimally comprised of multiple clinicians, clinical supervisors, legal counselor, and a client or student ombudsman or advocate be used when assessing students for potential violence and when making recommendations regarding potential interventions. Assessments and interventions by such violence assessment committees should always provide the greatest potential safety for all persons involved.

CHAPTER 7

Using a Systems of Care Approach With Post-Violent and Potentially Violent Students

When high-risk students are assessed as a clear and imminent danger to others within the school milieu, the response is clear. They must be removed until such a time as they present no imminent danger to others. More challenging, however, are students who present with mild to moderate violence potential, have previously been violent, and now wish to return to school. Decisions related to this population should never be made by one individual. Instead, a team approach that includes school counselors, administrators, teachers, systems of care services team members, parents, school safety officers, and potentially juvenile probation officers and judges is warranted. Only if the team can be confident that: (a) the student does not pose an immediate threat to self or others, (b) others within the school environment will be safe and not academically or interpersonally disrupted, and (c) sufficient structure and control can be arranged should the mild to moderate violence risk student be allowed to return to the school milieu.

SYSTEMS OF CARE (WRAPAROUND SERVICES)

Systems of care, also commonly referred to as *wraparound services*, is encompassing enough to provide broad-spectrum application to students who present with mild to moderate risk factors for violence yet who have been ruled out as requiring restrictive environments.[1] Additionally, systems of care is part of an overall effort to capitalize on more "seamless" care to students (Adams & Juhnke, 1998, 2001; Juhnke & Liles, 2000; VanDenBerg & Grealish, 1996). Thus, post-violent and potentially violent students, as well as their families, receive a unified provider front rather than compartmentalized treatment providers working from individual service silos with little if any service or goal commonalities. This chapter provides a systems of care approach that can be adapted, as necessary, to the individual student's needs and uniqueness.

Systems of care is a proven, evidenced-based treatment that has demonstrated efficacy (Friedman & Drews, 2005). The systems of care model has been identified as an innovative treatment and service treatment model that can be utilized effectively within both the juvenile justice and educational systems. This approach utilizes professional (e.g., school counselors, school psychologists, probation officers, etc.) and nonprofessional (e.g., grandparents, deacons, baseball coaches, etc.) persons identified by the student and the student's family as important to his or her successful counseling outcome.

Specifically related to reducing violence probability, mild to moderate-risk students identify persons they believe will be able to aid them in their goal of remaining violence free (e.g., school counselors, teachers, parents, coaches, etc.). The approach encourages the development of an individualized treatment plan. The plan is based on both traditional (i.e., individual, group, and family counseling) and nontraditional (e.g., photography, basketball, gardening, etc.) interventions. The goal is to help students become absorbed in nonviolent and nonviolent triggering projects. Thus, their attention will be diverted from violent behaviors.

Often students who have been violent or who have been previously identified as a significant danger to others within the school milieu receive mandated treatment, including case management services, from multiple mental health agencies and judicial systems. Instead of having these agencies and systems work independently with little coordination, the systems of care

---

[1]Such nonrestrictive determinations should be made by multiple mental health professionals who have: (a) administered appropriate psychological testing; (b) conducted face-to-face clinical interviews with the student, the student's family, peers, and teachers; and (c) determined that the student does not pose a significant threat of danger to self or others.

method establishes a joint treatment venture designed to meet students' needs 24 hours a day, 7 days a week, and 365 days a year. This includes both times when students are at and away from school. Such efforts require joint commitment and collaboration by mild- to moderate-risk students, their families, and school counselors.

STRENGTHS ASSESSMENT

Once mild- to moderate-risk students have been assessed by the team and the team believes that these students do not pose a threat to self or others and can be safely reintegrated back into a controlled school environment, the students and their families would participate in the systems of care strengths assessments. Here the school counselor, professionals representing other agencies providing services to the students (e.g., speech therapists, juvenile probation officers, etc.), family members, and persons identified by the students and their families meet.

The three primary strengths assessment goals include:

1. Determining how students and their families are meeting both the previously violent students' needs (e.g., providing a nurturing and safe familial milieu for the students) and their families' needs (e.g., sufficient food and dental care)
2. Identifying ways in which mental health professionals and nonprofessionals can be helpful to the students and their families (especially related to keeping the mild- to moderate-risk students violence free)
3. Providing students and their families kudos and positive feedback support for the effective behaviors they are implementing to both enable the students' nonviolent behaviors and promoting family functioning (VanDenBerg & Grealish, 1996)

The underlying purpose of the strengths assessment is to provide previously violent or potentially violent students and their families information regarding what they are doing well. Concomitantly, the intent is to help the family system build upon their strengths while reinforcing the students' nonviolent and pro-systems of care behaviors. Attending persons participate in their designated professional roles to fulfill this underlying purpose. Additionally, a spirit of collaboration and equality is fostered as nonprofessionals' suggestions and ideas are considered equal in importance to those rendered by professionals.

Initial Student, Parent(s), School Counselor Strengths Assessment Session

To help you better understand the systems of care strengths assessment process, the next vignette is provided. In this vignette, 12-year-old Maria presents as an intelligent sixth-grade student. She is an only child who lives with her 33-year-old mother and 58-year-old maternal grandmother. Maria is a second-generation Mexican American who resides in a medium-size southeastern city. Her family moved to this city when Maria was 3, and she has continued with her same immediate school peers from kindergarten into sixth grade. Approximately 25% of the students attending Maria's middle school identify themselves either as Hispanic or Mexican American, and 12% of the general school population has been identified as obese by the school system. Maria is markedly obese and has a history of fighting with those who tease her about her weight and diabetes.

During the last academic year, Maria was suspended twice from school due to initiating fights. She was later expelled for a third fight. During that third fight Maria initiated a physical altercation with a female student who teased her about her weight. Maria sat on the teasing student and repeatedly struck the girl's face, neck, shoulders, and arms with a sharpened pencil. The altercation resulted in severe facial lacerations to the other student and puncture wounds that required plastic surgery. Immediately after the altercation Maria was adjudicated and placed in a juvenile detention center. After three months in the detention center and two months at home with intensive case management, Maria and her mother petitioned the school requesting that Maria be allowed to return to school.

ENGAGING PARENT(S) AND STUDENT, DESCRIBING THE SYSTEMS OF CARE, AND IDENTIFYING POTENTIAL PARTICIPANTS

Similar to the ambience of a fine dining experience, this part of the strengths assessment process is vitally important to establishing a successful treatment outcome. Failing to adequately engage parents or students will inhibit commitment to the assessment process. Concomitantly, an inaccurate presentation of the systems of care process or failing to discuss the importance of appropriate significant others will lead to an unsuccessful treatment outcome. Thus, each is described in greater detail next.

Engaging

The first half of the strengths assessment vignette is conducted with Maria and her mother. Here the counselor simply meets with the post-violent or mild- to moderate-risk student and the student's parent(s). This is especially true when the student is mandated to attend counseling via the court or school system after a violent episode. In these situations, the student's violence assessment has already been conducted, and it has been determined by those assessing the student—typically a team minimally composed of a board-certified child or forensic psychiatrist; a clinical, forensic, or school psychologist; and a systems of care worker, counselor, or marriage and family therapist—that the student poses no immediate danger to self or others within the school milieu and is determined to be sufficiently invested in returning to school. Thus, the initial portions of the systems of care session vignette focus on engaging the mother and Maria, describing what will occur within the systems of care intervention, and helping them identify potential professionals and nonprofessionals to be included in the intervention.

> Counselor: Ms. Diaz, thank you so much for bringing Maria to today's meeting. Mothers are vitally important to the successful reintegration of students back into the school environment. Your being here today demonstrates to me that you are committed to Maria and invested in her school success.
>
> Mother: No problem. Maria and I want her to return to school and continue her education.

Before we continue, it is important to discuss the reason for addressing the mother first. Often, entry-level supervisees engage students first. Although there may exist some potential clinical advantage for doing so, we believe the more eloquent and sophisticated intervention is to first engage the mother. From a structural family therapy position, addressing the mother first confirms that mother's parental role. It further implies that Maria is the child. Talking to the mother first puts her in the "power seat." It confirms the mother's position at the top of the family power hierarchy and confirms that she is the person in charge within the family system. Had both parents been in the treatment session, the counselor would have said "Mr. and Mrs. Diaz" or "Mom and Dad." Hence, both mother and father would have been placed in the family authority positions.

Additionally, it is likely that Maria would neither attend nor engage in counseling had her mother not required it. In other words, the mother or whoever comprises the family's parenting team is critical to Maria's counseling engagement. Therefore, the more we praise the mother, the greater the probability that she will continue to require Maria's counseling attendance and ensure that Maria arrives at the counseling office. Should the mother disengage or sabotage treatment, the harm will be irreparable. Hence, the counselor needs to ensure that the mother perceives herself as a vital ally within the counseling and parenting process.

Furthermore, engaging the mother first has potential implications for this Mexican American family as well as many other families of diversity (A. Valadez, personal communication, May 18, 2009). Often within Mexican American or Hispanic cultures, the authority figure is the husband or oldest male figurehead (e.g., grandfather). In this case, the father is absent. Thus, the mother is the figurehead. Failing to engage the mother first would likely be perceived as disrespectful to her and possibly even to Maria. Engaging the mother first is the most clinically and culturally appropriate technique with this family.

Next the counselor engages Maria.

Counselor: Maria, how does it feel to be back at school?

Maria: It is good to be back. I missed my friends.

Counselor: I bet. It is always good to reconnect with friends. What do you wish to accomplish though these systems of care counseling sessions, Maria?

Maria: Beats me. My mom and our attorney just told me to meet with you just so I could get back in school.

Counselor: So, are you here because your mother forced you to come to these sessions, or because you really want to return to school, be with your friends, and most important learn?

Maria: Well, yes! I'm here because I want to be.

Counselor:	So, like an adult, you decided to attend these coun-seling sessions, because you want to learn ways that will help you stop fighting and focus on your learning?
Maria:	Yes. My mom did not force me to come.
Counselor:	Good, that says to me that you are mature. Lots of times little kids will simply come because their moth-ers force them to come. Unlike adults, they don't understand that learning in school is important to their jobs later in life.
Maria:	I know how important school is. I'm not a little kid.

Engaging Maria may seem simplistic to some, but it is critically important. Some entry-level counselors fail to provide communication balance. Despite having both parents and student present, they fail to equally engage one or the other. Maria needs to believe she is truly heard and understood. Given that the counselor has already spoken to the mother, it is important to provide Maria communication time as well.

In this case, the school counselor validates Maria's response but, instead of lingering on that response, immediately asks Maria what she would like to accomplish by attending the sessions. Maria's flippant response is met with a strategically placed "forced choice" paradoxical question: Either Maria was forced to attend or she wants to reengage in school and learn. Most tweens (i.e., students between the ages of 10 and 12) and adolescents refuse to admit that they are forced to do anything. Additionally, most want to prove they are adults. In other words, *they* make their own life decisions. *They* are not ruled by parents. Thus, the counselor's question provides an eloquent therapeutic paradox. Does Maria say her mother forced her to attend the counseling session? If she does, it suggests that her mother has power and control over her. Furthermore, should Maria indicate that her mother forced her to participate in counseling, it suggests that Maria is neither an adult nor capable enough to control her life. In other words, she cannot make adult decisions. Hence, we can anticipate that many students will deny that they were forced to attend.

Here is the paradoxical hook. If Maria truly chose to attend the session without her mother's coercion, she will have to prove that she is more adult-like than childlike. Thus, she will be forced to respond in a more adultlike manner within session as well as within the school and home milieu. This is exactly what the school counselor wants. Thus, Maria's response to this strategically placed forced choice paradoxical question catapults her toward healthier behaviors.

Describing

Now that the school counselor has engaged both mother and Maria in balanced communication, the counselor will ask what mother and Maria know about the systems of care counseling. In most cases, the student and parent(s) have little understanding of systems of care. However they may have heard of the process by either probation officers or others who have previously participated in such meetings and who believe the process is helpful. Remember, the intent here is not to *test* them. Nor is the intent to determine what they do not know. Instead, the school counselor wishes merely to provide an opportunity to successfully engage mother and student by praising them and providing positive strokes for whatever information they are aware of. Concomitantly, the counselor will help the two gain a fuller perception of the process and respond to any questions they might have.

Counselor:	Tell me a little bit about what you know about systems of care.
Mother:	The way I understand it, Maria and I will identify people who we think will keep Maria from getting in fights. We will ask those people to help us brainstorm ways to keep Maria out of trouble.
Maria:	Yes, so it's kind of like getting a group of friends and family and saying, "Help me so I won't get in fights."
Counselor:	It sounds as though you have done your homework. You are correct. Today we will create a list of professionals and nonprofessionals who Maria will invite to help her. Some people might not be willing or able to attend sessions. That will be okay. However, for those who agree to attend, we will be asking them to create new, nonviolent ways for Maria to interact. Remember those we ask are only helpers. The real work will be done by Maria. So, it will really be up to Maria to do the things she agrees to so she can remain violence free.

As demonstrated, the counselor simply asks what this family knows about systems of care. Mother responds first; then Maria adds her understanding. The counselor immediately compliments both mother and Maria, then describes key aspects of the systems of care process. Both of these points are critical to building rapport and ensuring successful counseling.

Reader, would you mind if we asked you a question or two? Do you like to feel capable and competent? Do you like people to give you appropriate compliments? My suspicion is that you answered yes to these questions. Guess what? The same is true for parents and students. Every time you provide positive reinforcement to their attempts to appropriately engage, the experience builds rapport. No parent or student desires to be corrected or embarrassed in front of family or friends. Parents often are anxious that others will perceive them as inept or, worse yet, *failures*. Often students are corrected so often that they turn off to anything said by adults and counselors. Simply stated, they turn off because they are tired of being corrected. So, whenever counselors have the opportunity to provide a compliment or praise to a student (or parent), they should do so. My belief is that only when the compliment-to-correction ratio is lopsidedly disproportionate on the compliment-giving side do parents and children later respond favorably to corrections.

Be careful not to overlook the school counselor's final potent statement within the last vignette. The counselor's statement reminds mother and Maria that no matter who is present or what is said or done, the true change agent is Maria. To emphasize Maria's responsibility, the counselor repeats this construct twice in succession.

Identifying the Number of Participants

Next, the school counselor helps mother and Maria identify potential systems of care counseling team members. Appropriate member selection is critically important to the success of the systems of care counseling and Maria's goal attainment. No more than 50% of the participants should be professionals (e.g., school teachers, speech therapists, counselors, juvenile probation officer, etc.). The other members should be nonprofessionals (e.g., grandparents, uncles, aunts, pastor or minister, family friends, etc.). Although the goal is to "wrap around" the family and students' every life aspect (e.g., school, home, community, etc.) to reduce the students' violent behaviors by increasing familial and community functioning and interactions, the systems of care counseling sessions can become very challenging if too many people participate. Based on our experience, meetings of more than eight members tend to become too chaotic. Thus, we would recommend between five and six highly committed participants.

Invested and Respected

Persons selected by the student and family for possible systems of care inclusion must be perceived as invested in the student and family's successful counseling outcome, and they must be respected. Nonprofessional student- or family-identified examples might include a revered teacher, respected coach, or favorite music instructor whom the student likes. It does little good to invite unknown persons who are unwilling to invest in the student's life. Students and family members will sabotage treatment if they perceive that the nonprofessionals do not respect and value them.

Contraindications

Persons who may be specifically contraindicated as systems of care members would include those:

- Whom the student or family dislikes or distrusts
- With an evident substance abuse or addictions disorder
- Who fulfill *Diagnostic and Statistical Manual of Mental Disorders, Fourth Edition, Text Revision (DSM-IV-TR)* criteria for personality disorders (e.g., Antisocial Personality Disorder)
- Who are actively engaging in criminal activities or have been recently convicted of criminal activities
- Who were previously convicted or arraigned due to sexual crimes or suspected of same
- Who currently or recently have evidenced or are suspected of psychotic features, such as hallucinations, delusions, and the like.

Additionally, persons who have demonstrated recent violent behaviors or who qualify for a *DSM-IV-TR* diagnosis, such as Intermittent Explosive Disorder, Oppositional Defiant Disorder, or Conduct Disorder, should be ruled out as potential members.

Participant Identification

To aid in understanding how this systems of care strengths assessment identification and selection process works, the next clinical vignette is provided.

Counselor: Mom, as both Maria and you already know, part of the systems of care strengths assessment process is identifying potential persons to invite to Maria's counseling sessions. Given that I will facilitate those sessions and that the court and school system have mandated both Maria's juvenile probation officer, Ms. Sanchez, and Maria's case manager, Mr. Osborne, be present, I believe it would be important for us to identify about four to six persons who Maria and you believe would be helpful in helping Maria be violence free.

Mother: Maria and I have discussed who we would invite. The first person we would like to invite is my 58-year-old mother, Rosa. She lives with us and helps me raise Maria.

Counselor: Grandmother sounds like an excellent suggestion, Ms. Diaz. Help me understand how you believe she will help keep Maria violence free.

Mother: She is very strict but loving. She loves Maria a lot and is home with her when I am working. Therefore, I believe Grandmother can set down the law when I am at work.

Counselor: What are your thoughts, Maria?

Maria: Grandma is already very helpful. She and I do things together like shop and make dinner and stuff. I would like her to join us.

Counselor: Who else have you thought about, Maria?

Maria: Ms. Elms. She is my favorite teacher.

Counselor: It sounds like you really want Ms. Elms to participate. Maria, tell me how Ms. Elms will help you eliminate your violent behaviors.

Maria: It used to be when kids teased me about being fat, I would beat them up. If Ms. Elms were helping me, I could talk with her rather than fight.

Counselor: Maria, that is an excellent idea. How did you come up with that?

Maria: My case manager, Mr. Osborne, and I thought that up.

Counselor: Well, you did a great job. Who else would be helpful to you?

Let us take a moment and review what occurred in this clinical vignette. Here the school counselor described those required to attend (e.g., Maria's juvenile probation officer). This is simply stated in the manner of Joe Friday from the old *Dragnet* television show, "Just the facts ma'am." There is no apology about required participants. The counselor simply states who must attend. Once these participants are named, the school counselor asks for names of three to five persons who will help Maria "be violence free." This is important for two reasons. First, by indicating the limited number of persons, it encourages mother and Maria to focus on those perceived as most helpful to Maria. Therefore, it helps truncate the identification of dozens of people who may only minimally be invested or helpful to this student.

Second, asking mother and Maria to identify those who will help Maria establish her violence recovery empowers them. It makes them the experts and implies that mother and Maria can make the best decision as to those attending these systems of care sessions.

Such empowerment is neither a gimmick nor a game. Who best knows the persons who can aid Maria in crystallizing her violent free behavioral patterns? Reader, have you ever gone on a diet? How do you typically respond when someone *tells* you what dieting foods you *must* consume? We do not know about you, but whenever someone tells us what we *must* do, we typically resist. In fact, we are going to prove them wrong. Instead, if someone provides us with the information necessary to make a wise decision (e.g., "You are at significant risk of diabetes, stroke, and heart attack unless you lose 15 pounds"), and we then decide it is in our best interests to diet, we are far more committed to dieting. In other words, when we make the decision to diet, we are successful. However, should someone attempt to force us to diet, there is significant probability that we will waste valuable time and energy fighting the mandate, and we likely will not stay on the diet long.

Incidentally, who best knows your most tempting high-caloric foods? Do you crave salty potato chips? Or are you more tempted by creamy, sweet milk chocolate candy bars? Also, who knows the times of day that you are most tempted to eat those high-caloric foods? We ask these questions to demonstrate that *you* know more about yourself than some diet advisor. For example, are you the type of person who can refrain from eating all day and then inhale everything in sight after 11 PM? Our intent here is to demonstrate that *you* know more about yourself and your eating patterns than anyone else. The empowerment we provide the mother and Maria, specific to their identification of trusted persons whom *they believe will be helpful* in Maria's violence recovery, is key to the systems of care's foundation: Students and their families know what they need most, and they know who can best help them secure those experiences or resources.

Next we see that when the mother suggests the grandmother, the school counselor lauds Ms. Diaz on her suggestion. As a school counselor who had coursework in counseling theories, what do you remember about behavioral therapy? Exactly! Positive, rewarding behaviors typically result in replication of the desired behaviors. In other words, the school counselor positively rewarded the mother for her suggestion and reinforces the mother's behaviors. Thus, we can anticipate that the mother will remain engaged in the treatment process and suggest other potential participants as well.

Failure to provide such positive rewards creates participant disengagement. We suspect some of you likely experienced such disengagement sometime during experiences. Professors often ask students to comment on a reading assignment or class-related topic. Ineloquent professors seeking a specific answer will briskly dismiss all student responses until they find the student who provides the desired response. After three student responses are curtly dismissed, a funny thing happens. Students stop responding, and the professors have to answer their own questions. When such dismissive behaviors occur over successive class sessions, students give up. They discontinue engaging with the professor. The same is true for students and their parents. We need to ensure that students and parents perceive they are adequately heard and understood whenever they offer the name of a potential participant.

The school counselor also asks Maria's thoughts about her grandmother's involvement. It is important here to allow Maria to see that she has input into the participant selection process. Should Maria perceive that the participants are her *mother's* participants, the girl will be more likely to sabotage counseling. However, if Maria is able to include persons she truly feels would be helpful to her, she will likely become more engaged in the counseling process. After all, how can you be dissatisfied with the participants if you were the one who chose them?

Furthermore, the counselor establishes a pattern of asking *how* the suggested person will help keep Maria violence free. By asking this question immediately after the proposed person's inclusion, both Mother and Maria will begin to think about it before they suggest other participants. Thus, once this pattern is begun, Mother and Maria will begin self-talk: "How will cousin Julie help keep me from fighting?" This will help increase the probability that they suggest persons they actually believe can help Maria maintain her violence recovery.

Throughout the clinical vignette, we witness the school counselor providing Mother and Maria continued praise. Maria thoughtfully described how Ms. Elms can help eliminate the girl's violent behaviors. The counselor commends Maria's response and asks how Maria *developed* this intervention. Although Maria gives partial credit to her case manager for helping her come up with the idea, the counselor moves the focus off the case manager and instead heaps more kudos on Maria. The intent here is not to fail to recognize the case manager but to provide Maria the maximum recognition for her plan.

Ruling Out Suggested Participants

After using the systems of care method with families in crisis and supervising doctoral and master's students utilizing systems of care interventions, we have come to understand that one of the most challenging situations occurs when students or parents suggest a potential participant who is clearly inappropriate. Persons inappropriate for inclusion are noted in the Contraindications section on page [180]. Surprisingly, we have found that such inappropriate suggestions are greatly reduced by asking *how* the suggested person will help eliminate the student's violent behaviors. This questioning is demonstrated in the last clinical vignette. However, in cases where the student or parents suggest that someone be included and that person is clinically inappropriate, we typically ask "how" that suggested person will be helpful. Often this is sufficient for the suggested participant to be removed from consideration. However, when it is not, we attempt to determine how the presence of this person is perceived as potentially helpful. Then we suggest other means to address this need. This is demonstrated in the next clinical vignette.

Mother:	The first person we want is our attorney, Mr. Vos.
Counselor:	Help me understand how Mr. Vos will be helpful in keeping Maria violence free.
Mother:	No, that isn't why I want to invite him. I want to make certain that Maria doesn't get pushed around by her juvenile probation officer.

Counselor:	I can certainly understand that you don't want Maria to get pushed around by her juvenile probation officer, Ms. Diaz. However, the persons we invite to participate should know Maria very well and be committed to helping Maria eliminate her violent behaviors. Would Mr. Vos's participation directly influence Maria to be safe and not fight?
Mother:	No, I guess it wouldn't.
Counselor:	I'm assuming that Mr. Vos agreed to Maria's participating in the systems of care so she could be allowed to return to school. Is that correct?
Mother:	Yes. He said the only way the school would allow Maria to return is if she participated in the systems of care counseling sessions.
Counselor:	Then your attorney thought it was in Maria's best interests to attend these sessions?
Mother:	Yes. He said that.
Counselor:	So, he wouldn't have suggested that Maria attend if he had not felt it was in Maria's best interests to attend.
Mother:	I guess you're right.
Counselor:	How about this, Ms. Diaz. Since I will be the person facilitating the sessions, should at any time within those sessions you feel Maria is getting pushed around or harmed in any way, will you promise me you will say something to me within the session?
Mother:	I could do that.
Counselor:	Frankly, it is imperative that you let me know within session if you feel Maria is being harmed in any way. Although we have just recently met, Ms. Diaz, I believe you are very dedicated to Maria. So, should you believe at any time that Maria is being harmed, I need you to immediately tell me. That way we can address your concern right then and there. Will you make that promise to me?
Mother:	Yes, I will do that.

Counselor: Good, then I believe we can initiate these sessions without Mr. Vos as long as you promise to let me know if something is not going well.

As we review this clinical vignette, we observe the school counselor doing a couple of very important things.

When Mother suggests that Maria's attorney be present, the counselor does not panic. Instead, the counselor remains in the cognitive realm and keeps the conversation on a cognitive level. The counselor does not foolishly respond in an emotional manner. To keep the interaction at a cognitive rather than an emotional level, the counselor simply asks: How will the suggested person help the student remain violence free? Mother responds by saying that the attorney is desired for a different reason: She wants to ensure that Maria is not "pushed around" by her probation officer. We believe this voiced concern is legitimate. It has been my experience that many who are mandated into treatment feel disempowered. Here the mother simply wants Maria's attorney to be present to empower Maria and herself against a system that requires their successful completion of a process they do not control.

I (Dr. Juhnke) do not know about you, but when I feel disempowered, I don't like it. Think about the last time you felt disempowered. Where were you? What happened? The last time I felt disempowered, a young store clerk was unwilling to refund my money for a pair of sunglasses I had purchased. The purchase had occurred the day before from the same store clerk. At the time of purchase, the clerk had clearly told me that I had 90 days to return the purchase for a full money refund should I not like the glasses. As a matter of fact, the store's full cash refund policy was clearly described on the cash register receipt. The situation got uglier by the moment as it became increasingly evident that no resolution amenable to both the clerk and me was going to come about.

Please note that this situation revolved around a pair of sunglasses. How would I have felt and behaved if the situation had revolved around a loved family member? Clearly, students and parents who feel disempowered can present in an "ugly" manner. This is not the case with Ms. Diaz. However, despite verbal threats or high risk violence behaviors by children, some parents believe their children are not threatening. These parents are frequently familiar with their children's mannerisms and ways of behaving. Thus, they don't perceive their children as threatening to others. As a matter of fact, some of these parents perceive their children as being *exploited* by an unfair counseling mandate. Mandated students and parents are often angry. They typically behave and respond on an emotional level rather than a cognitive level. When students and parents behave this way, it is easy for school counselors also to respond emotionally rather than cognitively.

Dr. William Purkey, the founder of Invitational Education and Counseling, illustrates how school counselors need to remain cognitive and professional via his anecdotal story about a Japanese samurai. The fictional samurai was employed by an emperor to behead persons who failed to pay their tax debts. As a professional, the samurai merely was fulfilling the charge assigned to him by the emperor. Thus, he had no malice or emotions toward those he was paid to behead. One day the samurai encountered a debtor. As the samurai drew his sword and prepared to behead the debtor, the debtor spit in the samurai's face and insulted the samurai's mother, wife, and children. Enraged, the samurai sheathed his sword and walked away. Later, when asked by the emperor why he had failed to behead the obnoxious and insulting debtor, the samurai simply explained it would be unprofessional to behead someone because of his emotions.

This story contains a parallel meaning for school counselors, who sometimes encounter angry students and parents. Often these students and their parents do not seek counseling to reduce their children's potential violent behaviors. Many times these students and their parents have learned that when they intimidate or act in a threatening manner, others leave them alone or require little of them. Thus, when the school system or courts require these students and their parents to participate in counseling, they may attempt to intimidate or threaten the school counselor. As professionals, counselors must remain at a cognitive level. They should never emotionally respond in anger toward previously violent or potentially violent students. Although this is sometimes difficult, it is critically important. Responding in an emotional manner will resolve little and often increases the emotions of the student or parents. One needs to remain professional and operate in a cognitive rather than an emotional or responsive realm. Thus, should the counselor perceive the student or parents are threatening or dangerous, he or she should ask how these behaviors are helpful and describe what will happen should they choose to continue the threatening behaviors.

Counselor:	Ms. Diaz, I guess I'm a little confused. I believe our goal is to be helpful to Maria, is that correct?
Mother:	Yes, that is correct.
Counselor:	I'm very committed to helping Maria stay violence free and potentially return to school as she demonstrates her commitment to staying violence free. I believe you are committed to these things too. Is that correct?
Mother:	Yes.
Counselor:	Then help me understand how it is helpful for Maria to hear you say things to me such as "I'm going to sue your butt off if you don't let Maria back in school" or "I should take you outside and whip your sorry rear end"?
Mother:	I'm sorry. I didn't mean it to sound that way.
Counselor:	Thank you for your apology. However, as you know, it is not up to me but rather up to Maria and you whether she is allowed back to school. If Maria continues to choose to act violently, as she has in the past, then you will end up needing to find and pay for a private school that will accept her. That will be very expensive for you. Instead, I hope that I have both Maria's and your commitment to behave in nonviolent, unintimidating ways that will demonstrate that Maria can return to the Meadowbrook Independent School System.

Thus, we can see that instead of ignoring Ms. Diaz's intimidating statements, the school counselor moves to a very professional and cognitively based interaction. Here the counselor cognitively restates the goal, asks if the mother is committed to this treatment goal, and describes what will happen should Maria and her mother not demonstrate commitment to Maria's nonviolent behaviors (e.g., mother will need to pay for private schooling elsewhere). After confronting the potentially intimidating statements made by the mother, the counselor then reextends the opportunity for Ms. Diaz to actively join her in seeking ways to solidify Maria's nonviolent behaviors.

Returning to the original clinical vignette, the school counselor agrees with the mother and joins in her noted concern. This is done simply by repeating the mother's voiced concern. Hence the counselor agrees that she does not want Maria "pushed around" by her juvenile probation officer.

The counselor also redirects the session back to the central theme: Will the presence of Maria's attorney reduce her fighting? Mother confirms that the attorney's presence would not keep Maria violence free. However, understanding that the mother feels empowered by her daughter's attorney, the counselor asks whether the attorney had suggested that Maria and her mother attend counseling sessions. In other words, the counselor perceives Ms. Diaz's confidence in the attorney can be used as a means to promote mother and daughter's engagement in counseling. Once the mother reports that the attorney had made this counseling recommendation, the counselor capitalizes on her faith in the attorney and the attorney's recommendations.

In addition, the counselor attempts to build rapport with the mother by indicating that the counselor will facilitate the counseling sessions in a fair and impartial manner. Most important, here the counselor asks the mother to join her in creating a safe session for Maria. This is indirectly done by asking the mother to inform the counselor within session should the mother feel that Maria is being pushed around or harmed. Mother agrees. However, the counselor does not simply discontinue the discussion. In fact, the counselor again praises Ms. Diaz and indicates that she appears "very dedicated" to Maria. Then the counselor asks the mother to "promise" to bring forth any concerns within the actual treatment sessions. This clearly denotes the counselor's commitment to Maria; further, it demonstrates that the counselor heard the mother's concerns.

CONTACTING SYSTEMS OF CARE PARTICIPANTS AND ATTAINING RELEASES OF CONFIDENTIALITY

In most cases, we believe it is important for the post-violent student to contact potential systems of care participants. There are three primary reasons for requiring the students to make the contacts.

1. We believe it is empowering for students to learn how to ask help of others and appropriately engage others without utilizing previously relied on bullying, threatening, or conning behaviors. As students gain this new, help-asking skill, they acquire more appropriate, nonviolent ways to interact.

2. Given that students know and reportedly respect the persons they identified, it is far more likely that the invited participants will respond positively to the student's request for participation rather than a request made by an unknown counselor.

3. We have found that counselors and parents are far more invested in change than students. When counselors do the majority of the therapeutic work, there is little positive impact on the students.

Hence, should students be unwilling to make the contacts and seem minimally invested in the systems of care process, they are simply referred back to the school district, judge, legal counsel, or agency that made the initial treatment request. Reports then would be sent to the initial referring sources (e.g., judges, probation officers, etc.). These reports would document the student's unwillingness to comply with the mandated counseling or describe his or her lack of investment in the counseling process. For formerly violent students, such reports likely will result in returning to a long-term juvenile detention facility and the cancellation of the opportunity to return to their former school milieu.

Of course, few things in counseling are inflexibly rigid. Therefore, in some atypical situations, the counselor may perceive the student as committed to changing violent behaviors but presenting as exceedingly dependent, ashamed, or depressed. In such cases, the counselor may determine that it is clinically appropriate for the counselor to make contact with potential systems of care participants. However, we suggest that the counselor and student jointly make the telephone contacts via conference calls. In this manner, the student is continually engaged in the process.

Telephone Call Instructions and Role-Plays

Given the importance of attaining systems of care participants, telephone invitations are vitally important. Next, we describe the instructions given to students. Additionally, we describe how to role-play making the telephone calls prior to the actual contact.

Instructions

Prior to the placement of telephone calls to potential systems of care participants, the counselor, student, and parents again discuss each potential participant invitee. Specifically, the discussion revolves around how the student knows the participant, previous helpful experiences the student had with the participant, and how the student believes the participant will be helpful in maintaining his or her freedom from violence. Then the counselor and student jointly complete a formal Participant Request Sheet (see Table 7.1). This sheet should be available to facilitate both upcoming role-plays and actual telephone invitations.

Students are instructed not to tell potential systems of care participants that their counselor is making them call. Instead, students are encouraged to contact potential participants and begin by reporting that the potential participant is valued, appreciated, and able to provide important help to them. Here the students can describe how the potential participant has helped in the past and how his or her participation will help the student continue

Table 7.1 Participant Request Sheet

Participant's Name: Prefix (Dr., Mrs., Ms., Mr.)

_____

How do you know the participant?

_____

_____

Previous helpful experiences with the participant:

When	Where	What Happened
_____	_____	_____
_____	_____	_____
_____	_____	_____
_____	_____	_____

Describe how the potential participant can be helpful to you in maintaining your freedom from violence.

_____

_____

_____

TELEPHONE CALL:

Hello _____,

The last time we talked, you helped me

_____

I've had some challenges related to _____ and am wondering if you would be willing to help me by meeting with my (parents, mother, father, grandmother, other) _____ and me at my counselor's office on (date) _____ at (time) _____. The office is located at 501 West Durango Street. I really would appreciate your help. May I count on you?

_____

violence-free behaviors. Students then ask the potential participant if he or she would be willing to attend an initial informational meeting with students and others who have been identified as "required attenders" (e.g., juvenile probation officer, school counselor, case manager, etc.).

Telephone Role-Plays

Practice telephone role-plays are then begun. During the first two role-play experiences, the counselor assumes the student's role and the student assumes the role of a potential participant being asked to attend the first systems of care meeting. To make the role-play more realistic, the counselor utilizes the information contained within the Participant Request Sheet. During later role-plays, the student role-plays him- or herself and the counselor assumes the potential participant's role.

Suggestions are made regarding the student's role-played verbal communications. After a student creates a fairly sincere and cogently stated request, he or she makes the first telephone call from the counselor's office with parents and counselor observing and supporting the student. Parents and counselor can coach the student as necessary from the sidelines. At the conclusion of the telephone call, the counselor will ask the parents to identify what the student did well during the telephone call. Once the parents have identified as many positive things as they can, the counselor typically adds more positive things and commends the student on an outstanding job. Again, suggestions are made.

If the student's telephone invitation was adequately stated, he or she conducts the remaining telephone calls. These calls are made while under the watchful supervision of the parents. However, if the student struggled or had difficulties verbalizing the request, further role-plays are practiced and the counselor and parents supervise another invitation call. Additionally, should the student be unable to contact the desired systems of care participant after multiple attempts, another contact will be identified and invited to participate.

Why Include Parents?

At this point, some readers may be questioning why we encourage parental involvement during the role-plays and the actual telephone calls. From a structural family therapy view, placing parents in an administrative role over their children reestablishes the parents at the top of the family power hierarchy. In other words, it demonstrates to the students (and parents too) that parents rather than children rule the family system and establish the appropriate family's rules and boundaries.

It has been our experience that Conduct Disordered, substance-abusing, and violent students often have dethroned parental authority within the family system. This typically results in a chaotic home environment where the violent child rules the home via intimidation, threats, and violent behaviors. When parental control is eclipsed, violent and potentially violent students have nearly free rein. This leads to the students' misperception that they have successfully emancipated from all adult authority (e.g., school, judicial, police, corrections, etc.). Nothing could be further from the truth. Reestablishing parental authority within the home is crucial to addressing a student's violent behaviors, especially with younger students who are ineligible to become emancipated minors and are a long way away from the age of majority.

Concomitantly, parents see their children far more often than do counselors. Even under the very best circumstances, where frequent counseling and case management is court mandated for formerly violent students, the number of interactions counselors and case managers can have with students pales in comparison with the number of times parents can interact with them. Clearly, some parents desire no interaction or are unable to invest time with in children. However, for the vast majority of students we counsel, parents want involvement. Such active parental involvement ensures that students are supervised and under the watchful eyes of parents. In conjunction with counseling and case management, this supervision can lead to more effective and lasting interventions.

Rejected Invitations

In cases where potential participants reject the invitation to attend the systems of care meeting, it is important to monitor a student's responses toward the invited participant. In particular, should a student become upset and frustrated, the counselor can utilize this opportunity to help him or her connect how internalized, cognitive self-talk influences violent behaviors. An example is provided next.

Maria: That damn Mr. Pruitt! I am so mad at him! I can't believe he won't come to my counseling session.

Counselor:	Sounds like you're feeling pretty angry at Mr. Pruitt.
Maria:	Damn right I am angry at him. He is a good-for-nothing, self-absorbed, jerk.
Counselor:	Maria, help me understand what you are saying to yourself—in your own mind—about why you are angry at Mr. Pruitt for not coming to the systems of care counseling session.
Maria:	What do you mean?
Counselor:	Well, you say you are angry at him for not agreeing to come to counseling to help you. Is that correct?
Maria:	Yeah, so what?
Counselor:	So, what are you saying to yourself about his not coming to counseling to help you?
Maria:	I'm saying he doesn't come because he doesn't like me.
Counselor:	And, if he doesn't like you, what does that mean?
Maria:	That means that he thinks I'm a loser.
Counselor:	And if you are a loser?
Maria:	It means I'm never going to amount to much.
Counselor:	And if you never amount to much?
Maria:	I'm failing my mom.
Counselor:	And if you fail your mom?
Maria:	(silence)
Counselor:	And if you fail your mom?
Maria:	She is going to leave me.
Counselor:	Maria, if Mom leaves you, then what?
Maria:	Then I will lose her love and I'm unlovable to anyone.

In an effort to help Maria better understand the connection between her internalized, cognitive self-talk and her violent behaviors, the counselor does three things: (1) comments on her perception of Maria's feelings; (2) asks Maria to consider her own self-talk; and (3) utilizes a linking technique to help Maria connect her self-talk with her negative behaviors.

First, immediately after the counselor hears and senses Maria's anger at Mr. Pruitt, the counselor makes a comment related to her perception: Maria is in fact angry with Mr. Pruitt. This allows Maria an opportunity to admit, deny, or modify the counselor's comment. In the clinical vignette, Maria verbally admits her anger.

Second, the counselor asks Maria to notice her internalized, cognitive self-talk. At first the girl does not comprehend the counselor's comment. However, instead of dropping the comment and pursuing other interventions, the counselor simply rephrases the earlier statement to make Maria's internalized self-talk more evident and comprehendible. Here Maria verbalizes why she believes Mr. Pruitt rejected her invitation to attend the systems of care counseling session. According to Maria's internalized self-talk, Mr. Pruitt does not attend because he "doesn't like" her.

Last, the school counselor utilizes a "linking" technique. The intent of this technique is to help the student gain insight into the underlying issues that cause the behaviors resulting from negative self-talk (e.g., violent behaviors). When utilizing this technique, the counselor simply uses the student's previous responses and asks something like "What does that [previous response] mean?" This is repeated until the student moves to the smallest identifiable feeling or thought. In Maria's case, if she fails her mother, her mother will leave. Mother's leaving would then prove that Maria is unlovable; thus the anger and violence toward others.

Should someone not agree to attend the systems of care session, we utilize the experience to increase insight and self-understanding. The hope is that we can then help students gain the self-confidence to contact others who will accept the invitation to attend. Most often those who are truly invested in the student's success will at least agree to attend the first meeting. Frequently, these persons are less concerned with the details of the appointment and are focused on helping the student. Despite their demanding schedules, they usually make time. Typically, they are revered by students.

Quite a while ago, a young male contacted a family member to ask for her participation in a systems of care experience. He had believed this family member's involvement was vital to resolving his addiction and intermittent explosive disordered behaviors. When the male made the telephone call to her from my office, she was at work. She pleaded with the young man not to leave my office until she could arrive and pledge her support in person. In other words, this family member was so committed to the young man that she wanted immediate, face-to-face interactions with him. Within 20 minutes she was at my office reporting to the young man that she had been aware of his alcohol abuse for years but had never taken the opportunity to speak with him about *her* recovery and *her* previously violent behaviors resulting from her drinking and drug use. The experience was quite moving for the male, who reported he had "never known" of her struggles with addiction and violence. Frankly, because of this family member's involvement, the male readily progressed through his addictions and violence recovery experience.

Hesitant Others

Most who are contacted agree to participate in the first systems of care meeting. Less common, however, are those who are hesitant to participate. In general, hesitant invitees have one or more of the following seven issues in common.

1. They are less familiar with the student and the student's family than the student believed.
2. They have witnessed or heard about the student's violent behaviors and feel potential jeopardy or danger related to participation.
3. They are angry with the student for something that he or she said or did to them (e.g., the student had stolen items from the invitee).
4. They perceive little benefit or reward for attending.
5. They are friends or aligned with others who do not have favorable impressions of the student.
6. They do not perceive that their involvement will be meaningful to the student or the student's family.
7. They are experiencing immediate personal or work-related needs that require full attention and the truncation of outside demands.

Because we often only need two or three nonprofessional invitees to participate in the systems of care experience and one or two frequently are parents or family members, we encourage students to contact the next person on their rank-order list when someone is hesitant to engage. In other words, if someone is reluctant to engage prior to the systems of care process, it is better to select another person who is more invested. Concomitantly, should invitees attempt to establish unrealistic parameters regarding their attendance (e.g., "I will not attend if you don't cut your hair" or "I can only attend on the third Monday of the month"), I believe we should identify another invitee.

Confidentiality and Attaining Releases

Because students are frequently minors under the age of legal majority, parents or legal guardians must approve the post-violent student's participation within the systems of care experience and approve those who are invited to participate. Typically, the rank-ordered list of invitees results from a mutual brainstorming session with parents and the student. So there are few surprises. However, it should be noted that *parents, not students,* approve who is ultimately invited to participate. Approval is typically not a problem. In most cases the parents or legal guardians desire the post-violent student to return to school and view invitees as helpful in attaining their desired outcome. However, counselors should never initiate counseling without full parental or legal guardian approval and signed paperwork outlining full support of inviting rank-ordered others to participate. As previously noted, participation by some is contraindicated and only persons believed as therapeutically appropriate should be allowed to participate.

Concomitantly, if the invitee peer is under the age of majority, his or her parents will also need to approve the minor's participation in the systems of care experience. Depending on the specific situation, some parents may not allow their children to participate in another child's therapeutic experience. The key factor is explaining to the invited peer child's parents that the post-violent student values the invited peer and believes his or her presence will be helpful in attaining nonviolent treatment outcomes. Sometimes statements like these are sufficient in helping the invited parents to feel comfortable allowing their children to attend. At other times, the invited peers or their parents have experienced or witnessed the violent behaviors of the student requesting the peer's attendance. Thus, rightly, neither peers nor the peers' parents will want to attend the sessions. Invited peers and others are not bound by professional ethics or confidentiality. Therefore, students and their parents should be informed of potential issues and implications prior to the first systems of care meeting with invited others.

For example, counselors should inform both students and their parents that although counselors will encourage those invited to keep everything said within the interview confidential, others still may reveal to nonparticipants potentially embarrassing or hurtful facts or occurrences. Additionally, before any peers or other invitees are contacted regarding possible interview participation, students and their families must sign release of confidential information forms.

Furthermore, individual releases should be signed by all participants (e.g., student, counselor, and all participating others), thereby providing participants permission to communicate with one another during the course of treatment. Counselors may also require participants to sign a pretreatment contract. This pretreatment contract, although not necessarily legally binding, relinquishes participants' rights to seek case records or attempt to compel the counselor or other participants to divulge information or events that occurred within the course of the assessment or during treatment.

Management of Noncompliant, Treatment-Mandated Students

Because the impetus for post-violent students seeking to enter treatment is so varied, it would be foolish to attempt to describe the management of each situation where a student may decline systems of care involvement. This is especially true for voluntary students (e.g., students not ordered into treatment by the judicial system or required to participate by school districts). Many times students who volunteer to participate in the systems of care process feel coerced to do so by parents. Hence, they discontinue early in the process, because of these feelings of coercion or the anger generated by feeling that they "must" participate.

However, the situation is somewhat different for students mandated to participate by courts or school districts. Mandated students provide a release of confidential information and request the counselor submit assessment findings to a specific court or school district. Depending on the specific circumstances of the student's refusal to be assessed and participate in the systems of care process, the counselor generally can indicate that nonparticipation will likely result in the elimination of previous agreements with the judicial system or school district. Here counselors should encourage students to speak with legal counsel should they either have legal concerns or refuse to participate.

The intent of this statement is not to threaten or intimidate. Rather, the statement merely reflects reality. School administrators and legal counsel frequently offer first-time violent students the opportunity to return to school if they participate in counseling. Those offered such opportunities generally have posed only minimal threat to others and are not viewed by school administrators as a viable threat to the safety of others. Therefore, should students breach their agreements by refusing to participate in the school violence assessment or systems of care counseling process, they likely will not be allowed to return to school. Once this is verified by students and their parents, students often wish to "voluntarily" participate in the school violence assessment or systems of care counseling process.

INITIAL SYSTEMS OF CARE MEETING WITH STUDENT, PARENT(S), AND IDENTIFIED PARTICIPANTS

Specifically, we demonstrate five components of the initial systems of care meeting. We describe:

1. How the counselor will welcome, address releases of confidential information and confidentiality, and establish procedural aspects for this and upcoming meetings.
2. How the student will introduce each systems of care participant member.
3. The sequence in which members identify the student's strengths.
4. The identification of student strengths.
5. Nonviolent "favorite" activities.

For reading ease, we continue utilizing Maria's clinical vignette. As you will recall, Maria presents as an obese 12-year-old who is in the sixth grade. She is a first-generation Mexican American who resides with her single, 33-year-old mother and 58-year-old maternal grandmother. Maria has a history of fighting with those whom she perceives tease her about her obesity. Maria was expelled from school after her last physical altercation; her last student victim required plastic surgery. Maria's mother now wishes for Maria to return to school. Maria and her mother have agreed to participate in the systems of care process as required by the school district as a "first step" in considering Maria's potential reenrollment.

Counselor's Welcome

The intent of the counselor's welcome is to: (a) reduce the first session's "uncomfortableness" and lessen the participants' anxiety, (b) promote verbal commitment to Maria, and (c) establish procedural aspects of the first and upcoming sessions. Typically, whatever discomfort or anxiety quickly dissipates as the counselor introduces self, welcomes those present, and describes what is going to happen in this and upcoming sessions. We suggest that the counselor begin with a *brief* self-introduction and welcome. Given that most participants are present to help the identified student, they are relatively indifferent to a detailed description of the counselor's educational background and school counseling credentials.

As well, we have found it helpful to compliment participants for their attendance and to characterize their role as that of being "expert consultants." Therefore, we commonly indicate that the purpose of the systems of care meeting is for invited participants to help us understand the student and learn how we can be helpful. Additionally, we encourage significant others to make a verbal commitment to the student and to each other. Therefore, a typical introduction may begin like this:

Counselor: Hello, my name is Jerry Juhnke. I am supervising school counselor at Meadowbrook. On behalf of Maria and Maria's mother, Ms. Diaz, I'd like to welcome and thank you for coming. Your being here today demonstrates your commitment to helping Maria and your willingness to support Maria as she works toward her goals of remaining violence free. The intent of today's first systems of care meeting is to describe the systems of care process and its rules and for us to better understand how we can be helpful to Maria in her goal of successfully completing school in a nonviolent manner. Specifically, systems of care, or wraparound services as it is sometimes called, is an evidence-based counseling intervention that has been found to be helpful with adolescents. Basically, students with the help of parents and invited persons *wrap around* the student and help her stop violent behaviors. The belief is that when persons like you who are important to the student become invested in the student's success, they can help the student make the correct choices and select the best behaviors to be successful. Your

being here suggests that you are invested and want to
help Maria.

As you can see, the introduction is not wordy and does not get into details
of Maria's past violent experiences. Instead, it is future focused. It describes
how those present will *wrap around* Maria and help her make improved and
nonviolent choices.

Typically at this point, we attempt to promote verbal commitment by
asking if anyone is not interested in helping the student. Given that persons
who are present have already taken the time to travel to the counseling
office and are physically present, it is rare for participants to say they are not
interested in helping. However, if persons indicate an unwillingness to help,
we simply thank them for their time and if possible reframe their unwillingness to participate.

Counselor:	Is anyone not interested in helping Maria?
Jorge:	I hate to admit this, but I don't think I can help.
Counselor:	Jorge, I know that Maria identified you as someone who could be helpful to her and really wanted you here. I'm sure your presence would mean a lot to Maria.
Jorge:	I just can't help.
Counselor:	Is it that you don't want to help, or is there some-thing else?
Jorge:	I just can't take the time off work to be here. My boss just won't let me do it.
Counselor:	No problem. What I'm hearing you say is that you want to help Maria. However, your work obligations won't allow you to come to sessions. Is that correct?
Jorge:	Yes. I want to help Maria, but I just can't.
Counselor:	That makes sense to me. I thank you for coming today, Jorge. Let's let you head back to work at this time.

Once those who are unwilling or unable to participate are thanked for their
honesty, we quickly allow them to leave. Then we focus on those who are
present. The goal becomes helping those present to verbally disclose their
commitment to Maria, her mother, and significant others and their commitment to helping Maria achieve her new violence-free behaviors.

Counselor: Maria has identified each of you as someone very
important to her and able to meaningfully contribute
to her attainment of a violence-free life. So, today,
Maria; Maria's mother, Ms. Diaz; and I are asking you
for your help. Your being here and not leaving means
that you truly are committed to helping Maria.

These statements symbiotically frame the participants continued presence
as demonstrating their true commitment to helping Maria. We believe such
a statement is important both for the student and those attending. In other
words, it suggests to students that "these people *want* to help you" and "they
are invested in your success." For those in attendance, it implies that their
involvement in Maria's life will be helpful to her.

Readers may wonder why such a symbiotic frame is important. The
answer is simple. Have you ever been involved in a project where you anticipated that few if any would benefit from your investment of time or energy?
Exactly! When people are involved in a perceived "useless" project, they
often have little enthusiasm and frequently fail to achieve project goals.
Conversely, have you ever been involved in a project where there was an air
of excitement and expectation of success? Undoubtedly you have! Typically,
the excitement increases as group members see positive indicators suggesting that the goal is being achieved and realize the project's ultimate success is coming closer. Additionally, few members discontinue participation
in anticipated successful projects. Instead, a robust loyalty develops. You
understand others are "counting on you." Thus, you make attendance and
completion of assigned duties a priority.

About this time someone typically makes a verbal comment regarding a
desire to help the student. However, if no one makes such a statement, we
simply ask each person within the systems of care group whether they are
willing to make such a commitment. If we noticed persons nodding affirmatively to the question suggesting they are committed to helping, we often
start with them.

Counselor: Ms. Sanchez, you are Maria's juvenile probation
officer. When I asked "Is anyone opposed to helping Maria," I saw you shake your head no. That said
to me that you are not opposed to helping Maria. Is
that true?

Ms. Sanchez:	That is true. I want Maria to get back into school and be successful.
Counselor:	Do you think she can be successful at school and not act violently toward others?
Ms. Sanchez:	I certainly do.
Counselor:	Are you saying that just because you are her juvenile probation officer and are being paid to be here?
Ms. Sanchez:	Listen, I get paid to be here, but I don't think every kid can be successful. In this case, I believe Maria can be successful at school and can stop fighting and threatening others.
Counselor:	Why do you say that she can be successful at school, and why do you believe she can stop threatening and fighting others?
Ms. Sanchez:	That's easy. Maria is smart. She is one of the smartest young ladies that I have ever worked with. She also wants to please her mother and grandmother. Basically, she is someone who can be a leader at the school if she wishes, and I believe she will do just that.
Counselor:	Maria, what did you just hear Ms. Sanchez say?
Maria:	She said I can be a leader at the school rather than a bully.
Counselor:	Do you think Ms. Sanchez knows what she is talking about?
Maria:	I don't know. Maybe.
Counselor:	Ms. Sanchez, how many kids have you worked with as a juvenile probation officer?
Ms. Sanchez:	Hundreds. This year alone I have served as a probation officer to 90 youth.
Counselor:	That sounds like a lot. How many of those kids had the intelligence and leadership skills as Maria?
Ms. Sanchez:	Very few . . . Maria is quite able if she wishes to be successful.
Counselor:	Maria, what did you hear Ms. Sanchez say?
Maria:	I heard her say that I can be a leader.
Counselor:	Do you believe her?

Maria:	I don't know. I guess.
Counselor:	Ms. Sanchez, were you lying to Maria and us when you said you think she has the potential to be a leader at her school? Because I get the feeling you are pretty honest with people and say what you mean.
Ms. Sanchez:	I don't lie. If I didn't think she had the potential to be a leader at her school, I wouldn't say so.
Counselor:	Who else thinks Maria has the potential to stop her violent and intimidating behaviors at school and start being a leader?
Ms. Diaz:	I know my daughter. She is a leader, and she can stop bullying others. I know we can help her become successful at school.
Counselor:	So, I'm hearing you say that you are committed to being here at the systems of care meetings and helping your daughter become a leader at school.
Ms. Diaz:	Very much so.

Let us briefly summarize what just happened. First, after seeing the juvenile probation officer's favorable nonverbal behaviors toward the counselor's stated question, the counselor immediately turned to her. The counselor then informed the group that the probation officer had favorably nodded her head, indicating that Maria can be successful. This is important. It suggests to Maria and those present that someone perceives Maria as having the potential to stop her violent behaviors and be successful in school. Additionally, by commenting on the probation officer's positive nonverbal behaviors, it implies to Maria that her probation officer is not "out to get Maria" and perceives the girl's strengths.

Next, the counselor confronts Maria's probation officer and asks the obvious question, about whether the officer is there because she is being paid to be there. Here the probation officer eloquently addresses the counselor's question. The probation officer states that she *believes* in Maria. This is a powerful statement. Maria is street smart. She knows how to con others, and she knows when she is being conned. When she hears her probation officer state that she can be successful at school, it encourages Maria to internalize the officer's positive belief in Maria. The counselor builds on this by asking the probation officer to describe Maria's strengths. The officer then describes Maria's intelligence and desire to please her mother and grandmother. My guess is that Maria is internally agreeing with the probation officer and say-ing to herself "That's right. I *am* smart. I *do* want to please my mother and grandmother!"

Next, the counselor asks Maria to state what she heard the probation officer say. This is done for four primary reasons.

1. It encourages Maria to pay attention to comments made within session.
2. It rewards Maria for successfully paying attention. Within solution-focused therapy, this is known as "catching the client doing some-thing right."
3. Having Maria restate her attributes promotes an internalized aware-ness of them. In other words, Maria has heard the probation offi-cer say that she is smart and able, but Maria may not be fully aware of these positive attributes. Verbally repeating these positive attri-butes does not necessarily cause the attributes to be internalized. Minimally, however, it requires the student to acknowledge aware-ness that others believe that he or she has these favorable attributes. Over time, the student may well acknowledge and internalize these positive attributes as "who I am."
4. The restatement is not made just for Maria. It is made to ensure that all members of the systems of care group understand that Maria has strengths that can be used to be successful in achiev-ing her nonviolent goals. Again, this instigates synergy within the group and promotes the perception that each member's investment in time and energy has potential to positively achieve the desired outcome.

For even greater therapeutic punch, the counselor asks Maria's probation officer how many probationees she has served. The counselor does not really care how many probationers the probation officer has served. Instead, the question's intent is to help Maria understand that she is perceived as unique compared to many of the others. Specifically, the counselor asks the proba-tion officer how many probationees had Maria's intelligence and leadership abilities. Maria's probation officer states, "Very few," and further responds by noting that Maria can be successful.

The counselor quickly turns to Maria and asks her to repeat what her probation officer said. This is done so Maria understands her unique opportunity for success and to emphasize that she has the potential to go down a different path from others. Then the counselor asks if Maria believes her probation officer's opinion that she can be a leader. Maria's halfhearted response is immediately addressed by the counselor, who asks the probation officer if she is lying. The probation officer states, "I don't lie." In other words, she is saying "I wouldn't say that Maria can be successful at school and be a leader if I didn't mean it." The counselor then asks the other systems of care members if they believe Maria has the potential to stop her violent and intimidating behaviors. This opens the doors for others to voice their beliefs. As more members voice their agreement with the probation officer's perceptions, it challenges Maria's internal beliefs about herself and promotes this internalization: "If they believe I can be a leader without acting violently, and then maybe I really can eliminate those violent behaviors. Maybe I *can* have a new identity as a school leader and get rewarded for those leadership behaviors."

Releases of Confidential Information and Confidentiality

After having the student and the student's parents identify those who will be invited to the systems of care group, student and parents must sign appropriate releases of confidential information. Without signing such releases, the counselor cannot invite others to participate. Potential invitees who agree to attend the systems of care group are forwarded releases and asked to complete same prior to the first systems of care group meeting. At the first systems of care group meeting, the counselor explains the importance of the releases of confidential information and makes certain all the necessary releases are signed, dated, and signed by two or more witnesses (e.g., the counselor and the students' parents).

Next, the counselor explains confidentiality and its limits within the group experience.

We indicate that the counselor is likely the only person present affected by professional confidentiality ethics and laws. We then report that juvenile probation officers and other officers of the court or school are not bound by confidentiality. Instead, these court- or school-appointed officers are required by their jobs to divulge any disclosed information about illegal behaviors. In addition, they are required to divulge information related to potentially harmful behaviors directed at the students, community, or school. These officers also must respond to divulged information related to the failure to uphold previous agreements between the student and the court or school.

Often at this point we ask such professionals to describe their roles and what types of topics they are required to divulge (e.g., drug use, truancy, failure to comply with random drug screens, etc.). Once the mandated professionals finish their overview of their charges and what might constitute reasons for revealing discussions occurring within the systems of care group, a dialog similar to the next one ensues.

Counselor:	Correct me if I am wrong, but what I heard you say is that you aren't going to be telling others what happens in group unless you perceive that Maria is a danger to herself, breaking the law, or failing to comply with her release agreement. Is this correct?
Probation Officer:	That is correct.
Counselor:	So, you wouldn't disclose information that was discussed within the group with your friends or if you saw Maria at Wal-Mart, you wouldn't reveal to others that she was previously expelled from school. Is that correct?
Probation Officer:	I would never do that. If I did those kinds of things, I would likely get fired.

The intent of this conversation is to help those present understand that professionals mandated to attend treatment are not going to gossip. Instead, they are required to report violations and potential behaviors that may be harmful to Maria or the community.

At this point, we typically describe how people are hesitant to speak freely if they believe others will gossip about them outside the group experience or if they feel information shared within the group is going to be freely bantered about. Often we turn to the student and ask if it would be important for him or her to learn that group participants wouldn't be sharing what they hear in the group with others outside the group. Most often the student *desperately wants* promises that information will not be shared outside the group. When we hear this, we simply ask if those present other than court- and school-mandated officers would be willing to make this promise to the student.

Counselor: Before we go any further, I need to bring up the
                  topic of confidentiality. It is important for you
                  to know that I cannot guarantee that everything
                  said in this meeting will be confidential. I am
                  unaware of any law which states that you can-
                  not share information or report to others what is
                  said or what happens in this meeting to persons
                  who are not present. In other words, you should
                  be especially cautious not to share sensitive infor-
                  mation or information that could be potentially
                  embarrassing or harmful. The law clearly states
                  that I am the only one here who is bound by
                  confidentiality. Therefore, I cannot discuss what
                  happens here outside of this room unless I either
                  have your permission to do so or I believe that you
                  or someone else is in danger. However, knowing
                  the importance of confidentiality and the need to
                  have faith in each other, I am wondering if the
                  group members invited by Maria would make a
                  confidentiality pledge to one another. Although
                  this pledge may not provide legal recourse for
                  breaking confidentiality and it may not be legally
                  binding, the pledge would state that whatever is
                  said in today's meeting stays in the room and will
                  not be shared outside this room to anyone unless
                  someone is being a danger herself or in danger of
                  being injured. Would this be acceptable to you?
Maria: I'd like that.
Grandmother: Yes, this makes sense.
Mother: Certainly
Counselor: Okay, Maria, Mother, and Grandmother, I am
                  hearing that each of you is pledging not to report
                  anything that is said or done in this room to some-
                  one other than yourselves or me. Is that correct?

Next, the counselor establishes the procedural meeting rules. Although
these rules can vary from counselor to counselor and are at his or her complete

discretion, we have found that seven basic rules are important for the meeting. These include:

1. Each person should be treated with respect.

   Participants should respect each other by treating others as they wish to be treated. No one should swear at another, call others derogatory names, or be caustically sarcastic. Threats of violence or implied threats will not be tolerated.

2. Each person agrees to speak truthfully.

   Participants promise to speak the truth at all times. No one should be accused of lying.

3. Each person agrees to speak for him- or herself.

   Participants may describe behaviors that they observed in others (e.g., "I saw Maria kick Joann"), but participants will not speak for others (e.g., "Maria is too scared to tell Oscar that she doesn't like him") or attempt to interpret observed behaviors (e.g., "I think Maria was crying because she thought John was breaking up with her").

4. Each person agrees to participate.

   Participants will contribute via their active participation. Nonparticipation suggests an unwillingness to support the student or an inability to provide necessary support. Thus, it is vital that participants invest themselves in the interview process.

5. Each person agrees to ask questions.

   Participants will ask questions and have the right to expect honest and thorough responses.

6. Each person agrees to remain for the entire informational meeting.

   Participants can leave the group for a personal break but must agree to return.

7. Each person agrees to support the student and participating significant others.

   Participants verbally agree to demonstrate their support of the student and others present by encouraging one another and helping in whatever ways deemed appropriate and helpful.

After the rules are discussed, clarified, and agreed to, the counselor asks participants if any concerns or questions exist.

Student Introductions

At this point, the counselor invites the student to introduce each participant, describing how the student knows each participant, and how the student perceives this participant will be helpful in achieving violence-free behaviors. For example, the counselor and student might interact like this.

Counselor: Maria, I'm wondering if you would introduce everyone here, indicate how you know the person, and how they can help you achieve your new violent-free behaviors?

Maria: Okay. Well, this is my mom. I think everybody knows her. I know her because she is my mom. And I think she can help me learn how not to get mad and fight.

Counselor: Thank you, Maria. Can you help us understand what kinds of things you believe your mother can do to help you "not to get mad and fight"?

Maria: I don't know. I guess like having her tell me when she thinks I am getting mad and telling me things I could do instead of fighting?

Counselor: So, what would that look like?

Maria: Well, when I'm starting to get really angry and my mom sees that I am getting angry, maybe she could say something like "You look like you are getting angry. Go to your room and calm yourself down."

Counselor: Would that really be helpful?

Maria: Yeah, I think so. Sometimes I don't even know I am starting to get angry until I just explode. If she told me that I was starting to look angry, then I could think about what I needed to do to calm myself down.

Counselor: Mom, is that something you would be willing to do?

Mother: Yes. I could do that.

Counselor: What kinds of things might you tell Maria she could do in her room that might help her calm down?

Mother: Well, Maria likes to draw or make things. Maybe I could have some beads and bracelet wire in her room, so when she gets mad, she can sit down and make some bracelets or something.

Counselor:	Maria, would that be helpful?
Maria:	Yeah, it would. I'd like that. Maybe Mom or Grandma could even go in my room and talk to me while we work on a new bracelet or something.
Counselor:	Why don't you ask your mom if she would be willing to do that?
Maria:	Now?
Counselor:	Yup . . .
Maria:	Mom, when you see that I am starting to get angry, can you tell me and then you or Grandma go with me to my room and maybe talk or help me make some new bracelets or something?
Mother:	Certainly, baby.
Counselor:	Just one question, Maria. Are you attempting to make your mom responsible either to identify when you are angry or to solve your anger?
Maria:	I don't get what you are saying.
Counselor:	Are you saying to your mom, "I don't know when I am angry. So it is *your* responsibility to tell me when I am angry and it is *your* responsibility" to stop me from fighting?
Maria:	No. I am not saying that at all. Sometimes I don't know how angry I am. Having my mom tell me that I seem really angry will help me figure out when I need to do something that will calm me down.

Within this clinical vignette, we notice some important interactions. First, given Maria's age and the fact she introduced her mother, we did not need to press Maria about *how* she knows her mother. Her response was age appropriate and fully acceptable. However, had Maria introduced an invited teacher, for example, we would ask her to provide more information. Here we might query regarding the course or grade the teacher had instructed Maria. We would further inquire how the teacher's past behaviors positively impacted Maria. Once Maria can identify and verbalize the teacher's past helpful and supportive behaviors, we can encourage replication of these behaviors in the future. Thus, the teacher can be a key group player by replicating previously prized behaviors toward Maria as the girl continues her violence abstinence.

This behavior replication potentially creates three important outcomes.

1. It creates security for Maria in the immediate systems of care group. Hence, her defenses will be reduced, and she will be able to interact more freely within the group experience. This also means that there is an increased likelihood that Maria will accept constructive comments by this valued systems of care group participant.

2. Replication of these teacher behaviors within Maria's immediate school milieu potentially reduces the girl's stressors within that environment. A stressor reduction within her environments decreases her violent behavior probability.

3. Given that Maria believes this teacher values her and is committed to her success, the probability is increased that should Maria consider acting violent, she would instead seek out this trusted teacher.

The vignette demonstrates another critical element: the therapeutic sense of "baby steps," sometimes known as the progression not perfection construct. The idea is that we are not seeking immediate perfection. Instead, we utilize baby steps to progress toward the student's desired outcome (e.g., sustained, nonviolent behaviors). As we notice, Maria is not soliciting her mother to implement overly demanding or gargantuan behaviors. Instead, Maria merely asks her mother for three relatively easy behaviors: (1) informing Maria when she is perceived as presenting with an angry affect, (2) asking Maria to go to her room to "calm down," and (c) talking with her while she and Mother jointly work on beading in Maria's room.

Some might argue this change construct is far too simplistic. However, our experiences suggest otherwise. When combined, multiple small changes typically result in far greater change. When the smaller changes become ingrained within one's recurring repertoire of behaviors, the larger changes become ingrained. This same progression rather than perfection construct is often used by successful dieters. Foolish dieters abstain from eating for a day or possibly two. Then they give way to their massive hunger and gorge on every edible food in near proximity.

Conversely, successful dieters understand that small eating habit changes bring about successful weight loss. Instead of eliminating all foods, successful dieters exchange high-caloric foods with lower-caloric foods. Often they begin walking to burn even more calories. Soon the many small changes reap big rewards on the scale. In the same fashion, we are merely attempting to create multiple positive changes for Maria that will jointly provide opportunities for sustainable violence-free behaviors. Having the mother contribute to Maria's success by implementing the requested behavior is logical and a surefire way to begin the change process.

Two concluding comments regarding the introduction vignette are warranted. First, we have found it advantageous for participants to practice asking for help within the systems of care group experiences. Many tweens and adolescents do not understand how to effectively seek help or make requests. Instead they have learned to bully or intimidate others to gain desired outcomes. Within this vignette, Maria reports that she would like to have her mother or grandmother participate in beading and conversation when she goes to her room to calm down. The counselor then asks Maria to formalize this request of her mother within session. Maria asks, "Now?" The counselor affirmatively responds and Maria asks for her mother's help. Having students making requests like this within the group is useful. Should the student report that she does not know how to ask for help or fail at the request, the counselor can demonstrate how such a request could be made. Doing this opens further opportunities to practice such requests within the group. We have found that understanding how to effectively make requests empowers students and often lessens their bullying and explosive behaviors.

Second, some within the mental health professions are hypersensitive to codependency issues. They view even the most appropriate requests for help as creating codependency or fostering continued codependent behaviors. Although we believe that codependency can be a significant clinical issue, we certainly do not believe this is the case within the last vignette. However, the counselor does address this concern by asking Maria if she is "attempting to make your mom responsible" for Maria's behaviors. In this case, Maria denies such an attempt, and the counselor believes her. Conversely, had the counselor believed Maria was attempting to make her mother responsible for Maria's behaviors, the counselor would have responded differently. For example:

Counselor: It seems that you are denying any responsibility for your violent behaviors and implying that your mother should simply tell you when you are angry and resolve your anger by paying attention to you. Is this what you are suggesting?

In most cases, such a statement is sufficient to change the dynamics and provide a more therapeutic interchange to occur.

Identifying Student Strengths

The three primary reasons for identifying student strengths is to have significant others:

1. Describe healthy ways in which the student is meeting his or her current needs.
2. Identify ways in which the counselor as well as other nonprofessionals can help the student secure his or her goal of being violence free.
3. Encourage continued significant other positive behaviors toward the student (VanDenBerg & Grealish, 1996).

This is done by providing students and their significant others feedback regarding what they are already doing well, reinforcing these healthy behaviors, and advancing student and significant others' understanding of even healthier, new behaviors that could be adopted (VanDenBerg & Grealish, 1996). The result is a collaborative assessment and data-providing venture in which significant others, counselor, and student jointly learn what is working and helpful and what is perceived to be helpful in the future. Such a collaborative and positively framed experience is foreign to most students who have violent behaviors.

Despite the support occurring within this session, the intent of the strengths assessment is not to gloss over or minimize student-presented concerns or difficulties. This would clearly be a harmful injustice to the student and systems of care group. Instead, the intent is to learn what is going well and identify how the student, counselor, and significant others contribute to this process. Thus, the identification of student strengths encircles the student within a powerful, systems-oriented treatment milieu that continues support opportunities for the student and significant others.

Finally, identifying student strengths provides an opportunity to establish rapport and trust among participants. Building such rapport and trust is important because later the student will likely be challenged to change formerly familiar violent behaviors and be held accountable by those within the systems of care group to abstain from violence. Thus the strengths assessment establishes the foundation on which the student can be challenged. Therefore, it is imperative that the counselor help the student and the significant others affirm and support one another during the student's strength assessment. This can be accomplished by asking the student to respond to supportive statements made by significant others. For example:

Counselor: Maria, what was it like to have your mother tell you that she loves you?

Maria: (Weeping) I can't fully describe what it was like, because it was so unbelievable. After all the mean things that I did to her and Grandma, to learn that she loves me means so much.

Mother: Maria, you know I love you.

Maria: I know that now, Momma, but I didn't know that you still loved me until you told me. I had thought you hated me, because I was so wicked and beat up other people.

Counselor: Sometimes when people love us, they don't know how to respond when we threaten, intimidate, or act violent. Mother, if you could say just one thing to your daughter about her committing herself to living without violence, what would you say?

Mother: You don't have to live this way. You are strong just like your grandma. I know you don't have to fight. More important, though, Maria, I'll do everything I can to support you in your counseling. But I won't lie to you. If you start fighting again, I'll get right in your face and call your probation officer. I'd rather have you in juvenile detention for fighting than in prison for murder.

Counselor: What do you hear your mom saying, Maria?

Maria: I hear her saying that she believes I don't have to fight.

Counselor: I hear her saying that, but I also hear her saying something else too.

Maria: What?

Counselor: I hear your mother saying that she loves you, that you can eliminate your previous fighting behaviors and she will support you. But I also hear her saying that

	she is going be truthful. If you start fighting again, she will call your probation officer. She will advocate that you be put in juvenile detention as a way of protecting you from potentially killing someone and going to prison for the rest of your life.
Maria:	I hear her saying that too.
Counselor:	Does that mean she doesn't love you or that she is not trying to be helpful when she tells the truth?
Maria:	No. It just means that she is trying to be helpful and knows telling the truth will help me.
Counselor:	Then you want your mom to be truthful even if you don't like what she says?
Maria:	I might not like what she says. But if she is telling me something, I need to listen.

This vignette demonstrates two central elements. First, the interaction promotes an opportunity for daughter and mother to further build rapport and establish trust. This is done by emphasizing mother's statement that she "loves" Maria and encourages Maria to report what hearing of her mother's love means to her. Second, it inoculates Maria from responding inappropriately to truthful statements during future systems of care interactions. Thus, not only is the mother indicating that she will make truthful statements, the daughter encourages such statements and indicates that the purpose of the mother's statements is to help Maria remain violence free and stay out of prison.

Nonviolent "Favorite" Things to Do

We have found one of the most important pieces of the systems of care method is helping students identify nonviolent "favorite" things to do. The next vignette demonstrates how to help clients identify such fun behaviors.

Counselor:	Maria, tell me about things you enjoy doing.
Maria:	I don't know. I really don't do much.
Counselor:	How about things you like to do with your mother or grandmother?
Maria:	Well, my mother and grandma sometimes take me to Fashion Beads and Jewelry
Counselor:	What do you do there?

Maria:	We sit and talk and make bracelets and necklaces and stuff like that.
Counselor:	Is it fun?
Maria:	Yes, it is a lot of fun.
Counselor:	How do you make it fun?
Maria:	What do you mean?
Counselor:	Well, I have this belief that people make things fun by saying things to themselves that make the experience fun. You know, like those kids who like to do math problems.
Maria:	I hate math.
Counselor:	Me too. But I used to know kids who really liked math. They even thought math was a blast.
Maria:	Not me.
Counselor:	Me either, but what do you think they were saying to themselves about the math problems that made doing math fun?
Maria:	I don't get it. What are you asking?
Counselor:	Well, I'm thinking to myself "I don't like math problems. Maria doesn't like math problems." What must these kids who like math be saying to themselves when they do their math problems?
Maria:	I have no idea.
Counselor:	I'm wondering if they are not saying things to themselves like "This math problem is fun because I know I can do it." And "Math problems are puzzles, and I can't wait to see how to solve this puzzle."
Maria:	Yeah, I can see that. It makes sense.
Counselor:	So what is it that you are saying to yourself when you are making jewelry with your mom and grandma that makes the experience fun?
Maria:	Oh, I get it now. I'm saying "I'm here talking with my favorite people. I'm having fun because I'm making something pretty that I can wear and show everybody."
Counselor:	Cool! So you are not saying "Mom and Grandma will not tease me about my weight or about not making a perfect bracelet?"

Maria:	No, I would never think that. I'm saying to myself "Mom loves me; Grandma cares about me. They will never tease me about my weight."
Counselor:	Good. So I'm hearing two things. First, when you are with your mother and grandma working on jewelry, you are making the experience fun by saying things like "Mom loves me and Grandma cares about me." Second, I'm hearing that you like being with your mother and grandma, and when you are with them, you are not thinking about fighting.
Maria:	Exactly.
Grandmother:	Well, then, I think your mother and I need to do more things with you.
Counselor:	Perfect! Because the more you are with her . . .
Mother:	[interrupting counselor] . . . the less she feels she is being teased and she doesn't feel she has to fight back.
Counselor:	You're good, Mom! Way to go. You and Grandma know exactly what needs to happen.

Let us analyze what happened in this vignette. The first thing the school counselor so eloquently does is directly ask about fun things Maria likes to do. The assumption is that if the school counselor can identify times when Maria is comfortable, her self-talk will be positive, and she is more likely having fun. The next assumption is if we can identify just one fun time, then jointly Maria, Mother, and Grandmother can identify or create other fun times. The final assumption is that if Maria can begin to increase the amount of her positive self-talk and have more "fun times" throughout the day, the probability of her violent behaviors will be reduced.

Once the question is directly asked, Maria responds like most students by saying "I don't know." Instead of stopping, the counselor immediately asks about things Maria likes to do with her mother and grandmother. In other words, the counselor does not accept "I don't know" as Maria's final answer. The counselor understood that if the counselor kept asking about things Maria liked doing with people, sooner or later the girl likely would identify something fun. The key is always to ask about fun things being done with those with whom the student likes or spends time. We have never met a student who hangs around other students simply to enjoy the misery of their company. Even as adults, few of us spend time with those we dislike if we do not believe the benefits outweigh the costs. Typically for students, if they are not having at least some minimal threshold of fun with peers or significant others, they would disengage and begin spending time with others who are fun.

Once Maria identifies that she enjoys making bracelets and necklaces with her mother and grandmother, the counselor switches the conversation. Specifically, the counselor asks how Maria "makes" the experience fun. In cognitive behavioral terms, the counselor begins to train Maria that her self-talk or internal conversations either makes experiences positive or negative. In particular, the counselor talks about something that we have found almost universally inconceivable to the students we counsel: Some students like math! This resonates with Maria, and her response is that she "hates" math. Instead of arguing that Maria should like math, the counselor immediately joins with the student and states, "Me either." In other words, the counselor is indirectly saying "Hey, you and I are alike. You hate math. I hate math." More important, the implication for Maria is that she and the counselor have something in common. This cognition promotes the perception "Hey, this counselor is rather similar to me."

Such therapeutic joining is imperative. It helps Maria, Mother, and Grandmother see the school counselor as invested and similar to each of them. My guess is that the grandmother does not have an internal discussion, such as "What? This school counselor doesn't like math? How dare she say she doesn't like math?" Instead, we would anticipate that the grandmother probably is thinking "That school counselor is more like me than I originally thought."

Next, the school counselor challenges Maria to understand "how" students who like math internally reframe math problems. Here the counselor suggests that students who like math experience math problems as enjoyable puzzles. In other words, the counselor encourages Maria to understand a parallel process. Here math problems are "paralleled" to making jewelry. In other words, one's self-talk (e.g., "I'm having fun finding the answers to this math puzzle," etc.) influences how one interprets the experience or task. Additionally, the counselor helps Maria understand her internal dialogue regarding her mother's and grandmother's thoughts about her.

Further, the counselor points out that Maria is not fighting when she is in the presence of her mother and grandmother and doing something enjoyable. Grandmother immediately understands this nonviolence construct and identifies Maria's need to increase activities with her mother and grandmother. Concomitantly, Ms. Diaz completes the school counselor's statement, making it apparent that she also understands that when Maria is with her and her grandmother making jewelry, Maria is not fighting. The counselor then praises both the mother and grandmother for identifying Maria's needs and for their willingness to agree to spend more time with the girl.

Commonalities Within Nonviolent Times Compared to Commonalities Within Violent Times

After we initially identify favorite things the student likes to do, we shift our focus slightly. In particular, we move toward other nonviolent times. Specifically, we want to identify persons the student is with, what the student is doing, where the student is, and what the student is saying to self during these nonviolent times. Here the counselor might initiate the next dialog.

Counselor: Maria, tell me about the times when you are not fighting.

Maria: What do you want to know?

Counselor: My belief is that you don't fight every moment of the day, right?

Maria: Yeah.

Counselor: So tell me about the times you weren't fighting yesterday.

Maria: Well, let's see. I was at soccer practice with my friends and I didn't fight.

Counselor: Okay, who was there?

Maria: Annie, Karl, Juan, and Olivia.

Counselor: Have you ever gotten in a fight with Annie or fought when you were with Annie?

Maria: (Giggling) Of course not. She is my friend. We never fight. We are having way too much fun together to fight.

Counselor:	How about Karl, Juan, and Olivia? Do you ever fight with them or have you ever fought when they were around?
Maria:	Never
Counselor:	I'm confused. How is it that you don't fight with Annie, Karl, Juan, or Olivia?
Maria:	That's easy. We are always having fun together. We don't argue or fight.
Counselor:	Maria, when you are with Annie, Karl, Juan, and Olivia during soccer practice, what kinds of things do you say to yourself?
Maria:	I guess I am thinking to myself "This is fun, these are my friends, they like me, and I don't have to worry that they are going to make fun of me."

Let us stop here. Maria has just reported four people she enjoys and with whom she does not fight. She also has told us what the five of them are doing when she does not fight: They are practicing soccer. Maria also reports her self-talk. At this point, the counselor may wish to engage Maria and the systems of care group members to identify noted commonalities occurring when she is not violent.

Counselor:	Maria, I don't know about others here, but I'm hearing some common themes related to times when you are not acting violently. Specifically, I am hearing that when you are with people you consider to be your friends, like Annie, and when you are places that are fairly structured such as Girl Scouts, church, and soccer practice, you frequently are telling yourself that you are "having fun" and "enjoying" yourself. What are the rest of you hearing?

After the group has thoroughly discussed perceived commonalities among nonviolent times with Maria, the counselor might continue in this way.

Counselor:	Maria, you specifically chose each person here. Tell us whom they would say you should interact with, the

> activities you should do, and the places you should go
> to decrease the likelihood of becoming violent?

The intent is to have Maria self-identify the people, activities, and places she should become more involved with.

Next, the counselor will investigate people, activities, places, and self-talk related to times when Maria is violent. Here the counselor might state something similar to the next dialog.

> Counselor: Tell me about the last time you fought. Who was
> there, where did the fight occur, and what were you
> saying to yourself?

Again, the counselor is going to be listening for commonalities in times when Maria acts violently. Once these commonalities become clear, the counselor will say something similar to the next dialog:

> Counselor: Maria, just like the commonalties you described during
> times when you choose not to fight or act violently, I'm
> hearing some other common themes related to times
> when you do act violently. Specifically, I am hearing
> that when you are around Chrissie and when you don't
> have much adult supervision, you tend to do things that
> get you in trouble. Are others hearing the same thing?

At the conclusion of the investigation of violent times, the systems of care group will make suggestions as whom Maria should stay away from, places she should not go, and things she should not be doing. The counselor should then ask Maria how committed she is to following through with the recommendation of the systems of care group.

> Counselor: This is what I heard people you value say today.
> I heard them say you should spend more time with
> Annie, Karl, Juan, and Olivia and that playing systems
> of care with your friends was important to do. I also
> heard the people you value say you should stay away
> from Chrissy and places where there is little or no
> adult supervision. On a scale between 1 and 10, how
> likely will it be that you do these things?

Should Maria indicate a high number, such as 6 or above, she should be praised and congratulated for choosing to do the best things. Conversely, should she provide a score of 5 or lower, the counselor may say:

> Counselor: You have said you would give yourself a 1 on the scale. Meaning that you likely aren't going to do the things this group suggested. How is it helpful for you *not* to do the things that this, your group of friends, have suggested?

As you have seen in the mini-clinical vignettes and discussions, the systems of care method provides opportunities for the student and the student's significant others to learn how to change. The intervention is relatively easy to implement, and the outcomes can produce significant results. The systems of care participants support the previously violent student with sincere and nurturing directions; in essence, they make up the coaching team. These directions provide new behavioral and cognitive patterns that ensure student success.

CHAPTER SUMMARY

Existing literature demonstrates the utility of systems of care interventions with students and their family systems. Concomitantly, the systems of care method seems to offer previously violent or potentially but not imminently violent students an opportunity to lessen the probability of violent behaviors via regular meetings with significant others. The approach seems well suited for multiservice interventions where professionals from various agencies jointly devise interventions with students, students' families, and significant nonprofessional others ways to impede potentially violent behaviors and increase desirable behaviors. Concomitantly, the use of trusted and respected nonprofessionals identified by the student as important ensures a treatment approach that is specifically developed to meet the unique needs and goals of each student, thereby enhancing student motivation and treatment compliance. Coordination of the systems of care approach with students potentially at risk for violent behaviors increases treatment provider collaboration and the promotion of integrated interventions with the purpose of preventing student violence and fostering prosocial, nonviolent modes of interaction.

8

Utilizing Psychological First Aid When Responding to School Violence Survivors and Their Parents

PSYCHOLOGICAL FIRST AID

Psychological First Aid has significant utility for school violence survivors and their parents. It provides a nonintrusive intervention that can be easily facilitated by counselors. The nonthreatening approach provides survivors and their parents the opportunity to engage in counseling following a violence experience. Yet, the approach does not require or force survivors into the counseling process. Instead, it welcomes survivors to join in an approach at a pace and level matching the survivors' comfort level.

General Overview

According to the *Psychological First Aid: Field Operations Guide* (National Child Traumatic Stress Network and National Center for PTSD [NCTSN/ NCPTSD], 2006, p. 1), "Psychological First Aid is an evidence-informed modular approach to help children, adolescents, adults, and families in the aftermath of disaster and terrorism." In a nutshell, Psychological First Aid was developed to reduce the emotional trauma experienced by disaster survivors and to promote "short- and long-term adaptive functioning and coping."

Professionally speaking, Psychological First Aid matches basic Professional Counselor tenets and underpinnings. Specifically, Psychological First Aid is health based and does not focus on psychopathology. In other words, those who developed Psychological First Aid believe most survivors are resilient. They believe many survivors will cope adequately with the experienced event without developing debilitating, long-term, trauma-related symptoms. Additionally, the Psychological First Aid developers believe that if trauma-related symptoms develop, the symptoms will fall somewhere on a broad continuum. Thus, symptoms would range between mild to severe. This broad continuum range is especially important to counselors. All trauma-related symptoms will *not* be experienced at the severe end of the spectrum. Hence, the model stands in stark contrast to those who view survivors as "broken" and in need of "fixing." Instead, the underpinnings of Psychological First Aid suggest that survivors respond according to multiple factors, depending on their perception of the experience, previous levels of emotional and interpersonal health, and perceptions of hope and the future.

Eight Core Actions, Goals, and Corresponding Mini-Clinical Vignettes

Eight Core Actions provide the Psychological First Aid foundation. Each Core Action has a corresponding goal. The Core Actions and their corresponding goals are described in greater detail in this chapter, along with mini-clinical vignettes based on this school violence scenario. Angel is a 13-year-old seventh grader who attends Cactus Bluff Middle School in a large southwestern city. She and her best friend, Katrina, play on the school's seventh-grade girls' basketball team. Both wore school basketball team spirit wear and cheered the seventh-grade boys' basketball team at school during a Thursday evening game. At the game, Angel and Katrina "talked smack," hurled trash talk, and made negative comments toward opposing players. A sister and two female friends of one of the visiting team's basketball players threatened to "beat up" Angel and Katrina if they did not stop their obnoxious talk.

Angel and Katrina continued their verbal bashing toward the opposing basketball team players and began taunting the sister and her friends. At halftime, the opposing team member's sister shoved Angel. Angel fell from the third row of the bleachers. This physical altercation ended when the school resource officer ejected the opposing team member's sister and her two friends from the game. After the game, Angel and Katrina exited the school building and began walking home. However, as they crossed the dimly lit school parking lot, the opposing team member's sister and two friends appeared. The sister had a knife and stabbed Angel in the chest, neck, and arms. Katrina escaped the assailant's friends and ran back into the school gymnasium and sought help. The school resource officer, vice principal, and several teachers immediately ran onto the parking lot and began looking for Angel. Once the opposing team member's sister and friends saw the adults coming, they ran away. Angel was taken by ambulance to a local hospital and received several stitches for the superficial cuts and stabs wounds inflicted. Katrina was badly shaken and tearful.

Core Action 1: Contact and Engagement

The first Core Action is Contact and Engagement. The goal of this Core Action is either to initiate contact with the violence survivor or respond to the survivor's contact. Key components of this Core Action revolve around demonstrating respect and compassion to those who have experienced violence and presenting in a calm manner. Often this first Core Action is initiated by the school counselor via a brief introduction. In the scenario just described, the school counselor was at the basketball game and was the first to respond to Katrina after the parking lot attack. The counselor might say:

Counselor:	Hello, Katrina. I am Ms. VanderPaul, your school counselor. I remember talking with you last week when you needed a hall pass. Do you remember me?
Katrina:	Yes, I know you. I remember you helping me get a hall pass.
Counselor:	Good. Are you okay?
Katrina:	I don't know. Angel and I were walking across the parking lot, and we were attacked.
Counselor:	I thought I would just check in with you to see if you're okay.
Katrina:	(Long pause) I don't know.
Counselor:	What can I do to help you right now?

Given that school counselors are often on campus when school violence occurs and because students are already familiar with these counselors, these professionals are most uniquely positioned to be "first responders" to school violence survivors. Typically, students immediately recognize school counselors. This familiarity often engenders a feeling of security and comfort for student violence survivors. In the last mini-clinical vignette, the counselor recognizes Katrina and reminds Katrina of their recent benign school interaction. This is done simply to connect with the student in a nonthreatening and nonintrusive manner. Katrina immediately acknowledges that she knows the school counselor. The counselor then simply affirms Katrina statement and states, "Are you okay?"

This statement is vitally important. The counselor does not gush, "Oh, you poor thing. I bet you are scared to death!" Instead, she provides the student the *opportunity to engage*. Stated differently, the counselor neither demands interaction from the student nor conveys that the student must have experienced severe psychological distress as a result of the violent event. Had Katrina responded, "I'm fine," the counselor would simply have asked if she needed anything (e.g., a ride home) or wanted to talk. The opportunity to engage is up to the student, and a school counselor should never force engagement to occur. Note that the counselor also asks what Katrina needs from her right now. This is important as well. A student may indicate a need to talk, a need for someone to talk with her parents about the violent event, or any of a million other things. The important thing is that the school counselor acts interested in the student and asks about the student's immediate need. Whatever needs requested by the student should be followed by at least an attempt to secure the student's request(s). For example, when survivors are provided Psychological First Aid, they often will simply request an opportunity to talk, bottled water, or some food. Giving student survivors bottled water provides opportunities for them to feel comfortable, talk with counselors in a nonpsychopathological focused manner, and respond to basic needs. These safe experiences create feelings of immediate normality and provide further opportunities to engage in discussions about what happened, what the student wishes to do, what the student needs, or feelings about the violence.

In the mini-clinical vignette, the school counselor initiates contact with the student. However, there are also times when a counselor will respond to a student violence survivor's contact. Here, for example, when Angel returns to school Friday morning, she may present at Ms. VanderPaul's office. In this case, Angel is seeking help from her school counselor.

Angel: Ms. VanderPaul, do you have a minute to talk?
Counselor: Certainly, Angel. Would you like to sit down here in my office? How about bottled water?

Angel: No, thanks.
Counselor: Angel, how may I best help you?

Again, notice what happens. The school counselor, Ms. VanderPaul, immediately invites the student to sit down in her office and offers bottled water. Then she asks how she can best help Angel. This interaction conveys the school counselor's interest in Angel and vividly implies that the school counselor wants to be helpful. Such interactions convey safety and provide opportunities for students to describe what happened, their concerns, or their needs.

Core Action 2: Safety and Comfort

The primary goals of this Core Action are "to enhance immediate and ongoing safety, and provide physical and emotional comfort" (NCTSN/ NCPTSD, 2006, p. 12). In particular, this Core Action is designed to let students know that they have survived the immediate violent event and are in a "Safe Zone" that is protected from immediate threat. Concomitantly, this Core Action allows school counselors to assess students impacted by the school violence for shock and threats of harm to self (e.g., suicidal ideation, etc.) or others (e.g., retaliation toward others, etc.). If such issues are noted, immediate intervention must occur. For example, should the school counselor assessing student survivors for shock note that a student presents with irregular breathing, dizziness, lack of bladder or bowel control, or clammy skin, the counselor would want to immediately contact emergency medical services personnel and ensure appropriate medical intervention is provided. Should the violence-surviving student report intent to retaliate and harm those who perpetrated the violence, the school counselor will need to intervene. Here, for example, should the counselor perceive the threat is an imminent danger, the counselor would need to immediately consult with a supervisor and the school district's legal counsel and then contact police authorities to ensure safety.

In the case of Katrina, the school counselor within this Core Action will establish an immediate safe zone away from danger. For example, the counselor might secure and cordon off a safe zone within the school library or teachers' lounge. Cordoning off such an area will keep everyone except the survivors, school counselor, and medical responders outside the safe zone and away from the surviving student(s). To accomplish this charge, the counselor will need to involve others. This might include assigning school resource or peace officers, vice principals, nurses, teachers, coaches, or custodial staff the task of creating a safe zone area where survivors can simply "be" without feeling mobbed by those who wish to help until police and loved ones arrive. Survivors' loved ones (e.g., parents) can then be escorted to an area within the safe zone to reunite with the individual student survivor(s).

Depending on the particular circumstances, including the violent event and the age and popularity of surviving students, school counselors may wish to allow one or two known close friends of the survivors to enter the safe zone. Once in the safe zone, friends can support the surviving students until their parents arrive. Here is a scenario using the previous example with Katrina.

> Counselor: Katrina, let's go to my office. School Resource Officer
>   Richards is going to stand guard outside my office
>   door to ensure that we are safe inside. From there,
>   I will contact your parents and ask them to meet us in
>   the safety of my office. Is that all right with you?
>
> Katrina: Yes . . . I just want to be safe. I don't know what to do.
>
> Counselor: Katrina, I'm going to stay with you until your par-
>   ents arrive. You will be safe with Resource Officer
>   Richards and me until your parents arrive.

Here the school counselor takes administrative control. She includes the school resource officer and ensures that Katrina understands that they will be safe until Katrina's parents arrive. When Katrina reports that she does not know what to do, the counselor again takes administrative control and reports that she (the school counselor) will stay with Katrina until her parents arrive. At all times, the gist of the school counselor's communication is "You are safe," "I am here with you," and "Your parents are on the way."

As previously indicated, the school counselor may determine it therapeuti-cally supportive to have one or two of Katrina's friends who attended the basketball game "be" with Katrina in the safe zone. Instead of unilaterally making this decision, however, the counselor would ask for Katrina's desires.

> Counselor: Now you are safe within my office with the school
>   resource officer standing guard outside the door to
>   ensure you are safe. Mr. Valadez, our principal, is call-
>   ing your mother and will make certain she gets here as

quickly as she can. In the meantime, I am wondering. I saw you sitting with Gina Gonzalez and Erin Jones in the bleachers at tonight's game. Would you like me to ask one or both of them to join us here in the safe zone while we await your mother's arrival?

This is an important interaction to comment on for three reasons.

1. Note that the school counselor continues to communicate Katrina's safety. She reports "you are safe" and augments that communication by reminding Katrina that the school resource officer is standing outside the safe zone door to ensure that no one can harm her.
2. The school counselor's statements apprise Katrina of what is happening outside the safe zone. The counselor indicates that the principal is contacting Katrina's mother and the mother will be arriving quickly.
3. The school counselor had seen Katrina in the bleachers with two other students believed to be Katrina's friends. However, instead of merely allowing them into the safe zone without Katrina's permission, the counselor gives Katrina a sense of control by allowing her to determine if both, one, or none of the students should be allowed to support Katrina in the safe zone until Katrina's mother can arrive.

In the earlier case with Angel, who presents at the school counselor's office the morning after the violence, the Core Action continues to revolve around safety and comfort. However, because the violence occurred the preceding evening and the vignette perpetrators do not attend Angel's school, the school counselor's response will be different. Instead of whisking Angel to a safe zone, the counselor will promote safety and comfort in a slightly different manner. Again, the counselor will consult with others, such as the school resource officer, to ensure Angel's safety within the current school milieu. However, this may require informing the school resource officer, principal and staff, and Angel's teachers of the previous evening's violence.

In Angel's situation, after the school counselor contacts the district's legal counsel for directions, her principal, and the school's resource officer, Ms. VanderPaul informs Angel of the exact school measures being enacted to protect Angel, describes what Angel should do if she feels threatened while at school or if she should see her alleged assailants elsewhere (e.g., at a store, movie theater, band concert, etc.), and discusses available services to help Angel cope. In particular, the school counselor will most likely meet with Angel and her parents to ensure that all have information regarding the previous night's violence and to explain how they should respond should the assailants reappear. Meeting with Angel and her parents also will provide an opportunity to describe the manner in which students Angel's age typically present immediately following experienced violence.

Counselor:	Mr. and Mrs. Jones, thank you so much for coming to discuss Angel's situation. Your being here conveys to Angel that she is very important to you and that you are committed to helping ensure her safety and needs are met.
Mrs. Jones:	Thank you for having us. We are very concerned.
Counselor:	Angel, have you told your mom and dad about last evening's events?
Angel:	Yes, they came to the emergency room while I was getting stitched up and the police told them what happened.
Counselor:	What did the police tell you, Mrs. Jones?
Mrs. Jones	The officer was very nice. He indicated that a verbal altercation had occurred. Apparently Angel and her best friend, Katrina, had argued with some girls from Smith Middle School. After the basketball game, the Smith girls attacked Angel and Katrina with a knife. Katrina escaped, but Angel was stabbed and needed about 13 stitches.
Counselor:	Did the police say anything else?
Mr. Jones:	They took Angel down to the police station, and she identified two of the girls from the Smith High School Yearbook. The assistant district attorney contacted us this morning and said charges would be filed against the girls. Their names were Penny Andersone and Veronica Wareht. They still didn't know the name of the third girl but thought they would have that information this afternoon.
Counselor:	Would you mind if I conveyed this information to our school resource officer and principal?
Mr. Jones:	Please do.

Counselor: This is what we are doing at Cactus Bluff to help ensure Angel's safety. First, the resource officer, principal, vice principals, and Angel's teachers have been informed of the situation. Specifically, a description of the alleged assailants has been provided to the resource officer, principals, and Angel's teachers. Should these girls come to Cactus Bluff, the school resource officer will arrest them for trespassing on school property. Second, Angel and I have devised an action plan. Angel knows what to do if she sees any of these girls or others who she perceives as a threat to her. Angel will immediately tell a faculty member, staff member, resource officer, or administrator should she feel in danger. Additionally, we have asked that Angel use the "buddy system" during the remainder of the semester and have at least one friend with her at all times. This includes coming to and leaving from school.

Let us review this mini-clinical vignette. The first thing the school counselor so eloquently does is thank Angel's parents for attending the session. She also frames their attendance aloud in very positive terms so Angel and her mom and dad hear very positive things about one another. This potentially promotes Angel's positive perception of her parents' attendance. In other words, rather than Angel perceiving that her mother and father are there to "control" or "sanction" her, the counselor suggests the parents' presence indicates that Angel is important to them and her parents are committed to ensuring her safety. At the same time, the school counselor has provided a positive complement to mother and father. Such a complement has the potential to reduce their potential defenses about "having" to attend this school requested meeting.

Next the counselor empowers Angel by sharing administrative control. Asking Angel if she has shared the situation with her parents promotes her active participation in the discussion and allows her to feel part of the conversation. Had Angel not shared information regarding the previous evening's events, this would provide an opportunity for her to describe what happened within a safe environment controlled by the school counselor.

For example, if Angel had not described the situation with her parents and her parents became angry because she had not provided such information, the school counselor might positively reframe Angel's noninforming behaviors.

Angel: No, I didn't tell them.

Mr. Jones: What! You were attacked at school and you didn't tell us!

Mrs. Jones: Why didn't you tell us? We are your parents. I can't believe . . .

Counselor: (gently interrupting Mrs. Jones) Pardon me, Mrs. Jones, I don't mean to interrupt but if you wouldn't mind, please allow me to provide my professional opinion here. It sounds to me as though Angel had been through a very traumatic event—someone attacked her with a knife with the intent of causing great bodily harm. Undoubtedly, Angel was in emotional turmoil from the event and responded like many 12- or 13-year-old students would. She bottled everything up. In psychological terms, she "compartmentalized" the situation, because it was incredibly scary for her and because she wanted to protect both Mr. Jones and you from worrying. Now, given that Angel probably did this subconsciously rather than consciously, she probably doesn't fully remember why she did this. All she knows is that the situation was emotionally overwhelming at the time and that it short-circuited her ability to respond. Again, as a 12- or 13-year-old, this would not be uncommon or atypical. I believe the important thing here is that Angel wanted both of you to be present here in my office so she could tell you about the events in a safe place where she knew both Mr. Jones and you would be able to feel safe and know that Angel is okay.

Here the school counselor respectfully interrupts Mrs. Jones, apologizes for the interruption, and inserts her "professional opinion." This interruption is therapeutically relevant. In layman's terms, the counselor gets between the dog and the fire hydrant. The school counselor diverts the mother's negative verbal salvo by reminding the parents of the severe trauma likely experienced by Angel. Without inappropriate harsh confrontation, the school counselor eloquently reminds Angel's parents that their daughter is merely a 12-year-old child, and her behaviors are consistent with those of most 12-year-olds who experience life-threatening trauma. The school counselor also reframes Angel's behaviors in psychological terms and then suggests that subconsciously Angel was attempting to "protect" her parents. Our experiences suggest that when such positive reframing occurs, the arguing or "attack" ends. Even a semiplausible explanation proposed by the counselor stops the negative discourse long enough for parents and students to thoughtfully consider the explanation. An interruption within the arguing sequence is enough to refocus the session and move back to the needs at hand.

Getting back to the original mini-clinical vignette where Angel had informed her parents regarding the previous evening's traumatic events, the school counselor again promotes the Core Action of Safety and Comfort by providing Angel and her parents a summary of what will be done at the school to protect the girl. This both reminds Angel of how she should respond if she sees the alleged perpetrators and encourages her to remember the action plan that she had developed to help ensure her safety.

During the Second Core Action stage, the school counselor continually reminds students (and parents, upon their arrival to the school) that the students are being cared for and are safe. If the trauma is over and there is no imminent danger, it is helpful to repeat frequently to survivors that they are safe. Doing so implies that the immediate danger has passed. Here the school counselor might say, "Angel, you are safe now. We are here for you. Everything is going to be okay." This affirming mantra is comforting to students. It reminds them and arriving parents that the immediate crisis has passed. Such reassurance is vitally important and can do much to quell the presenting anxious and fearful feelings.

Additionally, depending on the affected students' ages and the emotional stability of parents, it is helpful to describe typical trauma responses. Whenever working with students who have experienced a traumatic event, tell parents that students who experience trauma often respond and behave differently. Many times when multiple students experience the same traumatic event, their clinical presentations widely differ. In the post-violence period, some students will present with depressed affect and feelings of hopelessness and sadness, and will demonstrate fatigue or report low energy levels (Perry, 2002). Others respond to the traumatic event by becoming overly clingy on mothers and primary caregivers. They may have a heightened sensitivity to perceived rejection. Many times they will have difficulties separating from their mothers or primary caregivers, and they may be perceived as overly whiny. Some will regress, presenting and acting younger than their true chronological age. School violence survivors may present with enuresis (wetting oneself) and/or encopresis (feces soiling in clothes) (Krill, 2009) and want extreme parental coddling and nurturing. Others may present at the other end of the continuum. Here students who had previously presented without Attention Deficit Hyperactivity Disorder symptomatology may suddenly present as highly distractible, impulsive, or aggressive. Therefore, it is imperative that the school counselor tell parents about potential symptoms. It is our belief that informing parents decreases the probability that students will be punished for post-violence symptoms and increases the probability that parents will both attend to the symptoms and seek immediate mental health counseling should the symptoms escalate.

In Katrina's case, the dialog may go as follows.

Counselor: Over the years, we have found that students respond to violent incidents in a variety of different ways. Some experience few if any symptoms. Others will suddenly present as sad, depressed, or fearful. Some will become clingy or whiny and won't want to be separated from their mothers or family members. Still others will become angry, defiant, impulsive, or distractible. All these are normal trauma response behaviors.

Mother: Makes sense.

Counselor: This is what we would ask you to do over the next few days and weeks. Are you up to it?

Father: Yes.

Counselor: Good. First, keep an eye on Katrina. I realize that I don't have to tell you this, so I am preaching to the choir here. However, some parents punish their children should they begin to demonstrate some of the post-trauma symptoms. Instead, I know that you won't do that with Katrina.

Father: We would never punish her for experiencing trauma symptoms.

Counselor: I agree. After getting to know you for just a few minutes, it is strikingly evident that you both love Katrina.

Mother: Very true.

Counselor: Knowing what great parents you both are, I suspect that you will make special times for Katrina and the two of you to do things together. Maybe you will decide to take walks or play board games together. Or maybe you will do something else like make family dinners together or write stories together. The key is spending extra time with Katrina until she is back to her normal self. Can I count on you both doing this?

Mother: No question we will do that.

Counselor: Good. I've got just one more thing to say. Should you find that Katrina begins to get worse in any way, call me. Here is my number. (The counselor hands a business card to the mother and another to the father.) So, if she begins to demonstrate increased depression, anger, or an inability to concentrate, give me a call so we can meet.

Father: We certainly will.

Counselor: Katrina, this goes for you too. If you begin to feel overwhelmed, like hurting yourself or others, or feel really sad or depressed and you don't know why, come to my office or call me at this number. (The counselor hands a business card to Katrina.)

Let us review what happened here. First, the school counselor describes the types of symptoms Katrina may present or develop. This is rather psychoeducational and provides Katrina's parents a general description of potential post-trauma symptoms that Katrina *may* present. Next Mrs. VanderPaul invites Katrina's parents to respond to a potential therapeutic directive. However, instead of simply telling Katrina's parents what to do, the counselor asks them if they are willing to follow the directive. Although the implication is subtle, the inference is significant. Katrina's parents now agree to follow the counselor's instruction. Stated differently, Katrina's parents are buying into treatment. Too often counselors tell parents what to do. Many times parents agree without truly investing in their child's trauma recovery. In this instance, however, the parents had the option to refuse the directive. Instead, they didn't refuse. They pledged their commitment to comply with the expert's directive.

Immediately, the counselor both lauds Katrina's parents and establishes a paradox. The paradox suggests that inept parents punish children who experience post-trauma symptoms. Further, the paradox clearly differentiates Katrina's parents from the implied inept parents. Can you imagine any caring parent responding "No. I want to be an inept parent and inappropriately punish my child due to her genuine post-trauma symptoms"? Of course not! Katrina's parents are invested in helping their daughter. They quickly report they would never punish Katrina for legitimate symptoms. Such seemingly inconsequential communication nuances are in fact quite consequential. They promote appropriate responses by Katrina's parents.

The school counselor then provides a smorgasbord of potential ways in which Katrina's parents can engage their daughter in additional parent-child time. Thus, instead of providing one example describing how Katrina's parents could engage Katrina, the school counselor suggests four. More important, the counselor embeds the suggestion that Katrina's parents can come up with "something else." The suggested engagement activities are then capped with a question. Specifically, the school counselor asks if the parents will provide special engagement time. Who could possibly answer "No"? If they did, the school counselor might simply respond in this way:

> Counselor: I guess I am a little confused. How will it be helpful to Katrina *not* to provide special opportunities to spend time with you?

Two final powerful interactions are noted.

1. The counselor provides her business cards with telephone number to each person—the father, mother, *and Katrina*. This is important. No one is left out. If the counselor simply provided the mother and father cards and failed to hand a card to Katrina, it would suggest that Katrina is not part of the solution. It would further suggest that Katrina's parents control her recovery and that she is utterly powerless.
2. The school counselor asks each person—including Katrina—to call if Katrina decompensates. Again, making a special invitation for Katrina

to participate in her personal trauma recovery empowers her and suggests that she can positively impact the success of her treatment.

Core Action 3: Stabilization (If Warranted)

The primary goals of this Core Action stage are to calm and orient emotionally overwhelmed and disoriented violence survivors. This Core Action is often appropriate when students experience severe violent events (e.g., an on-campus shooting or explicitly graphic assault that results in the death or significant injury to a highly regarded classmate). Core Action Stabilization may be unnecessary if the violent event was less serious in nature (e.g., a single veiled threat made by a nonmenacing person) or outcome (e.g., no injuries were sustained). For example, if the violent event was a veiled threat made by a smaller, younger student, the threatened student may not perceive potential danger. Thus Stabilization may be unwarranted.[1]

However, should survivors' post-violence presentations be extreme, school counselors will need to stabilize the students or refer them for stabilization by other mental health professionals. Examples of such extreme presentations might include students who:

- Are unresponsiveness to verbal questioning.
- Demonstrate severe regressive behaviors, such as assuming the fetal position, aimless rocking back and forth, or thumb sucking.
- Cry, tremble, or shake uncontrollably.
- Rant or speak nonsensically aloud to themselves.

Remember the vignette about Katrina. She had escaped an attack in the school parking lot and, although emotionally shaken, had reported the incident so that her friend, Angel, could be rescued. Let us slightly modify that case vignette so that it is relevant to the Stabilization Core Action. This time when Katrina escapes, let us say that she was so emotionally distraught that she hid between parked cars in the school parking lot. Later that evening, she is found sitting with her lower back against the wheel of a parked truck. Her knees are drawn tightly to her body with her arms wrapped around her shins and her hands clasped around her ankles. She is aimlessly rocking back and forth, trembling, and just audibly crying.

---

[1] Note that just because a threat is not perceived as legitimate or because the person making the threat is of smaller stature does not mean that the threat is not real or potentially dangerous.

Her face is tear-soaked and her mascara is smeared from weeping. Katrina is unresponsive to the school resource officer who found her. Here it is quickly apparent that the Stabilization Core Action is relevant to the presenting case and necessary.

In such a situation and depending on the immediate presenting dangers in the parking lot (e.g., traffic, at-large assailants, etc.), the most therapeutic stabilization intervention will include going to the student rather than having the unresponsive student brought to the school counselor's office. Here, for example, the counselor may ask the school resource officer to summon additional staff or police to create a safety zone around the student. If possible, the student should have at least a six-foot radius around her where no one except immediately intervening persons can enter. In full view of the student, the school counselor would quietly and slowly approach. She would then ask if the student would mind if she sat next to her. The school counselor identifies herself as a counselor who is going to help the student. The counselor's voice is soft and caring. The tempo of the communications is very slow. The counselor speaks slowly and allows silence between questions or statements. Specifically, the school counselor might say something like this.

Counselor:	I'm Mrs. VanderPaul. (Pause and wait for student response. If no response is given continue.) I'm a counselor at Cactus Bluff. (Pause and wait for student response.) Would you mind if I sat by you and talked with you?
Student:	(Unresponsive; staring ahead with no direct eye contact; continuing to weep)
Counselor:	(After a minute or so of silence) Everything is going to be all right. You are safe. I'm going to take care of you. Can you tell me your name?
Student:	(Unresponsive)
Counselor:	You are going to be all right. Can you tell me your name?
Student:	(Unresponsive)
Counselor:	You are okay now. I am here to help you. You are safe. I won't leave you until I know that you are okay. Can you tell me what happened?

Student:	Uh-uh . . . (Katrina slowly and almost imperceptibly shakes her head side to side, indicating no.)
Counselor:	That's okay. We won't talk about what happened. It is over. You are now safe. I see you have a Cactus Bluff Middle School T-shirt. Do you attend Cactus Bluff?
Student:	Uuhhh-huh. (Katrina slowly nods her head, indicating yes.)
Counselor:	Who's your favorite teacher?
Student:	Ms. James (Almost inaudible)
Counselor:	Ms. James is one of my favorite teachers too. She is a good lady. Let's see if we can find her, okay?
Student:	Uuhhh-huh. (Katrina nods affirmatively.)
Counselor:	What classes do you have with Ms. James?
Student:	(Sits unresponsively)
Counselor:	We are looking for Ms. James right now and will try to get her here or get her on my cell phone. Everything is going to be all right. You are safe with me.
Student:	(Sits unresponsively)
Counselor:	Sometimes when I get really scared or bad things happen to me, I want to talk with my mom or dad. Can we call your mom or dad for you?
Student:	Yes . . . I want my mom.
Counselor:	Okay, we are going to get your mom. What is your name so we can call her?
Student:	Katrina. Katrina Marlboro.
Counselor:	"Do you remember your mom's telephone number?"
Student:	"222-5000"
Counselor:	Okay, Katrina, we are going to call your mom right now.

In this mini-clinical vignette, Ms. VanderPaul, the Cactus Bluff middle school counselor, was informed by the school resource officer that an unidentified student appeared unresponsive and emotionally overwhelmed in the school parking lot. For safety reasons, the school counselor goes to the student *only* after verifying that the parking lot is safe and makes certain that other persons go with her. Upon seeing Katrina, Ms. VanderPaul approaches the girl slowly and in full view. This ensures two things:

1. That the student is aware of Ms. VanderPaul's approach and is not startled
2. That if the student becomes agitated or hostile, Ms. VanderPaul can observe this change in physical or emotional presentation and escape if necessary escape

Next Mrs. VanderPaul identifies herself by name and position. This is important. It helps Katrina understand that Mrs. VanderPaul is not a stranger who is attempting to revictimize her. It is hoped that the statement triggers positive memories of seeing or interacting with Mrs. VanderPaul at school. Such memories may provide Katrina a sense of security and promote her engagement. Even if the student has not interacted with Mrs. VanderPaul, the counselor's introduction still may foster a positive sense of safety. This is because most students perceive school counselors favorably and believe that their jobs are to aid students (E. Zambrano, personal communication, December 23, 2009). Hence, listing her position and affiliation with Cactus Bluff Middle School demonstrates the counselor's attempt to connect or engage the student.

Mrs. VanderPaul also asks permission to join and speak to Katrina. Asking permission is an excellent therapeutic intervention with violence survivors. It provides them with a sense of control and indirectly indicates that students control whether this counselor can enter their space or not. Such perceived control by those in post-violence situations often engenders a sense of security. Typically, violence survivors literally had no control as they or others were helplessly violated. Verbalizing their current "control" of who is allowed to interact with them suggests that they are no longer helpless and denotes they have regained their control.

Here the student responds by not responding. Instead of immediately saying anything, Mrs. VanderPaul provides a period of silence. Again, this is an excellent therapeutic intervention. It empowers the student by suggesting that *she* controls the interaction. In other words, Katrina, not the adult, controls whether Katrina responds. Therefore, Katrina controls those with whom she verbally engages. Additionally, she controls the session's tempo. Such tempo control ensures that topics discussed occur at Katrina's pace, not the school counselor's pace. If questions or topics are too disconcerting or perceived by

Katrina as too "threatening," she can discontinue responding or slow her responses. This ultimately ensures that Katrina directs the tempo of the questions. Thus, the student has regained power and controls what happens next.

During this time, it is important not to continually stare at the student. Instead, it is best for the counselor to demonstrate that she is fully listening but to briefly and slowly shift eye contact. Often we teach our supervisees to sustain full eye contact when first asking questions. However, if the student is still unresponsive after a few moments, we instruct our counselor supervisees to slowly lower their heads and nonchalantly look at their hands in their laps. Once supervisees look at their hands, they are instructed to slowly rub their left index finger with their right thumb, then slowly look back at the student's eyes. If the student still does not engage, the counselor repeats the thumb-look-and-rub technique. The counselor completes this process two to three times as needed before making any further statements.

At no time should counselors look far away. In other words, they should not look at the distant school building or football field. The student may misperceive the counselor looking at distant or faraway objects as a desire to escape the student's presence. Instead, by slowly and briefly looking at their own hands, the counselor remains in the student's "relationship bubble." The action suggests "I am still here with you. I am paying attention to you. And I am not leaving this immediate relationship."

Next the school counselor tells Katrina that everything is all right; she is safe. The counselor also indicates that she is going to take care of Katrina. Stated differently, the school counselor is saying "I am here for you. I am committed to you." This conveys to Katrina that she has someone who is committed to helping her and that nothing is going to harm her while the counselor is present. Again, these statements promote the student's sense of safety and allow the counselor to ask the next question: "Can you tell me your name?"

Here Katrina is unresponsive. So, the counselor repeats that the student is safe and asks her name again. Instead of continually asking the same question over and over, the school counselor repeats the mantra, "You are safe" and changes the question to "Can you tell me what happened?" At no time does she challenge the violence survivor to respond (e.g., "Come on, answer my question. Who are you!?"). Instead, Mrs. VanderPaul gently continues the mantra "You are safe now." Often badly shaken violence survivors do not want to recall what happened. The memories are overwhelming and frightening.

Notice that when Katrina physically shakes her head no, the school counselor provides a supportive response: "That's okay. We won't talk about what happened. It is over." This response is key and states that the traumatic event is over. In other words, "You don't have to relive what happened." The response further repeats the safety mantra and clearly reports that the school survivor will not be forced to respond. Again this says to the surviving student "You do not have to reexperience the overwhelming memories. *You control* what topics are discussed."

The counselor then verbalizes a new question, which further indicates that the survivor continues to control the interaction. It suggests, "Okay, you don't want to talk about the violence. However, I am not going away. Instead, I am committed to helping you. I'm going to ask more questions to learn who you are. You are important to me." Here the counselor reports a benign observation and asks a different question ("I see you have a Cactus Bluff Middle School T-shirt. Do you attend Cactus Bluff?"). This question has nothing to do with the violence. Instead, Mrs. VanderPaul asks the student: "Who's your favorite teacher?" The question is totally safe. It has nothing to do with the experienced trauma. More important, it potentially introduces positive memories of someone who has cared about the student in the past—someone with whom the student undoubtedly felt comfortable and safe. The question produces Katrina's verbalized response.

The counselor then talks favorably about Ms. James, the student's reported favorite teacher. The school counselor's positive statements regarding Ms. James are an attempt to build rapport and continue the student's engagement. The statement that the school counselor will seek Ms. James is designed to imply "More safety is coming. Someone you like and who cares about you is coming." Additionally, by contacting Ms. James, the school counselor has a clue as to the student's identification if no further student responses are forthcoming.

The school counselor then reports that when she is scared she often wants to talk with her parents. She then asks if Katrina would like to speak with either mom or dad. Katrina immediately responds, and provides her name and mother's telephone number so the school counselor can call the mother.

Core Action 4: Information Gathering: Needs and Current Concerns

As this Core Action name suggests, goals of this stage revolve around identifying the violence-surviving student's immediate needs and concerns (e.g., "What does this student need right now?"). In particular, the school counselor determines how the student survivor perceives the severity of the violent experience. Remember, those who directly experienced the threat of death or severe harm have survived a potentially terrifying experience. Also, those who witnessed the death or trauma of close friends or peers may experience emotional trauma. Depending on the resiliency, coping mechanisms, and support of each individual survivor, their needs greatly vary.

When gathering information from students related to their violence experiences, school counselors will follow each individual survivor's lead. Some survivors may present as reluctant or reticent to engage. These violence survivors may provide terse or cursory responses to questions. Others may gush information and present as overly loquacious. Key for school counselors is a balanced response for those being questioned. Should survivors be hesitant to engage, allow the students space. Instead of asking further questions, simply provide contact information (e.g., handouts with emergency counseling contact numbers and directives for students and their parents) and mingle with other nearby survivors. In this way reticent students experience the presence of school counselors and have access *if needed*. Simply being in the presence of trusted counselors provides a sense of security and comfort to those who are reticent to engage.

In the case of a reticent high school student who witnessed the shooting of a friend at a school track meet, a school counselor might respond in this manner.

Counselor:	How are you doing?
Student:	I'm fine.
Counselor:	Did you know Johnny?
Student:	Yes. We were stretching out together and waiting to be called to the track relay race when he was shot.
Counselor:	Did you see him get shot?
Student:	You know I really don't want to talk right now.
Counselor:	Okay. Here is my office telephone number and a 24-hour school crisis line (hands the student a school counseling business card). If you want to talk, I will be close by. Just let me know.
Student:	Right.

Here the school counselor simply asks the high school student how he is doing. The student's response is terse. The counselor then asks if the student knew the violence victim. The survivor reports they were stretching out together when his friend was shot. The counselor then asks the survivor if he witnessed his friend being shot. The survivor tersely extinguishes the communications. Instead of the counselor pushing the survivor for further details of what was seen or how the survivor experienced the violence, the counselor matter-of-factly validates the student by stating "Okay" and complies with the student's request not to talk. However, before disengaging, the counselor provides contact numbers and informs the student that she will be available if the student changes his mind.

Notice the school counselor does not say something like "I understand." This statement would inaccurately convey that the school counselor knows exactly what the survivor has experienced. Such a therapeutic mistake can quickly result in a verbal assault on the counselor by a survivor. Survivors often feel angry that persons not present at the violent event could proclaim to understand the violence experience. Additionally, the school counselor does not say, "I bet that was awful to see your friend shot." This would imply that the survivor *should* feel "awful."

Conversely, student violence survivors who present as loquacious and seemingly wish to discuss every aspect of their experience need to be validated. However, they should also be informed that at this particular time, school counselors are merely gathering important "basic" information regarding survivors' potential pressing needs. Next, the survivor should gently be reminded that in a short time after the basic information is gathered, survivors will be given an opportunity to discuss their experience more fully. Utilizing the scenario presented in the previous example, the school counselor–loquacious student interaction might present like this:

Counselor: How are you doing?

Student: I have no idea. Johnny and I were stretching out and the next thing I knew there were gunshots. Johnny fell to the ground. There was blood everywhere. I didn't know what to do, so I ran and hid by the bleachers. Once the shooting stopped I ran over to Johnny, but he was already dead. I can't believe this happened. I mean, like, this was something right out of a movie. It was unbelievable. One moment I'm stretching out with my teammate and the next thing is he is dead. I was so afraid. I think everyone was very afraid.

Counselor:	Can I do something for you right now?
Student:	I wasn't the one who got shot. I'm perfectly fine, but it scared me. It scared me really bad. I was thinking "This can't be happening. This is like in the movies or something." I'm so glad you are here, Mrs. VanderPaul, because I've got so many things running through my head that I want to process.
Counselor:	What I am doing right now is merely trying to help understand what survivors need. Are you okay?
Student:	Yeah, I'm fine. I just really can't believe this just happened here at Jefferson High. But I'm so glad I can process this with you, Mrs. VanderPaul.
Counselor:	At this time I'm just gathering basic information. You've provided me with yours. Once things settle down and we learn what everyone's basic needs are, we will be coming back through. Let's talk more then. How does that sound?
Student:	I'd like that a lot.

As in the previous interaction with the terse student, the school counselor again simply asks how the student is doing. This time, however, the student rambles on, describing what he saw, thought, and felt. The counselor allows the loquacious student to ramble for a little while. As he takes a breath and slows, the counselor truncates the student's rambling account by rephrasing the original question. Now she asks if she can do something for the student "right now." This implies "Do you have an immediate need?" The student concretely responds with a desire to process the event with the school counselor. Instead allowing him to do so now and continue his loquacious rambling, the counselor explains that she is attempting to determine what survivors' immediate needs are. She then repeats, "Are you okay?" This final, direct, and closed-ended question is designed to stop the loquaciousness. The student has the choice to answer either yes or no. Stated differently, the school counselor gently closes the opportunity for loquacious rambling discussion. The student then responds he is "fine." The counselor reconnects with the student by reporting that the information he provided was exactly what she needed. Further, she implies that the student will have an opportunity to talk with her after she determines all survivors' pressing needs. She concludes with the question "How does that sound?" This final question is very empowering. It suggests that the student has some control in the school counselor's leaving or not.

Commonly asked questions within the Information Gathering Core Action stage revolve around the survivor's experience or needs. Questions might include "Were you injured?" "How well did you know the person who was shot?" or "Is your friend missing?" At other times survivors might be confused and not know what to do next. Here the school counselor might say: "How about we call your parents?" Still other survivors might be overwrought with feelings of guilt or shame, because they survived rather than their friend. Here the school counselor might say, "It sounds as though you believe you should have been the one who was shot rather than your friend." Notice each of these questions or statements simply attempts to gather information regarding survivors' needs or concerns. The intent is not to utilize the questions or statements posed to survivors as entrée into talk therapy. Instead, the intent is merely to allow survivors to voice needs, concerns, or feelings and to identify the specific needs of the survivors.

Core Action 5: Practical Assistance

Here school counselors offer practical help. Specifically, the Practical Assistance offered will relate to the information gathered in the last Core Action. Providing student violence survivors with help to pressing or anticipated concerns is paramount. Four steps comprise this Core Action:

1. Identify the most pressing need or concern.
2. Clarify the need.
3. Discuss an action plan.
4. Act to address the need.

First, from the list of needs identified in the preceding Core Action, help the client *identify the most pressing need or concern*. Identifying one's most pressing concern is therapeutically helpful. It helps survivors determine what is most important to them at this specific moment in time. It also helps them to articulate what they want and how that would look.

Before moving on, it is important to comment regarding age-appropriate needs and concerns. In general, elementary-age children will simply want their nurturing parents or caregivers to arrive on scene. In this case, once parents arrive, the school counselor will provide Psychological First Aid to both student and parents. Here it requires helping student and parents identify the student's most pressing need and responding to the parents' most pressing need regarding the student. Often parents want assurances that their child is safe and will suffer no lasting physical or psychological harm. The school counselor might say something like this to a young student and his parents:

Counselor:	Johnny, you are safe now. Mom is here.
Mother:	John-John, I was so very worried.
Johnny:	Mommy . . . it was horrible.
Mother:	I can't believe this happened. Are you hurt?
Johnny:	No.
Counselor:	Ms. Samuels, it is so good to have you here. Johnny really needs to hear you tell him that he is safe, everything is going to be all right, and you are with him.
Mother:	John-John, everything is going to be all right. Oh, I was so worried about you.
Counselor:	The thing we need to do right now is to help Johnny know that he is safe and that things are going to get back to normal as quickly as possible.
Mother:	Will he be all right? I mean, is he psychologically damaged because he saw that jerk attack his best friend Tommy with a knife? This whole thing is insane. I hope they kill that kid for doing what he did.
Counselor:	Mom, John-John really needs you to focus right now. Tell John-John he is safe. The attack is over, and Tommy is en route to the hospital where the doctors will do all they can to make him better. John-John needs you to tell him this. Hold him in your lap. Look him in the eyes. Tell him he is safe. You are here to protect him. And Tommy's going to the hospital and the doctors there are going to do all they can for Tommy.
Mother:	John-John, Momma's here. It's over. That bad man is gone. The police are going to put him in jail. Tommy's mommy is going with him to the hospital and everything is going to be okay.
Johnny:	Okay. (Crying softly)

Counselor:	Good work, Mom.
Mother:	But can you promise me that John-John is going to be all right?
Counselor:	The EMTs looked John-John over pretty carefully and didn't find any injuries. Isn't that right, John-John?
Johnny:	(Nods)
Mother:	But I mean psychologically. Can you promise me that he won't have psychological problems because of this?
Counselor:	One thing we know about young kids like John-John is that they are usually very resilient. Often when they have support from loving and devoted parents like you, they do very well. Of course I can't promise anything, but I believe the big thing right now is to get things settled down, get you back home, and make things as normal as possible. How does that sound to you?
Mother:	Pretty good. I just want to get John-John home.
Counselor:	How does that sound to you, John-John?
Johnny:	(Again, Johnny does not respond verbally but nods.)
Counselor:	"Good, then that's what we are going to do. Mom, I'm going to give you a couple of handouts related to emergency contact numbers should John-John begin to have some difficulties or if you have concerns or questions that pop up later. The handout also describes some typical behaviors kids can have after a situation like this. (The counselor goes on to explain potential psychological trauma responses of children.)
Counselor:	So, Mom, what is your most pressing concern?
Mother:	I just want to get John-John home.
Counselor:	Okay, let's do that. I'm going to walk you over to Command Officer Smith, who will have a couple of forms for you to sign, and he will make certain that you get to your car.
Counselor:	John-John, what is your biggest concern?
Johnny:	I don't know.
Counselor:	Okay. Do you need anything right now?
Johnny:	No . . . I don't think so.

Counselor: Good. So if you think of anything, tell your mom
              and have her or you call me, okay?
Johnny: Okay.

Let us discuss this mini-clinical vignette exchange in greater detail. As in previous vignettes, the school counselor again continues the mantra that the student is safe. The school counselor suggests that things are back to normal and the student is safe because the mother has arrived. This implies to the mother that she is in control and knows what is best for her son. It gives her power and authority. Thus, instead of stating or implying that the school counselor is in control, the counselor has placed the mother at the head of the immediate power hierarchy. From a structural family therapy perspective, this places the mother in authority over Johnny and suggests that Johnny needs to follow his mother's authority. The statement also suggests that things are back to normal. Mother is taking over.

Following the brief exchange between mother and Johnny, the school counselor therapeutically *joins* the mother by indicating it is good to have her at the scene. Then the counselor tells the mother some important things she needs to say. This establishes a tone for the mother's communication with her son. It suggests, "Mom, you've got to be strong for Johnny. Don't get overwhelmed by emotions. Tell Johnny he is safe. He will be all right. And you are going to ensure his safety." This statement informs the mother that she is critical for Johnny's healthy recovery.

When the mother asks if Johnny will experience psychological repercussions or dysfunction due to the violent trauma and then starts to emotionalize the situation by describing what she wants done to the perpetrator, the counselor refocuses her to the charge at hand. The counselor then tells the mother exactly what to say and describes how to physically place her child on her lap. Besides directing the mother on what she will say and do, the counselor's directives serve another important purpose. They tell Johnny what is going to happen. Knowing what is going to be said and done provides immediate structure with no surprises for the boy. Additionally, having the school counselor say that the attack is over and Tommy is on his way to the hospital, and having his mother repeat these same things signify that indeed Johnny *is* safe and all the things that can be done for Tommy are being done.

As an aside, did you see the slight but important rapport-building technique utilized by the school counselor? The school counselor initially called the student "Johnny." However, when the mother spoke, she used the name "John-John." Once the school counselor heard this, she immediately utilized "John-John" during the remainder of her interactions with student and mother. This is another way of engaging the student and parent(s) and suggesting that you are committed to their family.

Also important to note is the manner in which the school counselor responded to the mother's request for a *promise* that Johnny was not psychologically harmed. The counselor first describes the resiliency of children, then implies how his mother's love and devotion can favorably impact Johnny. Finally, the school counselor states, "I can't promise anything." This is important. Parents want reassurance that their child will be the same as before the violent trauma. Regretfully, no matter how much we wish this would be true, professionals cannot make such a promise. Instead, the best thing to do is simply state that one cannot promise this while providing hope and expectations that the student's resiliency will prevail.

Because this Core Action stage provides Practical Assistance to the previously reported pressing needs and concerns noted by mother and student, the school counselor next addresses their desire to return home. Specifically, the counselor describes what will happen next. The counselor does not simply leave this Core Action stage at the mother's discretion. Instead, the counselor invites Johnny's input as well. When the boy does not identify a pressing need or concern, the counselor praises him and gives him the opportunity to continue engagement with the counselor, should a concern arise. Finally, the counselor again empowers both mother and student by stating that either can call the school counselor should a future need or concern arise.

Prior to moving to the second step in this Core Action, it is important to discuss the difference between realistic and unrealistic pressing needs. Like the beauty pageant contestant announcing her desire for world peace, sometimes students or parents may identify unrealistic pressing needs. When such clearly inappropriate or unrealistic needs are presented (e.g., "We need the school to send us to Disney World for a month so we can forget about the experienced violent trauma"), it is helpful to respond in a manner that does not argue or engender contention. Here, one might say:

Counselor: You know, Dad, your idea of going to Disney World to help your son and family recover from this experience makes sense. Regretfully, I have never heard of a school system sending violence survivors to Disney World, nor do I believe the school system has the money to fund such a trip. However, I am wondering whether there might be another place that your family and you might consider going that would be afford-able and provide a respite for your son and family.

The intent of this communication is to validate the underlying purpose of the request and redirect it in a way that provides the parent a chance to consider and discuss other potential opportunities.

The next step in this Core Action stage is to *clarify the need*. In particu-lar, the school counselor will talk with the surviving student and likely his or her parents to clarify the identified pressing need. Then the counselor will help them realistically examine the need and understand its "underlying core." Thus, instead of chasing a vague and global need (e.g., "I want to feel better"), the school counselor works to help the student and family under-stand the crux of the need. Here it is important to help students behaviorally describe the need (e.g., "I want my mother here" or "I want to drink some Gatorade"). Behavioral-based need descriptions increase the probability that a successful outcome can be sought and secured.

Third, the school counselor will *discuss an action plan* with student survi-vors and their families. School counselors often are aware of available services to help survivors and their families. For example, students often want to know the condition of fellow victims who were rushed away by ambu-lance or who are being treated for injuries sustained in the violent episode. Depending on the specific situation, school counselors will want to utilize their clinical judgment regarding divulging information.

For example, in the Angel and Katrina clinical mini-vignette, the most pressing need identified by Katrina might be to learn Angel's whereabouts and condition. If the school counselor knew that Angel had survived the attack and was at a nearby hospital, it may be therapeutically logical to pro-vide this information to Katrina. As a matter of fact, if Katrina and Angel considered each other very best friends, and this was common knowledge to the school counselor, it might be therapeutically appropriate to reunite the two at the hospital if Angel was physically stable.

Conversely, if the school counselor was aware that Angel had been abducted and found murdered, the counselor will need to weigh the poten-tial therapeutic benefits of informing Katrina now as opposed to allowing her to learn of her friend's murder later. Many factors will need to be considered. For example, based on the school counselor's brief interaction with Katrina's mother, does the counselor believe that the mother has sufficient cognitive, psychological, and physical resources to adequately respond to Katrina's current post-violence trauma and her anticipated severe bereavement response to Angel's murder?

On the treatment side of the equation, if the school counselor is aware that other mental health providers on scene can offer immediate support with Katrina, that the school resource officer can provide transportation to a nearby hospital if deemed necessary, and that the hospital has indicated that psychiatric hospitalization is available, this may well be the best time to inform Katrina of Angel's death.

The final step of the Practical Assistance Core Action is *act to address the need*. Here, the counselor will assist the student and the student's parents respond to the most pressing identified need. Thus, if the student wants to know the whereabouts of other violence survivors, a plan is generated with the student to gain that needed information.

Typically, each of the four steps occurs in succession and moves rapidly from one step to the next with little hindrance. Using the previous vague example where the student's need is "I want to feel better," the school counselor might ask, "What would feeling better look like?" or "What would you be doing if you were feeling better?" In this case, this conversation might take place.

Counselor:	You say you want to feel better. I would like you to feel better too. What would feeling better look like to you?
Student:	I don't know.
Counselor:	Sometimes it is helpful to identify how you might be acting or what you might be doing if you were feeling better.
Student:	Well, if I were feeling better, I probably wouldn't be here.
Counselor:	So where exactly would you be if you were feeling better?
Student:	I would be at the basketball court shooting hoops.
Counselor:	That makes sense to me. So what would you have to do to go to the basketball court and start shooting hoops?

Student: I guess my parents would have to say it was okay for
                me to shoot some hoops so I could clear my mind of
                all the junk that happened today.

Counselor: Well, what would you have to do to ask your parents
                if you could go shoot some hoops to clear your mind?

Student: I guess I would just have to ask them.

Counselor: Might that be something you want to do?

Student: I think so. I think I just need to ask them.

Reviewing this clinical mini-vignette, we see the school counselor merely repeats the student-stated vague need (i.e., "You say you want to feel better"). Stating that the counselor would like this student to fulfill his stated need suggests to the student that his need is supported by the counselor and that the counselor is working with him to have the need satisfied. Next the counselor asks, "What would feeling better look like to you?" In other words, how would you be acting? Where would you be? What would you be doing? If the student can identify each of these above noted beliefs or perceptions, the counselor can begin creating a plan to satisfy the identified need. The student responds that he would not be "here." Instead, he would be at the basketball court shooting hoops. Again, the school agrees with the student survivor, then asks what he would have to do to allow him the freedom to do as he wishes. The student reports he would simply need his parents' permission. The counselor then asks if the student wishes to ask his parents to go to the basketball courts. Here the student believes he just needs to ask his parents for their permission and that playing hoops would eliminate a major source of discomfort and stress for him.

Core Action 6: Connection With Social Supports

The goal of this stage is to help student survivors and their families establish contacts with primary support persons and other potentially helpful resources. The contact degree and length may vary according to immediately presenting and developing needs. Both professional (e.g., professional counselors, clergy, physicians, etc.) and nonprofessional (e.g., family members, friends, neighbors, etc.) contacts are included. Specifically, survivors and their families will need connections that can provide psychological, physical, social, and spiritual support.

Of particular relevance to school violence survivors is parental and family support. With younger students, parents are key. Immediately after any threatened or realized violence, younger children want significant parental contact. Thus, school counselors should seek parental involvement immediately after any violent or potentially violent trauma. However, once students reach high school, the degree of desired parental support can fluctuate greatly. Some high school students will want substantial contact with significant peers (e.g., boyfriends, girlfriends, selected friends from band or sports teams, etc.) and limited contact with parents or family members. Although parental support should be sought, parents should be informed that older students may tend to seek most of their support from peers and that such peer support is common for this age. Here the counselor might say something like this:

> Counselor: Mr. and Mrs. Valadez, in situations such as this where violence was threatened toward your son, it can be particularly challenging for students, parents, family, and friends. Something that you may wish to be aware of is that high school seniors about Joel's age often want more peer support than parent support. This is sometimes difficult for parents, but desiring peer support is often developmentally appropriate for persons of Joel's age.

Here the school counselor positively reframes Joel's desire for more peer than parent support as age appropriate and normal.

Core Action 7: Coping Information Distribution

The primary goals of this Core Action are to provide student survivors and their families information related to potential adverse reactions to the experienced violence. Additionally, counselors will both suggest effective coping strategies should such reactions occur and help survivors and families determine which coping strategies *they* believe will be most helpful. This stage is psychoeducational in nature and often is conducted with both student survivor and parents. It repeats information previously discussed in greater detail and describes how students may respond to the violent experience.

All discussions related to potential adverse post-violence symptoms should be presented in an age-appropriate fashion to student survivors and their families. Stated differently, if the violence survivors are elementary age, create presentations specific to their cognitive, social, and emotional development. Utilize common, non–psycho-jargon words understood by students at the survivor's specific grade level. For example, do not say "enuresis" when explaining potential adverse reactions of younger students who have experienced violence. Young students certainly will not understand the word, which also may be unfamiliar to parents. Instead, the school counselor might say:

> Counselor: (Talking to mom in front of 5-year-old kindergarten student Melanie) Sometimes when 5-year-olds like Melanie witness or experience violence, they may begin a pattern of wetting their pants or beds. This is relatively common. If it happens, don't freak out. It is not unusual for 5-year-olds to pee in their pants or bed after seeing something really scary. Of course, not all 5-year-olds begin this pattern. But if they do, don't punish them. They simply can't help this unfortunate physical response and probably don't like sitting in their wet pants any more than adults would.

Here the school counselor normalizes post-violence enuresis by saying the symptom is "relatively common." Next, the counselor states, "If it happens, don't freak out." This statement is powerful. Notice the school counselor does not say "*When* [enuresis] happens . . . " Thus, Melanie is not banished to a lifetime of enuresis. However, mother and father are forewarned that it can be a symptom of the experienced school violence. Therefore, should Melanie wet her pants or bed, she is not *being bad* but is instead simply *suffering post-violence symptoms*. To further the point, the school counselor reports that, like adults, the student will not like sitting in wet pants. Also notice that the counselor begins by first saying "wetting" and then saying "pee." This ensures that parents and students truly understand the symptom.

Undoubtedly some counselors will be bothered by the fact that these statements are made with parents *and Melanie* present. They may be concerned that remarks made about enuresis in front of Melanie will result in her wetting herself intentionally. We disagree. Forewarning parents regarding potential enuresis prepares parents (and students) for what may happen. Thus, should enuresis occur, it is not experienced as a scary, uncontrollable, and unforeseen behavior that suggests students are intentionally being "bad."

When discussing potential adverse post-violent symptoms within this psychoeducational format, clearly describe symptoms common to the age of your student survivors. It makes little sense to talk about common reactions of adolescent violence survivors when one is speaking to 5-year-olds and their parents. Also, speak candidly. Do not utilize innuendos or insinuations.

Another helpful technique is asking younger students to explain what they "think" happened. Very young elementary school students may not understand the construct of death as being permanent or the injuries to friends as impacting future interactions. Thus, listen to how students describe the violence experience and answer questions as simply and honestly as possible.

If student survivors are very young, drawing may help them communicate what was seen or experienced more effectively. Conversely, should the violence survivors be high school students, create a presentation that takes into consideration their specific developmental stages and needs. Remember that adolescents typically want to be viewed as adults. Therefore, it is important to utilize age-acceptable communications. In other words, utilize clinical judgment when intervening. Varsity football players who wish to portray themselves as self-reliant, tough, and strong likely will not readily embrace crayons as a viable option for self-expression.

No matter what the school violence experience is, potential post-violence reactions should be discussed with both student survivors and their parents. At the least, six post-violence reactions should be included in the discussions:

1. Intrusive experiences
2. Avoidance and withdrawal
3. Physical arousal reactions
4. Repetitive play and social interactions
5. Grief and bereavement reactions
6. Anger

Intrusive experiences, avoidance and withdrawal, and physical arousal are often associated with Posttraumatic Stress Disorder. Intrusive experiences typically include distressing memories of the violent experience or associated images (e.g., a bloody knife, the face of the assailant, the scream of a fellow survivor). These memories or images continually return despite the survivor's active attempts to keep them from entering consciousness. Such memories or images are very frightening for younger students and can be disabling. Violence survivors often feel powerless to stop the recurring memories or images. Thus, they feel increasingly vulnerable to the feelings connected to these memories or images. Providing information regarding the commonness of such memories and images among violence survivors can help to normalize the intrusiveness of the post-violence symptoms and help survivors understand that they are not "crazy." Additionally, it is important to discuss survivors' potential feelings of vulnerability brought about by an inability to control such intrusive memories or thoughts.

One technique our post-violence survivors have reported helpful is the Hot Fudge Sundae Memory. Depending on the individual student's emotional, cognitive, and social presentation, age, and pressing needs, we might say something like this:

Counselor:	I'm hearing you say that as an honors high school senior who is also a strong and tough district champion wrestler, you *should* be able to stop the memories of the attack from coming into your mind. Is that correct?
Joe:	Right. I should be able to do that.
Counselor:	Would you be willing to help me for a moment?
Joe:	Sure. What do you want me to do?
Counselor:	Do you like hot fudge sundaes?
Joe:	Yes. But what does that have to do with anything?
Counselor:	Help me out for a moment. Will you promise me that you won't think about a hot fudge sundae for the next few moments?
Joe:	Sure, that's easy.
Counselor:	Good. Are you ready to start?
Joe:	Yup . . . I won't think about hot fudge sundaes.
Counselor:	Good. So, I don't want you to think about a hot fudge sundae. I don't want you to think about the vanilla ice cream in an ice cream bowl. I don't want you to think about the steamy hot fudge cascading down the vanilla ice cream. I don't want you to think about the whipped cream on top or the nuts or the cherry. So what are you thinking about?
Joe:	You got me. I was thinking about the hot fudge sundae.
Counselor:	So tell me, Joe. How is this visualization similar to the memories that keep coming to you about the attack?

Joe: They are not similar at all.

Counselor: Really. Were you trying *not* to think about the hot fudge sundae?

Joe: Exactly, I was trying not to think about the hot fudge sundae.

Counselor: The more you tried to not think about the hot fudge sundae, what happened?

Joe: Okay. I get it. The more I tried not to think about the hot fudge sundae, the more the hot fudge sundae was on my mind.

Counselor: Right. So, what did you learn?

Joe: The more I try not to think about the attack, the more I keep the memories coming.

In the same way that violence survivors attempt to exclude memories and images that continually bombard their consciousness, some survivors also attempt to avoid the vicinity of the violent episode, persons connected to the violence, and anything they associate with the violence experience (e.g., guns, clothes worn when the violence was experienced, songs played during the violence, etc.). In other words, survivors often attempt to shield themselves from memories of the violence by avoiding anything that reminds them of the experience. Thus, survivors may withdraw from friends who may wish to talk about the survivors' experience or even previously enjoyable hobbies or activities that survivors may believe are connected to the experience. Here, for example, if a student was attending a choir event when the violence occurred, he might stop participating in choir or even stop singing the songs that might engender memories of the violence.

Via the psychoeducational process, students and their families also should be informed of potential physical arousal actions that are associated to violent experiences. For example, students might be informed of their potential to develop "hypervigiliance." This occurs when students constantly scan their environment for real or imagined violent threats. In other words, some post-violent surviving students may constantly be on the lookout for another violent episode. Other common post-violence physical arousal responses include a heightened startle response, where a loud sound may cause the student to jump, or a sleep disturbance, where the primary presenting issue is an inability to relax. Additionally, some students may present an underlying anger and associated angry outbursts that appear inappropriately severe. Younger students may even enact repetitive play about the violent event and attempt to portray themselves as a hero disarming the violence perpetrator.

Many times younger students are unable to describe emotions they are experiencing. Instead of asking students about their experienced emotions, there exists greater therapeutic utility in asking them to describe experienced physical sensations and to utilize closed- rather than open-ended responses. Here, for example, instead of the counselor asking "What emotions are you experiencing?" the counselor may say:

> Counselor: Sometimes when students tell me how they feel after being shot at, they tell me things like their heart is beating really, really fast or they feel shaky. Other times they tell me that they keep hearing the sounds of the gunshots in their heads. Is your heart beating really, really fast or do you feel shaky?
>
> Joe: No. But I feel really strange, like I'm in a bad dream and I can't breathe.
>
> Counselor: What is that like for you?
>
> Joe: I don't like it. Sometimes it gets so bad I think I'm going to throw up.
>
> Counselor: What do you do when that happens?
>
> Joe: I get scared and think I'm going to get sick all over the place.
>
> Counselor: And if you got sick, what would happen?
>
> Joe: My teacher would send me to the school nurse.
>
> Counselor: And if you went to the school nurse, what would happen?
>
> Joe: I'd guess she would clean me up and send me back to class.
>
> Counselor: And if she sent you back to class?
>
> Joe: I would be right back where I started from. I'd be fine.
>
> Counselor: That makes sense to me. Sometimes students I know who start to feel like they are in a bad dream and scared like they can't breathe find it helpful to do

	something like count to 10, sing, or say something like "I am safe." Do you think any of those things or something else might be helpful?
Joe:	Hmmm. When I was a little kid and I got hurt, my grandpa taught me to say "estoy bien."
Counselor:	What does "estoy bien" mean?
Joe:	It means "I'm okay. I'm not hurt."
Counselor:	Did it help?
Joe:	Yes.
Counselor:	Do you think it would help you when you feel strange like you are in a really bad dream and can't breathe?
Joe:	My grandpa taught me that when you said "estoy bien" all your fear leaves. I will try it.

Let us review the three things that just happened.

1. Instead of asking Joe to discuss nebulous or difficult-to-describe feelings or emotions, the school counselor asks him to describe the physical sensations experienced. This is important. Even young students can accurately describe the physical sensations they are experiencing.
2. It is safe to describe one's physical sensations. No one can say your experienced physical sensations are "incorrect." A student knows his or her sensations. Although the physical sensations cannot be physically held in the student's hand or handed to the school counselor, the sensations are tangible to the student. They are real. Thus, the student's reported physical sensations cannot be incorrect. A student can say what he or she *feels*, and these feelings can never be suspect.
3. The language used is not psycho-jargon. The sensations described are presented in age-appropriate language that is easy to comprehend.

These three points provide safety for students. When students feel safe, they are more likely to engage in the counseling process.

Next, the school counselor describes some sensations reportedly identified by other students who experienced the same type of violence (e.g., being "shot at"). It is important to note that the school counselor does not describe sensations identified by fellow students who were struck by a car or who fell from a roof. Stated differently, the counselor states that students who experienced a similar situation identified these types of sensations. The counselor then focuses on three symptoms: heart palpitations, feeling shaky, and intrusive memories. This is a forced-choice response frequently described as a closed-response statement. Less experienced counselors might not understand the importance of utilizing such a forced-choice or closed-response question here. They might inaccurately believe that all presented questions should be open ended. Therapeutically, however, with younger students or persons exposed to violence, the use of only open-ended questions can be countertherapeutic. Often younger students and persons overwhelmed by a violent experience require the structure and safety provided by closed-ended questions. Limiting potential responses to three provides a feeling of control for the students and addresses potential concentration issues common to many violence survivors.

In the vignette, the student denies any of the three response options and instead reports different sensations—those of feeling strange, living a bad dream, and an inability to breathe.

Immediately, the counselor engages the student and provides an opportunity to further describe or comment on the sensations. The student reports not liking the sensations and reports a concern about vomiting. The counselor then utilizes a "linking" intervention in an attempt to help him realize the "final" outcome of the presenting concern. In this case, the student is encouraged to respond to the "next thing" that would happen until "final outcome" occurs (i.e., vomiting).

In this case, the student reports that if he actually vomited, nothing too overwhelming would occur. Eventually he would be safely returned to his classroom. Once this acceptable outcome is verbalized, the counselor introduces the idea of initiating a new behavior should the student experience noxious post-violence feelings like those previously experienced. Specifically, the counselor suggests counting to 10 or singing and provides a third "You Create It" option. The student goes for the third option.

The school counselor welcomes the student's response and learns his revered grandfather had taught the boy a Spanish phrase. Based on the student's comments, it seems the use of the phrase (positive self-talk) had been helpful in the past. When the school counselor asks if the student thinks utilization of the phrase related to post-violence symptomatology would be helpful, Joe embraces the coping option. Other potential coping options that might be suggested may include behaviors such as talking with trusted significant others (e.g., parents, friends, teachers, etc.), journaling, or engaging in counseling. Here the school counselor might say:

Counselor: I wonder what other coping behaviors you might wish to try.

Joe: What do you mean by that?

Counselor: Well, sometimes students who experience violence report that it is helpful to start not just one coping behavior, like saying "estoy bien," but to start a couple new coping behaviors, like writing in a journal and describing what you are thinking or sensations that you are feeling.

Joe: I don't like to write. Journaling wouldn't be good for me.

Counselor: I wonder what else might be helpful to you.

Joe: I like to play catch with my grandpa. He and I always talk. I bet that would be helpful.

Counselor: That sounds good. Let's talk with your grandpa and see if we can't make a schedule when the two of you could get together.

As you see, the school counselor attempts to engage the student in multiple coping behaviors. Journaling is proposed first. The student reports journaling is not a match. Instead of continually listing other potential coping options, the counselor asks what coping options the student believes would be helpful. This is an efficient intervention, and the student quickly identifies a behavioral coping option he believes best. Some students are unable to to identify potential coping options after a violent experience. These students and their parents typically want lists and ideas from which to choose. Others refuse all presented ideas and seem to find it important to create their own coping behaviors. Who suggests or creates the coping behavior is inconsequential. The important factor here is simply that students and their families utilize multiple coping behaviors and do what they believe most useful in helping themselves best respond.

Core Action 8: Collaborative Services Linkage

The primary goal within this Core Action is to link student survivors and their parents to preidentified person at agencies, programs, and institutions that provide needed survivor services. Many times these linked services include medical services for the treatment of physical injuries sustained during the violent episode or psychotropic prescriptions specific to post-violence anxiety or bereavement; counseling services for individual or family members related to post-violence symptoms or the pre-violence substance abuse that led to the violence; and legal services for restraining orders or petitions. Such petitions often revolve around the request for property confiscated in the violent event returned to the victim (e.g., bicycles, jewelry, clothes, etc.). School counselors will want to link students and their families to immediately needed services (e.g., medical services for a laceration sustained in the violent episode) as well as potentially needed future services (e.g., legal services for a possible future restraining order).

Within this final Core Action stage, school counselors discuss the opportunities to participate in an upcoming debriefing experience. No pressure is placed on student survivors or their parents to participate. Instead, school counselors simply provide the time and location of the debriefing with a little background specific to its intent. Participation in a debriefing is often influenced by people's perceptions of what the debriefing will do for them. It may be helpful if school counselors communicate that the debriefing experience is more about helping others process and cope with the violence than about helping themselves. In particular, school counselors may say:

> Counselor: Although the debriefing experience may be helpful to you, the debriefings are often more helpful to others who need to process what happened. Your presence and participation in a debriefing experience will likely be more helpful to others than yourself.

Hence, the stigma of attending is eclipsed. Survivors and parents can say they attended to help others rather than feeling that they need help with their psychological responses or symptoms to the violent event. In general, school counselors may wish to remind themselves of the 20-60-20 rule related to debriefing participation: Approximately 20% of those who participate in the debriefings find the experience to be of little help. Approximately 60% of the participants find the experience helpful or not based on perceived supportive interactions within the debriefing experience among themselves and others who participate. The final 20% of participants seem to find debriefings overwhelmingly positive no matter what happens.

CHAPTER SUMMARY

This chapter has described Psychological First Aid and each of the eight core actions and goals. Psychological First Aid presents as a relatively simple-to-implement intervention that may have utility depending on the specific needs of students and families involved. In particular, the intervention is presented as a general template that can be modified easily as necessary by school counselors to address survivors' needs. The proposed intervention, like others within the emergency response intervention category, lacks proven evidenced-based demonstration of effectiveness. Both the National Child Traumatic Stress Network and the National Center for PTSD (2006, p. 1) seem to address this lack of research-based efficacy demonstration by stating the intervention is "evidenced-informed." However, as is the case with all interventions, school counselors should strongly consider the potential positive and negative ramifications for implementing the intervention and ensure that it matches the survivors' needs and poses no significant dangers or threats for participants.

Adapted Solution-Focused Survivors–Parents Debriefing Model

Immediately after experiencing or witnessing violent events, student survivors and the systems in which they are members (e.g., school, family, friends, etc.) are catapulted into a swirling of physical, psychological, cognitive, and interpersonal needs. Of utmost importance is the need to stabilize physically injured students via immediate emergency medical treatment. However, once medical and physical conditions are stabilized, students and their parents warrant an intervention that: (a) promotes coping responses for those who witnessed or experienced violence; (b) provides assessment of potential post-violence symptoms and immediate referral of those in severe psychological distress who may benefit from psychotropic medications or warrant psychiatric hospitalization; and (c) restore previous functioning levels.

When I (Dr. Juhnke) began counseling violence and trauma survivors in the late 1980s, I searched for a post-trauma intervention "silver bullet." In particular, I sought an intervention that would address each area just noted. Originally I utilized individual and family therapies. These counseling therapies appeared to slow most survivor's swirling emotional vortex but were woefully inefficient when it came to treating multiple survivors and multiple families.

I also found that many survivors wanted connection or interaction with others who survived the same violent experience. Survivors frequently discussed other survivors' "needs" and yearned for interactions with those who had experienced the same trauma to "see how they were doing." Over time

I began to notice that significant treatment session portions revolved around discussions about other trauma survivors. Many times I utilized circular questioning as described in Chapter 7. This allowed survivors to compare themselves and their recoveries to other violence survivors, and it allowed survivors and their parents to verbalize concerns via a safe projection. In other words, instead of survivors saying "This is what is troubling me" or "This is what our family needs," they were able to voice their concerns indirectly by discussing what they believed others needed. This, of course, is akin to a skittish client who states, "I have a very close friend who is struggling with depression. She is my age, her husband is my husband's age, and we both are teachers. Actually, she is just like me. But I want you to know she is not me."

Additionally, although younger students responded well to individual and family counseling, older adolescents wanted peer survivor involvement. Much to their parents' dismay, these adolescents intensely desired peer interaction far more than parental interaction. This, of course, was developmentally appropriate but was something that individual or family counseling alone failed to adequately address. Thus, over time, I realized that conducting individual and family counseling survivor sessions separate from other survivors and other families seemed to limit therapeutic benefits and appeared to inhibit much needed peer and interfamilial support.

In the early 1990s, I read about Critical Incidence Stress Debriefing (CISD) and its use with natural disaster survivors. Later I received CISD training from a senior clinician and began participating in CISD interventions. During my first CISD experience, the team provided a debriefing with approximately 50 violence survivors. Many were overwhelmed with grief, fear, and raging anger. Immediately I observed the therapeutic synergy among survivors that had been missing in the individual and family survivor treatments I had conducted previously. I continued to participate in debriefings and enrolled in a CISD training seminar taught by the CISD founder and leading expert Dr. Jeffrey Mitchell (1994). Over time, I began to realize that much of what I believed my clients and their families had desired or found helpful was the foundational essence of the CISDs Mitchell had described.

Thus, the intent of this chapter is to familiarize readers with a post-violence intervention: the Adapted Solution-Focused Survivors–Parents Debriefing Model (Juhnke & Shoffner, 1999). Readers will gain a general overview of CISD and the distinct differences between CISD and the adapted Solution-Focused post-school violence debriefing. Readers will learn how to use the adapted Solution-Focused debriefing with students and their parents. Detailed mini-clinical vignettes are included throughout the chapter in an effort to demonstrate how specific phases of the model work and increase readers' knowledge specific to the model's use.

ADAPTED SOLUTION-FOCUSED DEBRIEFING MODEL

The Adapted Solution-Focused Debriefing Model provides counselors a means to further assess and intervene with student violence survivors. The debriefing experience can also provide an opportunity for added engagement with the survivor and the survivor's parents. Debriefings additionally allow counselors to actively monitor the survivor's immediate psychological and family systems needs. Thus, should the student or the student's family system decompensate shortly after the experienced violence, counselors can quickly intervene.

General History and General Overview

In the early 1990s, CISD was a widely recognized, small-group process originally developed to be used with adult emergency workers (e.g., fire fighters, emergency medical technicians, police officers, etc.) who encountered particularly gruesome and distressing emergency situations (Mitchell & Everly, 1993). The intent was to provide a debriefing intervention that would provide relief from psychological distress resulting from gruesome emergency situations and insulate emergency workers from the severity of extreme posttrauma symptoms. Since then CISD has been at the epicenter of debate, and professionals have argued about CISD's clinical efficacy (Everly, Flannery, & Mitchell, 2000; Leis, 2003; Lewis, 2003; Robinson, 2004; Rose, Bisson, & Wessely, 2003; Tuckey, 2007; and van Emmerik, Kamphuis, Hulsbosch, & Emmelkamp, 2002). Over the past 15 years, CISD has evolved into Critical Incident Stress Management (CISM). CISM in comparison to CISD is a far more sophisticated and thorough intervention that "represents a departure from early univariate crisis intervention models, and represents a new generation of . . . integrated, comprehensive multicomponent crisis intervention program that spans the complete crisis continuum from the precrisis and acute crisis phases through the post crisis phase" (Everly et al., 2000, p. 23).

When I (Dr. Juhnke) first began utilizing CISD with children and adolescent trauma survivors, it was considered as a viable intervention with school-age students who experienced violence or suicide (O'Hara, Taylor, & Simpson, 1994; Thompson, 1990). I found that CISD provided a therapeutic synergy among trauma survivors that individual and family therapies lacked. However, I had a number of concerns related to CISD. Five particular concerns were the impetus for my creating an Adapted Solution-Focused Adapted Debriefing Model specific to counseling children and adolescents (Juhnke, 1997):

1. CISD was designed for use with adult emergency services personnel.
2. CISD was designed as a single-session meeting.
3. The adapted debriefing process utilized professional counselors with emergency service personnel peers.
4. CISD focused primarily on psychopathology.
5. The personnel for whom CISD was designed thrived on adventure-seeking behaviors.

CISD was originally designed for use with adult emergency services personnel. Developmentally, adults are far different from elementary and middle school children. Specifically, CISD failed to adequately address the cognitive, physical, social, and psychological functioning of children. Frankly, it is hard to envision elementary or younger middle school students sitting in a circle and participating in a debriefing experience where they were asked to openly discuss the first thoughts they experienced when they realized they were in danger. Or students participating without both their parents' presence and their parents' support. Therefore, the Adapted Solution-Focused Debriefing process involved parents via both a parental debriefing and a parent-child debriefing. Additionally, the parent-child debriefing process utilized age-appropriate intervention techniques related to drawing, storytelling, and play.

CISD was designed as a single-session meeting. Frankly, given the psychological distress experienced by younger children exposed to trauma and their inability sometimes to verbally articulate their concerns, a single-session meeting lacked the clinical efficacy necessary for elementary and middle school students. Thus, the adapted debriefing required multiple meetings. These meetings were likely to be shorter in duration than the single-session CISD but better addressed younger children's attention needs. The additional meetings also provided a greater number of opportunities to observe and assess the children being served. They also allowed a longer period of time to observe and assess parent-child interactions and provide additional psychoeducational opportunities for them. Ultimately, the adapted debriefing process utilized a group family experience (Juhnke & Shoffner, 1999) that allowed parents of children trauma survivors to interact and learn from one another related to ways of handling everything from post-trauma nightmares to "secret cooking recipes."

CISD utilized professional counselors with emergency service personnel peers. It was my professional belief that children warranted a debriefing experience facilitated by nonpeer counseling professionals who had formal education and clinical experiences specific to the needs of the children they were serving. Additionally, I believed that school counselors must be a major part of the debriefing team. School counselors often know the students impacted by the violence. More important, the students know their school counselors and most already have at least a minimal rapport with them. School counselors also understand the idiosyncratic cultural, environmental, and language commonalities within their schools and among their students. Thus, they can intervene in ways that "outsiders" cannot.

In addition, it was my belief that CISD focused primarily on psychopathology. Little emphasis was placed on the therapeutic or healthy changes that survivors and their parents experience over time. As both a clinical supervisor and counseling professor, I have observed ineffective and inexperienced counselors promote client focus on client symptoms. I vividly remember one ineffective counselor-client interaction that went something like this:

Counselor:	How are you feeling today?
Client:	I feel very depressed.
Counselor:	How do you feel about your depression?
Client:	I feel very depressed about my depression.
Counselor:	So, how do you feel about your depression over your depression?
Client:	Look. I feel really sh#*ty. And I am not feeling any better talking about how sh#*ty I feel. So stop asking me how I feel!

Some ineffective counselors get their clients so overly focused on their presenting symptomatology that the clients fail to see progress or, even worse, spiral into the depths of despair by making their symptoms their only visible focus. Thus, I implemented basic Solution-Focused interventions to help student survivors and their families pay attention and note their positive changes.

Finally, the adult emergency services personnel for whom CISD was designed often thrive on adventure-seeking behaviors. Over time, they also experience indoctrination to life-threatening injuries and death. Emergency services personnel I knew had *chosen* to become emergency workers. They thrived on "hot calls." Despite the gore of horrific injuries, they enjoyed the adrenaline rush of responding to multiple vehicle accidents or shootings. Specifically, they liked being first responders. They became accustomed to responding to seriously injured persons. They had also encountered the deaths of persons they had attempted to revive. The students and families I served were not adventure seeking. They certainly had not chosen to be involved in the traumas they had experienced. Furthermore, other than viewing mostly sanitized injuries or death portrayed on television, the children and families I counseled had not been inured to injuries and death, as were the emergency workers for whom CISD was created.

Roles

The primary team member roles within the Adapted Debriefing Model are leader, co-leader, and doorkeeper. These roles correspond to the original roles assigned within the CISD (Mitchell & Everly, 1993). The leader briefly explains the debriefing process, creates a supportive milieu, identifies those experiencing excessive levels of emotional discomfort, and directs team members via nonverbal communications (e.g., hand signals, head gestures, etc.) to intervene with severely distraught students or parents. In addition, the leader discusses with parents and students common symptom clusters (e.g., diagnoses) experienced by school-age violence survivors (e.g., Posttraumatic Stress Disorder, adjustment disorders with anxious mood, etc.) The leader normalizes such symptoms and encourages parents to recognize more severe symptomatology that may require additional counseling (e.g., recurrent encopresis, persistent outbursts of anger, chronic hypervigilance).

Co-leaders add relevant comments during the session and support the leader. Most important, co-leaders give immediate support to students and parents who become emotionally distraught. They also help prevent disruption that may otherwise inhibit group dynamics. Co-leaders also can help redirect student attention and help leaders recognize when students' attention spans are nearing an end. Concomitantly, should two or more parents or students begin to socialize or initiate non–debriefing-relevant discussions, co-leaders can help truncate such behaviors and refocus all participants on the needs of survivors and the debriefing process.

The title of the third role is doorkeeper. Persons performing this important role prevent nonparticipants (e.g., reporters, other students) from entering the session. Doorkeepers also prevent severely distraught students or parents from bolting from sessions and encourage students or parents who take short breaks to return to sessions.

Before the Debriefing

Before the debriefing, team members should be apprised of the violent episode and its details. Answers to a number of questions warrant investigation related to the violent incident. For example, teams should learn whether the violence was random or specifically targeted toward the victims. Additionally, teams should learn whether the perpetrator(s) was apprehended. These factors will likely have an influence on participants' perceptions of the violent episode and the moods with which students and parents present. If the violent act was gang related or if retaliation toward the session's participants is suspected, the team must be assured that police or school security officers are outside the debriefing room during the session and that protection is present when participants both enter and leave the premises.

Separate Debriefings

Given the developmental and role differences between adults and students, the needs of participants within the debriefings are different. Each debriefing should address the specific concerns and needs of the members. Additionally, the debriefing experiences should have a single overriding objective—to help ameliorate the survivor's potential distress.

Parent Debriefings

Parent and student needs are often different and cannot be addressed adequately through a single session. Thus, the first session is conducted with parents whose children experienced the violent episode. Later sessions will be devoted to parents whose children witnessed but were not involved in the violent episode. It is important to keep the number of parents in these sessions small (i.e., fewer than eight). Parents most often express concern for their children's future safety and express anger at the school for not adequately protecting them from the violent episode. It is imperative that the team keep parents focused on the immediate needs of their children and not make promises related to future student safety. Such promises cannot be guaranteed and detract from the students' immediate needs. Parents need to be continually reminded of the three primary goals of the first parent session:

1. Educate parents regarding possible symptoms their children may exhibit.
2. Offer available referral sources.
3. Remind parents regarding their role in validating their children (which is not the same as validating possibly unfounded child presented concerns) and normalizing their children's concerns.

Parent-Student Debriefings

Students who have witnessed or experienced violence often are responding to their own perceived post-violence needs and concerns. Younger children, especially, are emotionally vulnerable and look to parents and teachers to protect them. Often they require reassurances of safety and indications from parents that the crisis is over. Therefore, the team must encourage a sense of security and calmness during the joint parent-student session. Team members can foster this by slowing their speech rates and lowering their voice tones. Whenever possible, debriefings should occur in quiet rooms away from hallway and playground noise. The use of movable furniture comfortable for parents and children alike is helpful.

During this joint student-parent debriefing, two circles are formed. No more than five or six students of similar ages sit in the inner circle with friends and peers who witnessed or experienced the violence. Parents sit behind their children. This parental presence promotes a perception of stability, unity, and support, which can be heartening to students. An additional gesture of support can include parents placing their hands on their children's shoulders. This should occur only when children are receptive to such gestures, however.

Seven Adapted Debriefing Model Steps

Introduction Step

During the introduction step, the team leader identifies members of the team and establishes rules for the debriefing experience. Participants are asked to identify persons who may not belong in the room (e.g., teachers, attorneys, students who want to observe but were not present, etc.), who are then asked to leave. Confidentiality and its limits are explained, and participants are encouraged not to discuss what is said within the session outside the debriefing room. All participants are encouraged to remain for the entire debriefing. The leader states that the primary purpose of the debriefing session is to help school violence survivors recover from the experience as quickly as possible.

Fact-Gathering Step

The second step of the process is fact gathering. Typically the leader begins this step by reporting that the team was not present during the violence and would like to hear about the episode from the students. Those speaking are encouraged to give their name and state where they were and what they did when the violent episode began. Emphasis is placed on telling the *facts* of what each student encountered. Team members should not push students to describe their feelings about the incident. However, should students begin sharing feelings, the team leader and co-leaders should acknowledge emotions expressed and indicate that these feelings are normal.

Thought Step

The third step is the thought step. This step is transitional and helps students move from the cognitive domain to the affective domain. The leader asks questions related to what students thought when the violence erupted (e.g., "What was your first thought when you saw her stab Angel?"). During this step, it is crucial to continue to validate and normalize each student's reported thoughts and perceptions.

Reaction Step

The thought step can give way quickly to the emotionally charged reaction step. Here the focus should be kept on participants' sharing their reactions to the violent experience. Typically, the leader will start with a question: "What was the most difficult part of seeing Angel being stabbed?"

Symptom Step

During the symptom step, the leader helps direct the group from the affective domain back to the cognitive domain. As emotionally charged reactions begin to subside, the leader asks students about any physical, cognitive, or affective symptoms experienced since the violent episode. If students remain silent or when their discussion of such symptoms subsides, the leader may ask what symptoms the parents may have observed in their children. Great caution must be used here. In the case of elementary and younger middle school students, parental discussion related to symptoms typically is helpful to students and especially other parents. However, in the case of older middle school students (e.g., seventh or eighth grade) or high school students, parental discussion can cause embarrassment to individual student participants, which may result in student disengagement. Thus, leaders should utilize their clinical judgment and knowledge of the participants to determine if it is best to engage parents within the symptom discussion. Often the leader will discuss symptoms such as nausea, trembling hands, inability to concentrate, or feelings of anxiety. Typically, the leader will ask those who have encountered such experiences to raise their hands. Such a show of hands helps normalize the described symptoms and often helps survivors experience relief that they are not "strange" or "crazy."

Teaching Step

A teaching step follows the symptom step. Symptoms experienced by group members are reported as being both normal and expected. Possible future symptoms can be described briefly (e.g., recurring dreams of being attacked, restricted range of affect, intrusive memories, etc.). This helps both parents and students better understand symptoms that may be encountered in the future and gives students permission to discuss such symptoms with parents and peers, should they arise. During this step the group leader may ask, "What little things have you done or noticed your friends, teachers, and parents doing that have helped you handle this situation so well?" This question suggests that the students are doing well and helps them begin to look for signs of progress rather than continuing to focus on the violent episode. Sometimes older students will express feelings of support from peers, teachers, or parents. Younger students may use active fantasy to help them better cope with their fears or concerns. An example of such active fantasy is a child pretending that he or she is a hero who disarms the perpetrator and protects other children from harm.

Reentry Step

The reentry step attempts to place some closure on the experience and allows survivors and their parents to discuss further concerns or thoughts.

The leader may ask students and parents to revisit pressing issues, discuss new topics, or mention thoughts that might help the debriefing process come to a more successful end. After addressing any issues brought forward by the students or parents, the debriefing team makes a few closing comments related to any apparent group progress or visible group support. A handout written at an age-appropriate reading level for students and another written for adults discussing common reaction symptoms can be helpful. Younger students who may lack the necessary reading skills necessary to understand such handouts may prefer drawing faces that depict how they currently feel (e.g., anxious, sad, frightened). Later, parents can use these pictures as conversation starters with their children at home. Handouts should list a 24-hour helpline number and include the work telephone number for the student's school counselor. Often it is helpful to introduce parents to their child's school counselor at the debriefing.

Post-Session Activities

After the initial debriefing, team members should mingle with parents and children as refreshments are served. Team members should be looking for those who appear shaken or are experiencing severe distress. These persons should be encouraged to immediately meet with one of the counselors who is present or be referred for counseling with someone who is available. The promotion of peer support (both parent and student) is important. Students and parents should be encouraged to telephone one another over the next few days to aid in the recovery process.

Additional Debriefing Sessions

Depending on the interactions of parent and student participants and the debriefing team's clinical judgment, additional debriefing sessions may be offered. Typically, such sessions are limited in number and closed to all persons except those who participated in the initial debriefing. Therapeutically, it makes most sense to offer additional debriefing sessions in two-session increments. In other words, agreeing to 12 additional debriefing sessions at the conclusion of the initial debriefing is therapeutically inappropriate.

Immediately following a school violence experience and the initial debriefing, parents frequently indicate a desire to participate in a long-term debriefing process. However, violence symptoms typically dissipate after the first debriefing, and families are so busy that many cannot fulfill their obligation to attend the requested additional debriefings. This limits attendance numbers. Those who make the effort to attend sometimes feel "betrayed" by others who fail to attend the agreed-on sessions. Thus, we believe that agreeing to long-term debriefings can be therapeutic aversive and actually may do more harm than good if limited numbers attend.

Instead, if additional debriefing sessions are desired by the majority of participants and are believed by the debriefing team to be clinically appropriate and not contraindicated (e.g., only one parent reports a desire to participate, students were disenfranchised from the debriefing process, etc.), an additional two sessions should be offered. If the majority of participants attend and participate in those two sessions and desire future sessions, the debriefing team will again need to reconsider the potential clinical benefits. If future sessions are perceived as therapeutically appropriate, an additional two sessions would be offered. This process would continue until such a time as the debriefing team perceives the clinical benefits are minimal. When this is the case, if one or two persons or families wish to continue, the debriefing team may wish to refer them to individual or family counseling options.

One or two school counselors typically can facilitate the additional debriefings. The intent of these additional debriefing meetings is to:

- Provide additional observations to assess students' recovery and parent-child relations.
- Provide additional psychoeducation related to trauma recovery to parents and children.
- Focus parents and students on the progress they are making and their healthy trauma recovery.
- Provide referral resources to students, parents, or families that appear to be having difficulties.

Hence, these sessions typically start by thanking participants for their attendance and asking a question, such as "Tell me how things have improved since our last meeting." In particular, school counselors will want to observe the interactions and learn how individual and family members report improvement. Based on the severity of the school violence events, the initial noted improvements may be small. Consider the next vignette.

Counselor: I would like to thank everyone for returning today. Your being here suggests that you are invested in helping yourself, your family, and your friends get through the events of last week. Additionally, I would like to ask a question. In what ways have you been seeing things improve or get better for you, your family members, or your friends since last week?

Katrina: I haven't seen things get better. I'm still very sad that my best friend Angel was stabbed last week.

Counselor: It sounds like it has been a difficult time.

Katrina: It has. I'm still having nightmares and see those girls trying to kill me.

Counselor: Are the nightmares occurring nightly?

Katrina: No. I had the nightmares the first couple nights, but I haven't had any for three days.

Counselor: So, it sounds as though the nightmares aren't occurring as often as before. What do you think that means?

Katrina: I think it means I am getting better, but that I am still not 100%.

Counselor: That makes a lot of sense to me, Katrina. How about others? Have others noticed a decrease in your nightmares or other symptoms?

Angel: Well, I'm not over the nightmares either. But I'm not shaking like I did the first couple days after the attack.

Counselor: Tell us about that.

Angel: The first couple of days, my hands shook so bad I couldn't even drink a Coca-Cola or write with a pen. Now I'm not shaking at all and my nightmares aren't as bad.

Counselor: Moms, I'm hearing Katrina say her nightmares have lessened and Angel say her nightmares have lessened and she isn't shaking anymore. Help us understand what things you as parents have seen that say your daughters are doing better and that your families and loved ones are going to make it through this experience.

Let us review what happened in the mini-clinical vignette. First, the counselor thanks everyone for attending the debriefing and frames their attendance as a way of helping self and others. Providing a compliment at the beginning of the session lessens participants' defenses. This in turn encourages those present to actively participate.

Next the counselor asks the question: "In what ways have you been seeing things improve or get better for you, your family members, or your friends since last week?" The manner in which the question is stated makes an important inference. It implies that participants *have seen* improvements. Concomitantly, these improvements are related to self and individual family members and friends. Do not be fooled. This is not word trickery. It is using an embedded suggestion that improvements are occurring and is encouraging participants to think about the positive changes they have experienced or witnessed.

Katrina responds that she has not seen improvements. Instead of arguing with Katrina, the counselor empathizes with her, listens to her symptoms, and then asks if her reported nightmares are occurring nightly. This is a very important therapeutic interaction. It validates Katrina and indicates that the counselor has heard her. When Katrina reports that her nightmares have lessened in frequency, the school counselor maintains discussion on the lessened nightmare frequency and asks a projective question. The projective question gives Katrina the freedom to interpret the lessened frequency of nightmares as she wishes. Katrina responds that she is "still not 100% [better]." The counselor does not argue that the lessening nightmare frequency suggests improvement. Instead, she asks if others have experienced a decrease in nightmares.

Notice how eloquently the counselor opens the question by saying "nightmares *or other symptoms*." In other words, the school counselor is opening the door not only to lessening nightmares but to any post-violence symptom improvement. Angel reports that she no longer shakes. The counselor asks Angel to explain her shaking in greater detail and then summarizes the improvements Angel noted. Finally, the counselor expands the improvements noted by Katrina and Angel and asks the mothers who are present to describe symptom reductions or improvements they have noted.

The additional debriefing sessions also provide increased opportunities to observe and to provide additional psychoeducation related to post-trauma symptoms and referral options. In the next mini-clinical vignette, the mother reports Angel's argumentative behaviors as occurring after the violence and as being disruptive to the family. The school counselor provides further psycho-education related to post-violence symptoms and suggests a potential referral option.

Mother: I get so upset with Angel. It seems that since she was stabbed, she mopes around, doesn't want to do anything, and is argumentative. So, I just grounded her for life!

Counselor: Sounds like you are pretty upset.

Mother: I am. I think she is simply making this whole stabbing thing into an excuse to be mean to me and her brothers.

Counselor: First, let me say that I am very impressed with you, Mom. It would be easy for you to simply ignore Angel's behaviors and say, "Who cares?" Instead, you want what is best for her and you are indicating that as the parental authority in the house, you require Angel to behave in a manner consistent to the rules and regulations you have established for your children.

Mother: Thank you. It is hard being the only parent in a home with three teenagers.

Counselor: Yes it is, but you aren't giving up. You are making them toe the line. You are demonstrating to them that they must obey rules. It sounds like you are doing a good job, Mom. Don't give up. Being a mom is a tough job. Being a single mom is even tougher. Hang in there.

Mother: I will.

Counselor: That said I want to repeat something that I said in our first debriefing session. Some of the post-violent symptoms that adolescents and teens demonstrate after trauma revolve around depression. Teen depression can present itself in a lot of different ways . . . not just sadness. Often teens can mope around or be argumentative. However, lots of teens who are not depressed or who have not experienced violence mope around or are argumentative too. Mother, any chance you would do something for me?

Mother: It depends.

Counselor: I know a psychiatrist who specializes in depressed adolescents. If I give you her name and telephone number, will you contact her for an appointment? Specifically, let's have her talk with Angel to determine if Angel is depressed or if Angel is merely moping around and being argumentative as part of her adolescent years.

In this mini-clinical vignette, we note a number of things. First, the mother reports Angel's behaviors—those that are consistent with post-violence behaviors in adolescents and teens. Instead of recognizing these behaviors as symptoms of Angel's post-violence experience, the mother says she grounded Angel. The counselor does not scold the mother. Instead she validates the mother by saying "Sounds like you are pretty upset." The mother confirms her feelings and reports that she views Angel's behaviors as suspect and an excuse for acting however Angel wishes.

Immediately, the counselor gives Mother a compliment. She reframes the mother's behaviors as an indication of her commitment to her daughter. Then the counselor further praises the mother. These complimenting and praising behaviors by the counselor are crucial. If the counselor had instead merely stated that the mother was "wrong" and the behaviors exhibited by Angel were symptoms of the violence, the mother would likely be forced to take an argumentative stance. If this happened, neither counselor nor mother would "win" and the ultimate loser would be Angel. Instead, the counselor again repeats the potential post-violence symptoms and provides a referral source for the mother. Thus, the counselor is providing further psychoeducation training to the mother and potential treatment referrals for Angel.

CHAPTER SUMMARY

This chapter has described how school counselors can effectively utilize Juhnke's Adapted Solution-Focused Debriefing with school students who experience violence and their parents.

Readers gained a general understanding of the history and development of CISD and CISM, the concerns Juhnke had specific to the CISD, and how he addressed these concerns via the Adapted Solution-Focused Debriefing. Mini-clinical vignettes were utilized to aid readers in their understanding of the Adapted Debriefing and how they may choose to implement the intervention. Again, as is the case with CISD, CISM, and other proposed crisis intervention models, Juhnke's Adapted Solution-Focused Debriefing does not possess clear evidenced-based research demonstrating clinical efficacy. Thus, the proposed intervention should be used only when, in the school counselors' judgment, the intervention may have clinical utility for the population in need. The specific needs of the students are the foremost consideration when selecting an intervention. We strongly believe the best intervention will provide a therapeutic quilt consisting of multiple assessments and interventions of which Juhnke's Adapted Solution-Focused Debriefing may be just one part.

Legal Issues and Preparation

CHAPTER
10

Ethical and Legal Issues

Recently I (Dr. Juhnke) watched a television interview with Michael Brewer and his mother. Michael is a 15-year-old Florida middle school student. Peers doused him with rubbing alcohol and then set him ablaze. Apparently, the attack was related to a dispute over a video game and owed money. According to Michael's mother, Michael had been "petrified" to attend school prior to the attack. He was aware that the peers who ultimately attacked him were intent on harming him. However, even veteran police officers were appalled by the viciousness of his attackers.

Thus far you have read about school suicide and violence assessment and intervention topics. However, this case reminds us of two important points: (1) No matter the amount of assessment and our best efforts to intervene before suicide or violence occurs, suicide and violence always can happen; and (2) we must be aware of ethical and legal ramifications for our professional decisions.

What would you have done had you been Michael's school counselor, and he had confided his concerns of danger to you? Your response would have significant ramifications for Michael, your school, and you. The incident with Michael occurred off campus. However, had he been attacked on campus after voicing safety concerns, we anticipate that an investigation would occur with the potential for ethical and legal charges. Depending on those investigational outcomes, rulings would likely be made that could have very severe penalties for school counselors and others who were aware of his concerns yet failed to act sufficiently. Given the ramifications of this case, we can understand the importance of ethical and legal issues specific to school suicide and violence. In an effort to provide the necessary foundation to discuss these important topics, we begin this chapter with a general discussion regarding professional ethics codes and laws.

PROFESSIONAL ETHICS CODES AND STATE COUNSELING LAWS

Professional ethics codes are vitally important to counselors helping students who have experienced school violence or to those who may present potential violence risk. In such cases professional ethics codes provide a broad template to interpret a threshold of care and the necessary boundaries for proposed interventions. These codes, then, help counselors chart appropriate boundaries and behaviors to insure that students receive appropriate care.

Professional Ethics Codes

It seems that every professional counseling organization has its own professional ethics codes. Some codes seem especially relevant to professional counselors and school counselors in particular. For example, the 45,000-member American Counseling Association (ACA), the 26,000-member American School Counselor Association (ASCA), and the 42,000-member National Board of Certified Counselors (NBCC) each has its own ethical code (ACA, 2005; ASCA, 2004; NBCC, 2005). The ACA Code of Ethics indicates five primary purposes (ACA, 2005, p. 3). These include:

1. The Code enables the association to clarify to current and future members, and to those served by members, the nature of ethical responsibilities held in common by its members.
2. The Code helps support the mission of the association.
3. The Code establishes principles that define ethical behavior and best practices of association members.
4. The Code serves as an ethical guide designed to assist members in constructing a professional course of action that best serves those utilizing counseling services and best promotes the values of the counseling profession.
5. The Code serves as the basis for processing of ethical complaints and inquiries initiated against members of the association.

As one reviews the various codes, it becomes strikingly evident that each was written specifically to promote protection for students and counselor alike. This observation is further supported by Koocher and Keith-Spiegel's (2008) review of mental health providers' ethical codes. Koocher and

Keith-Spiegel found a number of commonly recurring themes in existing mental health codes, including:

- Doing no harm to students.
- Acting professionally and ethically.
- Counseling within the scope of one's professional training and competence.
- Protecting students from unethical practice.
- Protecting students from exploitation.
- Protecting students' confidentiality.

Counseling-related ethical codes are most often presented as general templates that do not necessarily address specific questions. In other words, instead of telling counselors "this is what counselors should do in this particular situation," the codes provide general guidelines related to broad topic areas, such as confidentiality or avoiding student harm. Thus, it is imperative that counselors become familiar with ethical codes specific to the professions to which they belong and understand how to apply these general templates to situations that may arise within their professional practice. We believe that as school counselors become familiar with ethical codes related to their particular professional organizations, they will utilize ethical code decision-making models more frequently. Such use will promote broadly appropriate ethical behaviors and increase the probability that state counseling laws will not be broken. Thus, it is hoped that knowledge of professional ethical codes and familiarity with their use will reduce the frequency of more common ethical and legal breaches.

State Counseling Laws

Similar to professional codes of ethics, state counseling laws were written to protect the citizens of individual states from harmful, disadvantageous, or prejudicial counseling practices. Each state establishes its own licensure laws pertaining to the educational, training, and clinical supervision requirements of professional counselors and school counselors. Thus, if one wishes to practice school counseling within a state, one must comply with existing school counseling practice laws.

Although most states have central core requirements reflective of the eight Council for Accreditation of Counseling and Related Educational Programs Common Core Areas (CACREP, 2009)—including Human Growth and

Development, Social and Cultural Foundations, Helping Relationships, Group Work, Career and Lifestyle Development, Appraisal, Research and Program Evaluation, and Professional Orientation and Ethics—individual states often have somewhat different licensure requirements. For example, some states may require those seeking a particular counseling license to have specific courses that the state deems important to the practice of counseling and the safety of their citizens. For example, the State of Florida may require graduate coursework in human sexuality, substance abuse, and human immunodeficiency virus (HIV) whereas the State of North Carolina may not require these specific courses. Such graduate course requirements are determined by the individual state and mandated within that state's counseling licensure laws.

Similar differences between states occur related to required supervised postgraduate clinical hours. Some states may require more postgraduate clinical hours than others. For example, the State of Ohio requires 3,000 hours of postgraduate supervised experience whereas the State of Minnesota requires only 2,000 postgraduate supervised hours. Additionally, some states mandate that required postgraduate supervised clinical hours be completed within a defined time frame (i.e., five years). Therefore, unlike professional ethics codes, which often serve as general templates, state licensing requirements typically are very specific. State licensing requirements tell counselors exactly what must be done to attain the privilege of practicing counseling within that state and how counselors must act to keep their state-issued license.

ETHICAL DECISION MAKING

We believe that it is critical to understand both one's professional ethics and one's state professional counseling laws. However, in those sticky situations where state laws fail to address specific situations, knowing how to utilize ethical decision making helps increase the probability that the most ethically appropriate decisions are made. Selecting or creating the most ethical decision has greater potential to protect students, benefit society, and keep the counselor away from liability risk.

Biomedical ethics in particular has increasingly been viewed as the premier field for mental and physical health professionals to seek ethical decision-making practices and guidance (Michael Sunich, personal communication, January 28, 2010). Beauchamp and Childress (2009) are two prominent biomedical ethicists who have authored one of the most widely known ethical decision-making guidance texts on the market today. This text is currently in its sixth edition and is referred to frequently within the biomedical ethics literature. In particular, Beauchamp and Childress defend and advocate for a practice commonly referred to as the four-principles approach to biomedical ethics (Gillon & Lloyd, 1994). This ethical decision-making approach is founded on four pillars include:

1. Respect for autonomy
2. Beneficence
3. Nonmaleficence
4. Justice

Respect for Autonomy

Respect for autonomy is the first principle of bioethics discussed by Beauchamp and Childress (2009). However, they state: "Although we begin our discussion of principles of biomedical ethics with Respect for Autonomy, our order of presentation does not imply that this principle has moral priority over other principles" (p. 99). Apparently, previous reviewers had misinterpreted the fact that respect for autonomy was listed first as meaning that Beauchamp and Childress intended for it to be the foremost principle of the four-principle approach to biomedical ethics. In fact, each of the four principles within the model is equally weighted and should be reviewed when considering ethical assessment and interventions with students presenting risk for suicide or violence.

In particular, respect for autonomy indicates that one should have the ability to rule one's life and make personal decisions. According to Beauchamp and Childress (2009): "The autonomous individual acts freely in accordance with a self-chosen plan, analogous to the way an independent government manages its territories and establishes its policies" (p. 99). Counselors who show respect for autonomy recognize that students have the right to self-rule or make decisions based on personal choices. Respect for autonomy also affords students the right to maintain their views and "to take actions based on their personal values and beliefs" (p. 102).

For counselors and their students, respect for autonomy is vitally important to the ethical decision-making process. How many of us have not had incredibly bright and able students ignore our encouragement to take advanced courses—courses in which they had significant probability of excelling? Have you ever had graduating students refuse significant financial packages offered by highly visible universities? For example, a student was offered a financial package that would have completely paid for the first two years of her degree including all tuition, course fees, and books. The only requirements were that she complete the application package and enroll in the program. Despite our best efforts to encourage this student, she did neither. No one could force her to attend. Our ethical responsibility was to provide the options we were aware of in the most respectful way possible. Then, according to respect for autonomy, we were to *allow her to make her own decision*. Were we happy with her decision? Frankly, we were frustrated with her decision. We did not believe her decision was in her best interests. However, *the decision was not ours to make*. The decision was hers. After she weighed the options and considered the perceived costs and benefits, she made a choice that she believed best for her. This is the foundational principle of respect for autonomy.

As counselors, then, we must ask ourselves: Do I acknowledge my students' rights to choose as they deem best? More important: Do I respect them no matter their chosen decisions? Quite some time ago, when I (Dr. Juhnke) was counseling a divorced father and his son due to the son's Conduct Disordered behaviors and frequent alcohol abuse, the two told of an experience that I often think about when I lecture on counselors' respect for autonomy. The father and son had decided to participate in an overnight campout. Although the temperatures were relatively mild during the daylight hours, the father knew that once the sun went down, the night temperatures would be quite brisk. So, the father directed his son to pack a jacket. The son argued with his father, who allowed his son to choose whether to take his jacket or not. The son purposefully left his jacket at home and told his father that he "refused" to take his jacket. The father told his son that the ultimate choice of taking or leaving his jacket was up to the son.

That evening, in the chill of the night air, the son wanted to explore the woods. Unfortunately, he was jacketless. It was too cold to venture far from the campfire or tent. He remembered his father's directions to pack a jacket and did not want his father to say "I told you so." However, once it became too cold for comfort, the son swallowed his pride and asked to borrow his father's jacket. The father declined his son's request and instead encouraged his son to zip himself into his sleeping bag and go to bed early that night rather than explore the forest or view the stars. Although the son was in no danger of dying from exposure, the experience was not pleasant for him. And the son was mad at himself for not listening to his father's wisdom regarding the need for a jacket.

During our counseling session the following week, I asked about the camping experience. The father described the experience as very helpful for his son and reported, "My son is finally becoming a man and he is becoming responsible." When I pressed the father about his response, he reported that since the camping incident, his son was following the father's directions without arguing and was taking more "initiative" around the house. When I asked the son to help me more fully understand what the father was stating, the young man stated something like: "I learned a lot [during the campout]. I learned my dad asks me to do certain things, because it is best for me. I also learned he won't force me to do things I don't want to do. If I fail to follow his directions, I will have to live with the consequences. He is treating me more like an adult, and I like it—even if it means I have to live with my mistakes."

At the onset of the counseling session, I found myself thinking this father had really failed to support his son. Wouldn't it have been easier to simply throw his son's jacket into the truck? After all, the father knew his son would be cold without it. However, after hearing the two describe the experience, the therapeutic potency of allowing the son to choose whether to bring his jacket on the campout hit me like a basketball to the head. Unintentionally, the father had utilized part of the ethical decision-making model by respecting his son's autonomy. Even if the father didn't like his son's decision to leave his jacket at home, he allowed his son to choose whether the jacket would be brought. More important, the father respected his son despite the decision to leave the jacket at home.

There are times and situations, however, when this first pillar of the ethical decision-making process must be overruled. Specifically, if students are perceived as imminent dangers to self (e.g., suicide) or others (e.g., assaultive), counselors must act to protect the endangered. Beauchamp and Childress (2009, p. 105) state:

> Our obligations to respect autonomy do not extend to persons who cannot act in a sufficiently autonomous manner (and who cannot be rendered autonomous) because they are immature, incapacitated,

ignorant, coerced, or exploited. Infants, irrationally suicidal individuals, and drug-dependent patients are examples.

In these cases, counselors will need to intervene to ensure the safety of all. When such cases arise, it is important to utilize professional codes of ethics and understand the laws of the specific state.

Beneficence

Beneficence is the act of benefiting others rather than self. According to Beauchamp and Childress (2009), the principle of beneficence represents a "moral obligation to act for the benefit of others" (p. 197). They identify five general moral rules related to the principle of positive beneficence. These include (p. 199):

1. Protect and defend the rights of others.
2. Prevent harm from occurring to others.
3. Remove conditions that will cause harm to others.
4. Help persons with disabilities.
5. Rescue persons in danger.

Clearly, there exists a strong correlation between these general moral rules related to the principle of beneficence and the American Counseling Associations Codes of Ethics. In each case, the underlying concern is practicing in a manner that is morally responsible. Thus, school counselors are required to put their students' needs at the forefront of every aspect of the counseling charge.

A slightly different lens in which to view beneficence is presented by Carter (2002). She reports that the overriding question when analyzing this second pillar of the ethical decision-making model is: "Who benefits from my action and in what way [do they benefit]?" In other words, when addressing issues of school suicide or violence, the counselors' actions should be thoughtfully constructed to benefit the students at risk of harm as well as the school community itself. As a counselor who has practiced and specialized in life-threatening behaviors since 1986, I have seen school counselors go to inordinate extremes to protect their students. Sometimes these school counselors have endured ridicule, administrative persecution, and personal danger because of their commitment to ensure their students' safety. These counselors' vulnerable students have benefited because of these dedicated professionals. And, the overwhelming majority of the times, these school counselors have thoughtfully constructed interventions that benefited all involved.

Nonmaleficence

Simply stated, nonmaleficence (*primum non nocere*) means *first and foremost, cause no harm* (American Medical Association, 2008). Within this discussion of the four-principles approach to ethical decision making for school counselors, we must ensure that when we attempt to help those who might be endangered by school suicide or violence, our interventions (or non-interventions) cause no harm. Or that we do not cause more harm than good. Sometimes potential harm is readily identifiable. At other times, it is not. This seems especially true for school counselors. Often school counselors are placed in the precarious position of having to decide on a course of action quickly.

If, for example, a school counselor overheard a middle school student reporting clear suicidal ideation, suicide intent, and a thoroughly detailed and specific suicide plan, and the counselor did nothing to intervene and the student committed suicide, it is unmistakably evident that the counselor *did* harm. Her failure to act despite the presence of clear suicide markers resulted in the student's unimpeded suicide.

What is more difficult to anticipate is potential harm done despite our best intended professional intentions. Here, if a school counselor believes a student *may* be at suicide risk, completes an assessment, and is uncertain about the student's immediate suicide risk, it may be common practice to encourage the student's parents to hospitalize the student briefly for observation and potential protection from self. However, what happens if this involuntary hospitalization results in unintended harm to the student? The student's psychiatric hospitalization may result in ostracism by friends or forced relationship breaks due to friends' parents keeping their children away from a "psycho." Concomitantly, the student may encounter ridicule or mocking by peers. Thus, in an attempt to bring about good and keep the student alive, the outcome has produced unintended harm to the student.

Some might argue that a living student is better than a dead student. In other words, if one suspects a student is a potential suicide danger—no matter the level of immediate risk—one should hospitalize the student. However, any experienced school counselor understands the importance of friendships and socializing among middle and high school girls. Such social interactions are of significant importance to middle and high school girls. If a student is involuntarily hospitalized and is later ostracized by peers because of that hospitalization, the student may well believe the involuntary hospitalization caused more harm than good. Thus, despite our best intentions, the student suffers. Here the question is whether we as counselors caused more harm than good to the student. Hence, it is imperative that school counselors consider potential negative consequences to their best intentioned interventions. If at all possible, before intervening, we should attempt to mitigate and identify potentially unintended harm or noxious side effects that might be caused by the intervention.

Justice

The final pillar of the four-principles approach to biomedical ethics is justice. Justice implies that all persons are treated equally, fairly, equitably, and according to their presenting needs (Beauchamp & Childress, 2009). The term "justice" further suggests that one is not unfairly discriminated against and that exploitation, especially among vulnerable groups (e.g., the impoverished, the very young and very old, etc.), does not occur. For school counselors, justice means that we do not prevent the less affluent, younger, physically or mentally challenged, or less academically gifted students from receiving the same consideration and counseling services. Stated differently, we fairly provide counseling services to all students no matter who they are or their presenting needs.

Clearly, the four-principles approach to biomedical ethics has significant utility for school counselors facing issues specific to school suicide or violence. Understanding each of the four pillars (i.e., respect for autonomy, beneficence, nonmaleficence, and justice) and carefully considering each prior to making an intervention seems a logical way to protect one's students as well as oneself. Failing to consider each of the pillars places one in jeopardy of creating an ill-planned, impulsive, and ineloquent intervention that may do more harm to the students we are serving than good.

THE FOUR OUT OF FIVE CONSULTATION

The four out of five consultation provides school counselors with direct feedback from professional colleagues and encourages eloquent and effective interventions related to school suicide and violence. Concomitantly, the four out of five consultation potentially insulates school counselors from liability issues, because it demonstrates that the intervention implemented reflects a common standard of care among fellow professionals within the field. Here the school counselor identifies and contacts five fellow school counseling professionals, each having approximately the same educational background (i.e., a master's degree in school counseling), work experience (e.g., eight years of counseling middle schoolers), and professional certifications and licenses. Upon making contact with the first consultant, the school counselor asks if he or she could describe a pressing case, seek ideas and suggestions regarding the proposed intervention to ensure the most effective intervention, and document the telephone consultation so that, if necessary, the consultant could be contacted in the future. Next, the school counselor provides an overview of the case including all relevant and important details regarding the situation. Although the case should be depicted as accurately and fully as possible, it is also important to maintain student confidentiality. The school counselor responds to any questions posed by the consultant. If the consultant does not ask questions, the school counselor would ask if further information or clarification is needed or if the consultant has specific questions related to the case. After all consultant questions are answered, the school counselor describes the intended intervention and asks whether it seems appropriate and what parts of the intervention should be altered to ensure that the most thorough and appropriate intervention is made. Appropriate and helpful suggestions that would result in a more effective intervention are integrated into the intervention until it seems most clinically sound to both the school counselor and the counselor consultant.

Once the two school counselors believe the very best intervention has been created, the school counselor contacts the next consultant. The process is repeated until all five school counselors have heard a thorough description of the case and the planned intervention. The school counselor then contacts each of the consulting school counselors again, describes the integrated intervention that includes the recommendations from all the consulting counselors, and answers further questions. If further suggestions are noted, the school counselor repeats the process until four of the five believe that the intervention is clinically appropriate, ethically and legally sound, and provides the student(s) sufficient physical, emotional, psychological, and social safety. However, if those consulted believe the proposed intervention failed to adequately surpass a standard of care threshold, the proposed intervention should not be enacted, and a new intervention should be decided on.

CLINICAL SUPERVISION

As counselor educators and supervisors who have over 40 years of combined clinical supervision experiences, we have encountered our share of unusual supervisee-student situations. Throughout the supervision process, we believe it is imperative that supervisees follow their supervisors' directives and keep supervisors current on all cases. This is especially true in cases where suicide or violence risk is potentially present. Whenever school counselors believe a potential ethical situation may be budding, it is crucial to inform one's clinical supervisor immediately. One's clinical supervisor is an important insulating line of defense who should understand how to best ensure that all ethical, legal, and clinical issues are adequately addressed.

Supervisors should have appropriate certifications, such as the National Board of Certified Counselors Approved Clinical Supervisor credential and any required state supervision licenses or certifications. Counseling supervisors also may have counseling doctorates, which require that they successfully complete advanced graduate coursework in supervision or ethics or specialty coursework related to advanced clinical topic issues such as suicide or violence. Thus, these certified, licensed, and degreed supervisors should be keenly aware of potential ethical or legal issues that must be addressed by the school counselors they supervise.

Besides the importance of keeping counseling supervisors abreast of current students, it is important for school counselor supervisees to follow directions and instructions related to student cases. In most cases supervisors have encountered situations similar to those currently experienced by the school counselor and know precisely how the supervisee should respond. If supervisors have not encountered similar situations or are ignorant about the specific clinical interventions to use with an unusually difficult or demanding case, the supervisors should know how to attain the necessary information to help the school counselor provide the very best interventions for the potentially suicidal or violent student.

Whenever possible, supervisees should carefully and thoroughly follow the supervisor's directives and instructions. If the directives or instructions seem inappropriate or wrong, it is possible that there has been a communications breakdown. Supervisees should work as a partner with their supervisor to clarify the supervisor's directives. Supervisees should ask the supervisor for help in understanding the intended purpose of the intervention and how the supervisor's directed intervention has played out in the past. Stated differently, supervisees should use this opportunity to learn from their clinical supervisors. Typically, we have found that once supervisees gain clarification of the directive or understand the reasons for the directed interventions, their concerns diminish and the interventions work.

If after seeking clarification from the supervisor the directives clearly contradict state counseling laws or professional counseling ethical codes, supervisees may wish to consider other options. First, and foremost, one should always go to the clinical supervisor. Bring the ethical code or professional counseling law to the supervision session and have the supervisor explain how the directive follows the ethical code or professional counseling law in question. If the supervisor cannot explain how the ordered directive aligns with the ethical code or professional counseling law, yet continues to direct the school counselor to break or disregard the code or law, other options will need to be sought. These might include seeking consultation with a more senior clinical supervisor or contacting the national or state professional counseling association and speaking with an ethics specialist. If after speaking with the more senior clinical supervisor or ethics specialist, one believes that an ethical or legal violation exists, it would be important to document the concerns and record the supervisor's responses. If the concerns are ignored by the supervisor or if the supervisor continues to encourage the school counselor to break the professional counseling ethical code or law, one then needs to contact the state or professional board to determine the best procedural options specific to filing a professional complaint. Fortunately, it has been our experience that such situations are extremely rare. Most clinical supervisors with whom we are familiar truly want what is best for supervisees and clients alike and understand professional ethics and laws sufficiently.

SCHOOL DISTRICT LEGAL COUNSEL

Not long ago, my (Dr. Juhnke's) 14-year-old son ordered a fried fish sandwich at a local breakfast restaurant renowned for its incredible strawberry and rum blintz soufflés. How do you think he liked his fish? Exactly . . . it was horrible. Why? Because that particular restaurant's cooking staff members are breakfast food experts. They thrive on creating delectable strawberry and rum blintz soufflés, fancy omelets, and breakfast pastries filled with whipped cream and topped with sugary fruits. Sure, they will make a fish sandwich—just as they will make a requested peanut butter and jelly sandwich—but that is not their area of expertise.

Let's assume that you are a school counselor or mental health counselor with interest in providing effective clinical interventions for potentially suicidal or violent students as well as student survivors and their families. Probably your focus and concern is more on effective prevention, intervention, and postvention than on school law. Of course, you must be knowledgeable regarding ethical codes and legal issues, but you likely are focused on being the best school counselor, not the best legal counselor. Is that correct?

If we need ethical or legal counsel specific to schools, the person we want to depend on is a trained legal expert—someone who has a juris doctorate and a specialization in school law. We want someone who thrives on legal cases in the same manner we thrive on clinical cases. Given how litigious our society is and how quickly legal precedents may change, we want immediate access to a legal expert who can tell us exactly what actions are best in protecting the students we serve, our school, our community, and ourselves. If you work in a school district, you likely have free access to such experts via the school district's legal department. Use them. Before implementing any intervention, consult with legal counsel to ensure that the intervention fully addresses potential litigation issues.

When I (Dr. Juhnke) was clinical director of a counseling training and research clinic at the University of North Carolina at Greensboro, I consulted with the university's legal department. They were some of the finest legal experts I knew. Although they were not school counseling experts, we worked together to create the very best interventions that addressed students' clinical needs and pressing ethical and legal issues. Frankly, I enjoyed my interactions with each of them and found them to be quite invested in students.

In all candor, if you are counseling, I believe it is critical to have good professional liability insurance as well as legal expert access. Should a school suicide or act of school violence occur, someone is most likely going to bring litigation. Blame will be cast. And you will be in for an emotional roller coaster that is one heck of a ride. Having the best legal counsel will ensure that you have the protection you need.

RISK MANAGEMENT CONSULTATION

Interestingly, most professional liability carriers that I (Dr. Juhnke) am familiar with have risk management programming and consultation access. The risk management programming often consists of a course that includes pertinent litigation topics (e.g., confidentiality issues, disclosure statements, counseling records, etc.). The intent of these programs is to reduce liability claims by addressing high-probability scenarios before they occur. Training is often via DVD or online programming and can be very good.

These professional liability carriers typically provide a free consultation line. Thus, should a potential high-risk issue occur (e.g., a suicidal student), they can provide direct instruction on how to minimize potential liability risk. Of course, their intent is not specific to the clinical needs that need to be addressed. However, they can provide important information to school counselors who believe that they may be facing a potential litigation claim or concern.

CHAPTER SUMMARY

This chapter has provided a general overview of the ethical and legal issues that school counselors will want to be aware of. We have discussed the importance of professional ethics codes, state counseling laws, and the four-principles ethical decision-making model. Readers have learned how to utilize the four out of five consultation model and how to utilize clinical supervision, school district legal counsel, and risk management to help create both ethically and legally sound clinical interventions. Above all, we have advocated that school counselors *never* implement an intervention without consulting with other professionals including legal counsel. The Lone Ranger was not a counselor. He was a fictional character. Yet even he had a trusted consultant with whom he shared his plans before implementing them. Never be the only school interventionist. *Always* consult with professional peers, supervisors, and expert lawyers.

11

Wrap-up
Preparedness and Promising Future Interventions

Given the need to provide students a safe environment in which to learn and socialize, and given the frequency of student suicide and violent behaviors, school administrators, principals, counselors, teachers, staff, and parents will undoubtedly wish to work collaboratively to ensure that their schools are best prepared to respond effectively to potential crises and trauma events. Clearly, the time to review preparedness is prior to the occurrence of suicide or violence. Thus, the intent of this chapter is both to discuss ways to provide such preparedness and to aid readers in developing a general template to ensure such preparedness before such crises occur.

Regretfully, no amount of suicide or violence preparation can anticipate each potentially needed crisis response scenario. Neither can practice drills provide training for every potential type of needed school violence or suicide response. Therefore, this chapter is designed to help school counselors thoughtfully contemplate the general types of high-probability suicide and violence events that most likely may occur on their specific campuses and generate a practical template that will best suit their school's particular needs. Undoubtedly, each school will have idiosyncratic factors that should be taken into account when creating such a template. The template can be modified or adapted to meet individual school factors.

CRISIS PLANNING

According to Jimerson, Brock, and Pletcher (2005), schools responding to crisis need a "shared foundation of preparedness" (p. 275). Given the professional diversity among school personnel (e.g., school counselors, psychologists, social workers, etc.) and the different types of professional philosophies and training among school personnel, Jimerson and colleagues' statement seems especially true. If we are to anticipate successful school-related suicide and violence interventions, responders must share a mutually agreed-on foundation from which to serve.

The U.S. Department of Education provides such a shared foundation guide (2007) in its publication "Practical Information on Crisis Planning: A Guide for Schools and Communities." Although this guide is general in nature and was created to assist school professionals in preparing their schools for everything from natural disasters to school violence, it has specific relevancy to this chapter. According to the guide, there exist four connected school crisis management phases: (1) Mitigation/Prevention, (2) Preparedness, (3) Response, and (4) Recovery. Prior chapters have outlined how to respond to and recover from school-related suicide and violence. However, we have not yet discussed two very important phases: Mitigation/Prevention Phase and the Preparedness Phase. Both are especially relevant to this chapter.

Mitigation/Prevention Phase

The Mitigation/Prevention Phase is essentially designed to engender thought and discussion among school administrators, faculty, staff, police and school resource officers, nursing and medical team members, parents, and students that school suicides and violence *could* occur on their particular school campus. According to the U.S. Department of Education Model, awareness of the potential for these crises is crucial to this phase. The idea is this: Discussions on how to reduce or eliminate risk to life and property will result once school suicide and violence are discussed by school counselors, faculty, staff, emergency responders, students, and parents.

U.S. Department of Education Model

The U.S. Department of Education Model advocates that crisis response planning begins among those in top leadership posts (e.g., district super-intendents, principals, agency directors, mayors, police chiefs, etc.) and ensures the allocation of time, resources, and authority for cross-agency and cross-district grassroots planning. Eloquent interventions and clinically appropriate responses require such cross-germination of ideas and discussions as well as a common crisis response language. In particular, these discussions should foster new joint crisis partnerships with emergency medical services including hospitals, law enforcement, mental health, and community groups that describe how each agency will respond and support the others as they meet the needs of students who experience school-related suicides or violence.

Failure to Create Crisis Partnerships and Establish Clear Response Jurisdictions

By far the largest-scale crisis intervention in which I (Dr. Juhnke) have professionally participated was related to Hurricane Katrina. In the fall of 2005, approximately 14,000 Katrina survivors were brought to San Antonio, Texas. Most were shuttled via airplane or bus through the former Kelly Air Force Base. Chaos abounded. Children had become separated from parents. Family members desperately searched for loved ones. My fellow counseling department faculty, counseling master's and doctoral students, and I did everything from setting up cots and sleeping quarters for incoming survivors to counseling distraught children who had witnessed the deaths of loved ones. I mention this experience because it perfectly reflects the importance of the U.S. Department of Education Model.

Despite the dedicated efforts by many, some in top leadership posts seemed to have failed to consider such a large-scale evacuee population arriving in San Antonio. Concomitantly, few if any joint crisis partnerships were established for such a large-scale service need, and the services to those most in need were compromised. At one point as I was counseling in a makeshift triage area, a change in administrative operational leadership occurred. Service providers and volunteers were ordered to immediately discontinue counseling services and vacate the building. The experience was exceptionally disheartening both to those being counseled and those providing services.

Within two hours, the new leadership had either reverted or had changed again. I do not know exactly what happened. But I found myself once again counseling in the same building I had been ordered to leave. Regretfully, despite significant efforts, I never found those I was in the process of counseling. My hope is that they were able to begin counseling with another counselor. However, I will never know. In either case, an unnecessary administration dictate greatly diluted the efficacy of the counseling rendered. At best, the experience was frustrating for the clients. Such experiences emphasize the need for those in top leadership posts within the school district, community, and school to allocate time and resources for the creation of school-related suicide and violence response plans. Responders need to understand what specific agencies will do, who has ultimate authority, and how services will be jointly rendered. Without clear agreements and specific service demarcations, students and their families will be retraumatized. School counselors and those ready to provide assessment and counseling services to students and their families will waste energy and lose valuable treatment time. And the physical safety of everyone may be jeopardized.

Meeting Individual School and Student Needs

No matter what crisis plan is agreed on by chief administrators, the plan must meet both the idiosyncratic needs of each individual school and the needs of all children served within the individual schools. In other words, given the significant differences among students at elementary, middle, and senior high schools, plans should be devised that address their general age-related language and needs. Specifically, all distributed materials must be written in an age-appropriate manner.

Also, schools with students whose primary language is not English should be informed of crisis plans with directions spoken or written in their native language. Concomitantly, should schools have physically, emotionally, or mentally challenged students, intervention plans must include clear and concise methods to respond to them and their individual needs. My belief is that those working with these students likely will be more cognizant and aware of their individual needs than the "chief administrator" charged with managing the entire district or system or even the individual principals at each school. Thus, chief administrators need to provide vital support, resources, and time for those serving these special populations. Each one is necessary to ensure the creation and development of truly workable crisis response plans that meet the needs of all students in individual schools.

Crisis Response Plan Accessibility

Additionally, such crisis response plans should be readily accessible for administrators, teachers, staff, students, and responders. Few things are worse than being unable to access the crisis response plan. Understanding crisis response times prior to the crisis is important. Regretfully, my experience is that many persons fail to *know* their school's crisis response plan intimately. Instead, these persons believe they know crisis response plans *well enough* and will access the plans *if* ever needed. When access to response plans is hindered or if response plans cannot be found quickly, these persons and the students they serve are vulnerable.

How many times have you been a passenger aboard a commercial airlines flight and watched fellow passengers seemingly disregard flight crew instructions of what to do *if* an emergency happens? Of course, I (Dr. Juhnke) fully realize that *we* would never do such a thing. However, I strongly suspect you have witnessed others—at least on one occasion—not giving full attention to such instructions. My guess is that the day after Captain "Sully" Sullenberger crash-landed US Airways Flight 1549 in the Hudson River on January 15, 2009, people paid greater attention to flight crew emergency instructions.

So, why do passengers not pay attention? Because they do not believe their flights will really end in crash landings. If they did, they would not board their plane in the first place. Are you asking the relevancy of this discussion? Of course not! The relevancy *is* clear. Like persons boarding commercial flights, the vast majority of us do not believe *today* will be the day we need to respond to a school suicide or school violence incident. If we did, we would review our school crisis plans the night before and contact the victims, principal, emergency response team, and local police. In essence, we would interrupt the crisis before it could come to fruition.

Unfortunately, this is not reality. Typically, the day starts like most other days in our professional careers. We talk with our loved ones during breakfast. Then everyone hustles off to work or school. We drive the same roads to school. En route we purchase coffee at the same gas station and park in approximately the same location. The day seems mundane and typical until we realize we are in the midst of a crisis. At that moment of realization, we can no longer prepare. Events are in motion. Our students' emotional and physical safety now depends on multiple factors. Some factors are completely out of our control. Others depend on our school suicide and violence preparation and training, access to emergency plans that remind us of our game plan, and our abilities to respond quickly and rationally.

Procedures, Policies, and Programs

Thus, the Mitigation and Prevention Phase is especially important to school counselors. Investment at this phase reduces the likelihood of crisis catastrophes (e.g., homicide-suicide by a jilted eleventh grader). The Federal Emergency Management Agency (2003) states: "[Mitigation is] any sustained action taken to reduce or eliminate long-term risk to life and property from a hazard event. Mitigation . . . encourages long-term reductions of hazard vulnerability" (p. 20). The phase requires school personnel to thoughtfully consider and implement school procedures, policies, and programs—each specifically designed to inhibit, interrupt, and intervene before a school suicide or violent act occurs. Access control and contraband procedures are prime examples. Here only administrators, faculty, staff, or students with valid school identification cards or screened visitors can access the school campus. Access is also contained. Thus, no one should have carte blanche to roam the campus at will. If access is permitted, access is contained to general areas or is granted with escort to specified areas.

The second area, contraband, is equally important. Guns, knives, and potential weapons are considered contraband and are confiscated immediately. Thus, addressing who has access to the school campus and what can be brought onto campus are important. The intent of such procedures, policies, and programs is to control as many factors as possible and reduce both the probability and the degree to which students are vulnerable. Some have asked me if the implementation of such procedures, policies, and programs will guarantee safety and eliminate all school-related suicides and violence. Regretfully, the answer is no. However, failure to implement such access and contraband procedures, policies, and programs puts students at far greater risk, which is unconscionable to any counseling professional.

Those who typically ask these types of questions often do not want their freedoms curtailed. They perceive such procedures, policies, and programs as a personal imposition and inconvenience. Yet even if it were not unconscionable to place students at greater risk, it is illegal. School administrators and professionals who do not do everything within their power to protect students, faculty, and staff from potential dangers and risks can be held negligent. Thus, the true intent of such procedures, policies, and programs is to reduce risk exposure before potential suicide or violence occurs and to ensure that if such risks come to fruition, the degree of severity is limited.

Part of the Mitigation and Prevention Phase further requires school personnel to move beyond procedures, policies, and programs such as access and contraband control. School personnel also must be familiar with and regularly inspect their buildings and campuses. Specifically, school personnel should understand where potential risk areas are located and implement measures to decrease or eliminate risk within those areas. Here, for example, a remote and infrequently utilized corridor may be identified as a potential high-risk crime area. Students or faculty entering that area may be at increased exposure to potential assault or robbery due to its remoteness and lack of lighting. Thus, to reduce risk exposure, the corridor may be locked or additional lights with video-camera monitoring equipment might be installed. Again, the idea is to know one's campus and *proactively* reduce or eliminate potential risks via procedures, policies, and programs.

Preparedness Phase

Despite the very best attempts to mitigate and prevent all potential school-related suicide and violence acts, the probability is high that somehow and at some time one or the other will occur. Preparedness is the second phase. Unlike the Mitigation and Prevention Phase, the Preparedness Phase suggests that *when* school-related suicide or violence occurs, school counselors and personnel are prepared to respond to the *worst-case* scenarios. Stated differently, the Preparedness Phase indicates that after a school-related suicide or violence event occurs, *this* is what we do. The phase further suggests that school counselors should be prepared for the worst envisioned school-related suicide or violence scenario. Thus, if school counselors are prepared to respond to the worst-case scenario, it is probable that they will be able to respond to the actual events.

Worst-Case Scenario

Recently I (Dr. Juhnke) spoke to a Texas high school football player after a particularly hot, long, and grueling game. I had sat in the oppressive Texas heat under an oversized umbrella that had supposedly shaded me from the brutal sun. He had played nearly the whole game with no break. Later, I nonchalantly quipped that playing in such a game in the oppressive late-summer heat must have been difficult. The player's response surprised me. "No sir. Because we practice two times every day all summer long, and we practice in the blazing summer heat, game days are a cinch. Games only last about an hour. Practices last forever!" In other words, game days were a cakewalk in comparison to the grueling practices that he and the other boys experienced.

Certainly responding to any school-related suicide or violence will not be a cakewalk. I know of few things worse. However, preparing for the worst-case scenario primes us to respond to the far more likely and less severe types of school suicide and violence scenarios that we likely will encounter.

Preparedness Timeline

Before moving into further Preparedness Phase discussion, additional comment is warranted related to the establishment of a realistic Preparedness Timeline. After working on committees charged with responding to potential catastrophic events, I (Dr. Juhnke) have observed even the most able and intelligent persons suddenly wither. Often these titans of intelligence freeze when they realize how ill-prepared their institutions are to respond to large-scale catastrophes or even smaller on-campus crises. Frankly, on more than one occasion, such meetings reminded me of my first meeting with a retirement advisor. I was about 20 years old at the time and had little retirement forethought. Yet I was somehow trapped by a person I did not know well who had a sales pitch that gained my attention. In a nutshell, he had me identify the lifestyle I wanted at retirement. Then he calculated the amount of money I would need to invest each week. This amount supposedly would lift me to my retirement standard of living goals.

Of course, the lifestyle I wanted far exceeded my current means. When he calculated the monies I would need to invest in his sure-fire retirement plan, the amount would have consumed my entire monthly paycheck. What was the result? Exactly: I did nothing. Short of not eating and living on the streets, I saw no viable way to afford the enormous required weekly retirement contributions. Additionally, I felt like a failure. Why in the world had I waited until age 20 to consider retirement? Given what this advisor was saying, I should have started my retirement planning at age 13 or maybe birth!

So, what am I suggesting? When creating a school suicide and violence plan, it is important to be realistic. Do not freak out by focusing on what has not been done. Instead, create a realistic timeline to implement your school's Preparedness Plan. Undoubtedly everything related to the plan should have been done yesterday. However, it was not. You cannot change the past. Instead, focus on what is needed for the future. A realistic timeline puts planning into perspective.

A second word of warning: Do not anticipate that administrators will quickly embrace requests for preparedness planning resources (e.g., money, time, meeting space, etc.). Administrators have a challenging task. Often their minds and budgets are bound. They have limited resources to dispense among many pressing needs. Preparing for something that has not happened is likely not high on their funding list. However, it is important to petition your case continually and to document such petitioning. Even if sufficient funding fails to be provided, create a preparedness plan based on whatever limited support or funding exists. Our students' lives depend on our preparedness. Once school-related suicides or violence occur, any blame most likely will be focused toward those whose responsibilities included counseling services. This means *you*. Thus, it is extremely important to maintain hard copies and backup records of your continued preparedness petitions and the administrators' responses. Concomitantly, generate appropriate documentation related to what you were able to do, given the resources provided. This means generating and keeping preparedness planning meeting agendas and meeting action plans or summaries and any interactions with others (e.g., police, fire, hospitals, etc.) regarding response agreements.

Simple, Inexpensive, and Easy First

We believe the greatest return on your Preparedness Timeline will occur by identifying and implementing the simplest and least expensive activities that have the highest probability of contributing immediately to your students' safety. In other words, jointly having a cup of coffee with the local police chief, fire chief, principal, and parent teacher association (PTA) president to discuss the preparedness plan timeline would be easy to implement and cost less than $10. The potential benefits returned would be great. Much of this first easy step depends on whom *you* wish to bring to that first meeting. Stated differently, if your school principal and PTA president are supportive and get along well, invite them. If not, you may select to inform your superiors of the meeting and not invite the principal. No matter your decision, be wise. Do not step into a political firefight by bringing together two or more people who are distinctly at odds. Also, make certain that the political powers in authority above you know your intentions. Such poor politics may place you in harm's way and therefore ultimately sabotage forward movement. This, of course, would result in a disservice to your students and a headache for you.

Should you have access to student parents who are physicians, hospital administrators, police officers, firefighters, emergency response workers, nurses, mayors, county commissioners, or others who have expertise or who know others who have direct access to political figures who could help, invite them to aid in the establishment of such a timeline or plan. Frankly, you cannot create either the timeline or the response plan in a vacuum. Neither will be successful if you fail to get others involved. Your enthusiasm and the creation of a committee to help create such a timeline and plan will ensure that the entire burden does not fall on you and that a realistic timeline is both created and implemented successfully.

If your school is not flush with professional parents, reach out to PTAs from more affluent schools within or outside your school district. Some of the more affluent school districts I (Dr. Juhnke) am familiar have "sister schools" or "adopt a school" campaigns. Thus, their PTAs contribute resources to nearby schools that have fewer resources. Local television, radio, and newspaper personalities also may be helpful. Typically these folks know many high-profile persons, such as mayors, county commissioners, affluent business owners, and others who can both help devise a successful Preparedness Timeline and participate in the timeline's successful completion. Additionally, do not forget to contact area college and university administrators and faculty. University presidents, provosts, deans, and department chairs often wish to develop relationships with local school districts and schools. Concomitantly, faculty teaching in areas such as educational leadership, counseling, psychology, social work, criminal justice, nursing, social work, and other areas can help develop Preparedness Timelines. Later, they can be included in the development of outlined response specific to their area of expertise.

More Than a Timeline

An interesting thing occurs during the development of the Preparedness Timeline. Suddenly, it will become apparent how many different agencies and people will need to work in unison to respond successfully to a school-related suicide or violence experience. From police to principals and counselors to clergy, a truly helpful response will require a preplanned working agreement among many. Specifically, the scope of individual responder groups (e.g., school counselors) and agencies (e.g., firefighters) will need to be established clearly and thoroughly. One responder group cannot do it all. Like a football team, each responder group will need to understand its specific charge and how its duties fit into the overall response.

Given that most schools and supporting agencies (e.g., police, fire, etc.) already have established at least some form of emergency response protocols, it would seem most logical to review those protocols and determine the players involved and their existing charges. Here, for example, if a school has an emergency response protocol for a fire or a bomb threat, the fire department and school personnel likely could build on existing emergency response protocols. Revisiting these established protocols within a group of all invested players will provide an opportunity to clarify, enhance, and integrate responses for school-related suicide and violence responses. Specifically, existing and new roles should be defined and a chain of command should be established so that when a suicide or violent act occurs, each of the responding units and their personnel understand who is in charge and what their specific responsibilities are.

Communications

Schools, Responders, Students, Faculty, Staff, and Family

Additionally, schools and responders must identify clearly established communication methods. How will school counselors communicate with emergency medical services personnel if a student has hanged herself in the school locker room? How will school counselors communicate with arriving police during an ongoing campus shooting? Chaos will result if clear answers to these communication questions are not identified prior to an on-campus suicide or violent act. Therefore, it is imperative that school counselors and responders agree how such communications will occur (e.g., telephone, school intercom, etc.), potential contact persons, as well as school telephone numbers with room extension numbers and personal cell phone numbers.

Communications with faculty, staff, students, student families, and media also must be considered. In particular, a plan should be devised that will describe how information will be conveyed (e.g., telephone calls to families of student school violence survivors), who will make the communications (e.g., lead school counselor, principal, etc.), and when those communications will occur (e.g., immediately upon learning of the situation, after the immediate crisis has been resolved, after the students' safety has been secured, etc.). Given that news releases to media and letters to parents whose children directly experienced or witnessed the suicide or violence as well to parents whose children were not directly involved will likely be required, the time to write the general news releases and parental letter templates is before the crisis occurs. Thus, whoever is charged with actually writing the releases and letters will just have to insert information specific to the actual event rather than having to create the releases or letters from scratch.

News Releases and Parent Letters

The news releases and letters should do four key things:

1. Report the general facts.
2. Indicate that the incident is over.
3. Not glamorize those involved in the incident.
4. Indicate where students should go for classes.

The releases and letters should provide sufficient general facts related to the incident without getting into minutia regarding the event or disclosing confidential information. Facts would include an abbreviated incident description (e.g., a school shooting, a death from suicide, etc.), when the incident occurred (e.g., "9:45 this morning"), where the incident occurred (e.g., "in the school cafeteria"), and who was involved (e.g., "a ninth-grade student in Cook Middle School").

The news release and parent letters should report that the incident is *over*. If true, they should convey that safety has been restored. Thus, returning students will not be in danger nor presented with any additional risk. Remember, one cannot guarantee returning students' safety. Even in the safest schools with limited school suicide or violence risks, student safety cannot be promised. Instead, the news releases and parent letters should report what has been done (e.g., counselors' office hours have been lengthened and a school suicide hotline has been created; additional school resource officers have been deployed for the upcoming school week, etc.) to reduce risk or remedy the situation.

Suicide victims and shooters should never be glamorized or immortalized. The last thing needed is for a copycat suicide or act of violence to occur. Releases or letters that focus on the suicide victim's outstanding qualities (e.g., "Sam was a loving and kind person who will never be forgotten," etc.) and perceptions of being unseen and disregarded by peers (e.g., "Although Mary attempted to engage with us, we failed to adequately engage her") should never be discussed. Also, shooters or perpetrators of violence should never be presented in glowing fashion (e.g., "The cunning and intelligent student shooter amassed a remarkable array of weaponry that he skillfully used against victims and police alike").

Finally, news releases and parent letters should tell where and when students should report for upcoming classes. Here, for example, a parent letter might state: "Classes will resume at their regular time tomorrow at 8 AM." Again, the intent is simple. The new releases and letters must convey that school is resuming normal operations.

Lockdown, Open Containment, Evacuation, and Reverse Evacuation

Different crises demand differing responses. Should a threat be external to the school campus and building (e.g., a potentially violent person attempting to gain access onto the school campus and into school buildings to harm students), a lockdown would be warranted. The intent of a lockdown is to stop the potentially violent person from gaining access to students, faculty, staff, and visitors inside. In this situation, all campus and building access points (e.g., doors, windows, etc.) would be locked. No one would be allowed to either enter or exit the buildings or the campus. Additionally, students would be contained in their rooms with doors locked and windows covered. Here door windows as well as interior and exterior wall windows would be covered to inhibit a potentially violent person from seeing students inside. Depending on the intent and anticipated length of the lockdown, hallways, corridors, rest rooms, and other areas (e.g., teachers' lounges, cafeterias, etc.) would be locked, and barriers designed to inhibit access to students may be enacted (e.g., chained gates, closed fire doors, etc.). Securing an entire campus is a greater challenge than securing individual buildings. However, major external points of entry, such as driveways and gated areas leading to building access areas, should be guarded and secured.

Whereas lockdown is designed to keep potentially violent persons or external threats from gaining access to the building and ultimately to students, open containment suggests that the threat is already inside the building. In this case, the threat is either attempting to leave the building or highly confused and looking to exit the building. One example when open containment might be appropriate is if one student assaults another and is attempting to escape the building. In this case, similar lockdown procedures are used (e.g., students remain in their locked classrooms with windows closed and covered). However, hallways leading to major exits and external doors are opened wide. Thus, the escaping student can immediately see the open doors and potentially exit the building without danger of harming additional persons.

Evacuation is used when it is believed that students, faculty, staff, and visitors would be safer outside rather than inside the building. Thus, the intent is to quickly vacate the building due to internal danger, such as fire or bomb threat. In these situations, school officials may believe that the violent person has started a fire within the school or that an explosive device may be located within the building. Therefore, it is imperative that students, staff, and faculty know exactly what evacuation routes should be used to exit the building quickly. Additionally, evacuating persons need to be aware of safe places to gather and be accounted for once outside the building.

A reverse evacuation is designed to get students into the safety of their school building due to an external threat. For example, students on recess or outside at lunch would be notified of the reverse evacuation and would enter the building quickly. Once students are safely inside, appropriate lockdown procedures would be enacted to then keep the external threat from entering the school (e.g., school lockdown). Again, once students, staff, and faculty return to the safety of the school building, they should understand where to go and how to be accounted for.

No matter the method used (e.g., lockdown, open containment, etc.) to protect students from potential danger, accountability and post-crisis debriefing methods should be developed and enacted. Related to accountability, methods should be developed and practiced that would allow quick identification of students present as well as unaccounted-for or missing students, staff, and faculty. Post-violence debriefings previously discussed in the book can be altered to address the needs of students who experience a lockdown. One would follow the same seven steps described. Students would describe their thoughts and feelings specific to the lockdown, and school counselors would describe age-appropriate residual effects that may be experienced or expected.

Practice, Practice, Practice: Make Safety Procedures a Habit

A long time ago, as jazz trumpet players, my buddy and I (Dr. Juhnke) were invited to perform at an event. The music we were requested to play was *easy*. We played the requested songs a couple of times. Quickly we determined that the gig would be a cinch. When the time came to perform, we were all smiles. We had no worries. What possibly could go wrong?

The outcome was a disaster. As we stepped onto stage and suddenly saw hundreds of people staring at us, our anxiety peaked. Our once-nimble fingers froze. Our lips tightened. The sounds emanating from our trumpets mimicked dying elephants, and the crowd had a good laugh. What was wrong? We had failed to practice sufficiently. Sure, we had played the seemingly easy songs a couple of times prior to the performance. However, we had not practiced the music to a degree of excellence—a degree where the music had become habit. Aristotle said it slightly differently: "Excellence is not a singular act, but a habit." Instead of practicing the songs until they became an ingrained part in our musical repertoire—a habit, if you will—we had simply mimicked the singular act.

The implications of practice related to this book are enormous. School counselors and emergency responders can have the very best plans and interventions specific to responding to school suicides or violence. However, these plans and interventions are relatively useless without sufficient and frequent practice. The plans and interventions must become habit. Roger Federer and Serena Williams are famous tennis champions. They did not hit a tennis ball once and think they were ready to play in the U.S. Open. They practiced and practiced and then practiced more. Simply put, they practiced for years until they had perfected their games and their tennis techniques became perfected habits.

As my trumpet-playing buddy and I found out, when the supposed preparation occurs without the stressors of the actual event, one can be foolishly lulled into the belief that one is adequately prepared even when one is not. School counselors, emergency responders, staff, and students need to practice each of the potential interventions and responses until the behaviors are an ingrained habit. People need to know exactly what to do. They need to understand where to go. Errors in the plans and interventions must be identified and corrected. And the updated and revised plans and interventions must be practiced frequently. Once this happens, the habit is in place, and your students, faculty, staff, and responders will be ready to respond as necessary.

TEMPLATE

The following is a general template to consider. This template describes specific plans, response policies, and promising future policies that may be helpful to your school.

Plans

School suicide and violence prevention action plans and policies address risk factors and serve as preemptive means to reduce on-campus suicides and violence. The emphasis is on creating effective pre-interventions before student suicide or violence occurs. Thus, these five preventive actions and plans should be implemented. Additionally, they should be distributed via Web sites, e-mails, and posted flyers to administrators, teachers, counselors, students, parents, and potential first responders.

1. **Suicide and Violence Prevention Meetings**

   These monthly suicide and violence prevention meetings should be well publicized and open to the public. The meetings should be facilitated by a committee composed of interested parents, students, teachers, administrators, police, mental health providers, and community leaders (e.g., business owners, clergy, alumni, etc.). The intent of these meetings would be to:

   - Identify creative ways to decrease suicide and violence risk among students.
   - Increase awareness of suicide risk factors and referral options.
   - Increase school safety awareness and school safety.
   - Identify potential suicide or safety concerns (e.g., report students who repeatedly indicate feelings of hopelessness or thoughts of suicide, report environmental areas that might pose concern [unlit school hallways, etc.]).
   - Propose possible interventions to address possible safety concerns.

   Such a committee would not necessarily establish rules and policies but rather work in an advisory capacity to provide recommendations to school administrators, who could then jointly work with local law enforcement or mental health personnel to address suicide and violence needs within the school or on the school campus.

2. **Personal and Environmental Searches**

   Administrators, faculty, staff, students, parents, police, and school counselors should understand how searches for weapons, drugs, stolen property, and other potential contraband will be conducted. These policies should describe:

   - When such searches will be conducted (e.g., random searches, searches resulting from anonymous tips, etc.).

- Who will be present during such searches.
- The rights of those persons being searched.
- Items forbidden from being brought onto school grounds or in the student's possession on campus (e.g., guns, illicit drugs, etc.).
- The appeals processes available to those who have been searched or whose property has been confiscated.

Furthermore, these policies should describe when and how vehicles brought onto school grounds might be searched.

3. **Conduct and Behavior Expectations**

Administrators, teachers, staff, students, and parents need to be aware of both appropriate and unacceptable behaviors. This policy would explain expectations of appropriate conduct, describe how unacceptable conduct will be addressed, and describe any appeals processes. Related to suicide, conduct and behavior expectations would describe what students, faculty, staff, and student parents should do if a student reports suicidal ideation or a student is suspected of considering suicide.

4. **Systems of Care Individual, Group, and Family Counseling**

Students deemed as at potential risk for suicide or violence need preventive counseling services. They also may warrant psychotropic medications, such as antidepressants, or social learning educational components, such as conflict resolution training. Policies related to the expectations and requirements for potentially suicidal or violent students and their families to participate in counseling can help reduce the probability of suicidal or violent behaviors.

Concomitantly, treatment sessions provide counselors additional assessment opportunities and a baseline from which to evaluate student safety and progress. Over time, such assessments provide additional information regarding other counseling related services that may be warranted (e.g., substance abuse treatment). Additionally, assessments can alert school counselors to at-risk students who begin decompensating or who report increased suicidal or violent ideation and behaviors. Therefore, the probability of successful interventions before the student attempts suicide or violence is increased.

5. **College Faculty and Students**

Many times faculty with specific expertise related to suicide or school violence are within a short driving distance to schools that have encountered suicide or violence incidents. Often these faculty members are training entry- and doctoral-level students in prevention, intervention, and post-survivor methods and could be helpful to school suicide or violence interventions and survivors. Establishing contacts and working policies with such faculty and their students would likely be mutually beneficial. One of the significant benefits of such policies is that faculty in professions such as counseling, social work, psychology, family therapy, educational leadership, and criminal justice can assist by quickly bringing a sizable group of volunteer graduate students to help in whatever manner necessary. This can range from sitting and talking with students who had a peer commit suicide to cofacilitating debriefing groups with student survivors and their parents. Additionally, faculty and students from specializations in art, dance, or recreation management can creatively work with school suicide and violence survivors to create post-crisis experiences. Such experiences can aid in the students' healing process. Here, for example, art instructors could encourage younger students to draw pictures of their experiences, or recreation management students could create ropes courses on the school grounds. Students and faculty can then conjointly research effectiveness of various interventions and apply derived knowledge to prevent further school suicide and violence and enhance the recoveries of students who have been negatively impacted by either.

Response Policies

The next five response policies should be posted on school Web sites and distributed in print at the beginning of each school semester (Fall, Winter, Summer). Response policies are designed to engender helpful behaviors in the event of suicide or school violence. These policies are indicated next.

1. **Suicide and Violence Prevention Drills**

    On preidentified days at the onset of each semester, teachers, administrators, mental health providers, fire, police, and mental health providers should create and respond to different simulated student suicide and violence scenarios at each school campus. The intent of such simulations is to ensure that all personnel will be adequately familiar with response interventions and procedures (e.g., identifying which rooms can be used for post-violence debriefings, identifying how mental health providers will be transported from their various locations to the school to conduct post-violence interventions, etc.). Concomitantly, monthly lockdown, open containment, evacuation, and reverse evacuation drills should be conducted. Participation in these drills will ensure that students as well as faculty, staff, and administrators are familiar with how to implement and respond quickly and efficiently to events.

2. **Suicide and Violence Response Training**

   Administrators, principals, counselors, teachers, and support staff should receive ongoing suicide and violence assessment and response training. Here school mental health professionals and violence safety specialists would be brought to campus to give practical seminars about how to assess and respond effectively to various school suicide and violence scenarios (e.g., a student threatening to kill self, gunshots heard in the school hallway, etc.) and would facilitate discussions in which participants would describe how they would respond to scenarios involving suicide or violence. For example, after the seminar, participants might be asked: "What would you do if a student reported that another student had a gun in her backpack and had been threatening to kill her former boyfriend, her teacher, and then herself?" The intent, then, is to prepare faculty, staff, and students to respond in a manner that would lessen the probability of school suicide or violence and provide the greatest safety to all involved.

3. **Media Response Unit**

   Following a school shooting and suicide that I (Dr. Juhnke) responded to in the late 1990s, local and regional television news reporters descended on the campus and began randomly interviewing students, parents, and teachers. Emotionally charged parents and traumatized students responded as best they could to sometimes-leading questions. Some who were interviewed provided incorrect information related to those believed to have been shot or involved in the shooting. Others mistakenly reported events in a manner that portrayed others in an inappropriate manner. Clearly, it is important that individual administrators, teachers, staff, and students should be dissuaded from speaking independently to media personnel. Instead, school administrators should identify a single spokesperson for each school, and local news media should be informed how to contact that spokesperson in an actual emergency. Policies prohibiting media personnel from trespassing on school property and dissuading the interviewing of administrators, teachers, staff, and students (i.e., all persons other than the designated spokesperson) should be presented to media outlets. Administrators, staff, faculty, and students should be reminded each semester of the person charged with this responsibility.

4. **Violence Response Decision Trees**

Clearly written and up-to-date student suicide and violence response policies are vital. Policies written in a decision tree format are helpful. Such policies clearly delineate exactly who will perform what functions under specific conditions (e.g., student who committed

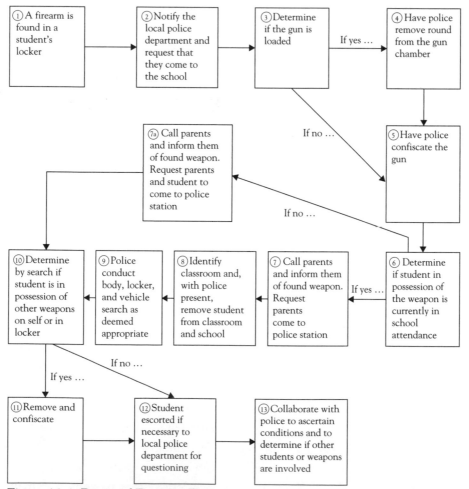

Figure 11.1 Proposed Decision Tree

suicide in a crowded lunchroom, gang-related shootings on campus, student hostage occurring on campus, faculty hostage occurring on campus, etc.). Such policies should be easily accessible by administrators, teachers, police, and mental health providers. Figures 11.1 and 11.2 present examples of decision trees that can be adapted as necessary for specific schools.

5. **Hospital/Emergency Medical Services/Physicians/Mental Health Personnel**

    Establishing policies with those agencies and professionals who would be needed in the event of school suicide or violence is

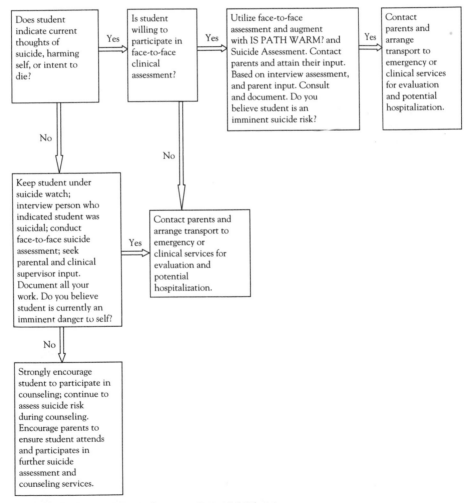

Figure 11.2 Student Indicating Suicidal Ideation

important. Specifically needed are policies that specify to which hospitals students would be sent, how large numbers of students would be transported, and the types of services that local mental health personnel would make available.

PROMISING FUTURE INTERVENTIONS

Clearly, the harm resulting from school suicide and violence are disturbing. Administrators, teachers, counselors, students, and parents struggle to ensure that schools are free from suicide and violence. Yet school suicide and violence likely will not disappear in the near future. Promising new projects that establish community-wide prevention and intervention are needed. Next we describe new initiatives that demonstrate potential promise. We believe these initiatives present the opportunity for second-order changes that protect and insulate our students and ourselves from school-related suicides and violence. It is our hope that such changes will alter the fundamental beliefs regarding school suicide and violence.

Suicide and Violence Prevention and Intervention Training for School Counselors

Many school counselors are frontline workers. They know their students, the jargon used by their students, and the stressors that students face. Few professionals are as trusted by students as these counselors. Yet, for the most part, school counselor training has changed little during the past 15 to 20 years. Formal graduate school education for new school counselors must include suicide and violence assessment, prevention, and intervention training. Specifically needed are courses that address these areas:

- Systems of care interventions
- Assessment of potentially suicidal, violent, and substance-abusing students
- Violence mediation
- Family counseling
- Cognitive or cognitive behavioral interventions coupled with social learning models

Experienced school counselors should be encouraged and rewarded for participating in practical seminar programs on these topics.

Suicide and Violence Prevention Officers

Given the number of funding agencies that offer financial support for research in the areas of school suicide and violence, school districts and administrators should look at working collaboratively with hospitals, law enforcement, universities, social service agencies, and local parenting groups to seek funds for the training of suicide and violence prevention officers within each school. Professionals with specialized training in suicide and violence counseling, childhood and adolescent development, and assessment would seem appropriate for such positions. These professionals would provide counseling services to at-risk students via individual, group, and family counseling.

Extended-Day Programs for Students

Positive peer relationships seem to play an important role in reducing the probability of suicide as well as non–gang-related violence. Thus, it would seem vitally important for extended-day programs to be established. Here students would be encouraged to participate in organized sports and extra-curricular peer activities (e.g., Spanish club, band, etc.). The more time students spend in a supervised and structured environment without alcohol and other drugs, the less time they will have for suicidal and violent activities. Concomitantly, structured environments increase the probability of accurate assessments, thereby affording school counselors more time to accurately assess students who are decompensating or becoming more suicidal or violent.

Parent, Grandparent, and Extended-Family Training

Parents, grandparents, and the extended family play a vital role in keeping students suicide and violence free. Past interventions often devalued the roles of these significant childhood influences and reduced the effectiveness of their supervision by diluting their power. Actively involving these vitally important persons in the lives of students and their peers creates a greater sense of community and can increase prosocial behaviors.

Training families to establish family rituals is also vital. Gurian (1999) states, "All areas in a boy's life are enhanced by family rituals" (p. 140). Rituals that require daily family interactions (e.g., the requirement that the entire family socialize over supper) and established weekly rituals (e.g., mother and father alternating Saturday morning McDonald's breakfasts with each of the children) increase opportunities for belonging, support, and discussion between parents and children, thus reducing the probability of suicide and violence and enhancing the likelihood that children's concerns can be addressed at the family level rather than at the school level.

Nonpunitive, Nonmandatory Religious and Spiritual Opportunities

Providing increased student opportunities to freely choose to participate in supportive, nonpunitive religious and spiritual experiences is another promising intervention that warrants additional investigation. Garbarino (1999) states: "Spirituality and love can fill in the holes left in the story of a boy's life and help him develop a strong positive sense of self and healthy limits, thus forestalling the need to compensate with grandiose posturing and deadly petulance" (p. 155). Garbarino suggests that religion, "when it is grounded in spirituality and love," gives life purpose and provides a context for daily experiences.

Specialized School Programming for Boys

Given that boys and adolescent males are at greatest risk of using the most lethal suicidal means and that they compose the clear majority of young violent offenders—thus far all student shooters in mass student shootings have been males—it seems important to establish specialized school programs for males. Murray (1999) states: "Schools are 'antiboy.' Elementary schools emphasize reading and restrict the activity of young boys, who are generally more active and slower to read than girls. Teachers often discipline boys more harshly than girls. Sensitivity isn't modeled to boys so they don't learn it" (p. 1). Garbarino (1999) and Gurian (1999) also note similar stressors and problems typically experienced by boys and male adolescents (e.g., increased frequency of attention deficit disorders for boys compared to girls, the social expectations not to display feelings of pain or hurt, etc.). Programming that addresses these important issues is important.

Additionally, based on Bowen and Bowen's (1999) findings, which appear consistent with existing literature (Berman, Kurtines, Silverman, & Serafini, 1996; Jenkins & Bell, 1994; Richters & Maxtinez, 1993), non-European American boys and male adolescents living in urban environments with greater exposure to violence and neighborhood dangers may benefit most from programming that addresses such violence and victimization exposure.

Increased Community Service Opportunities

Programs that encourage student participation in community service projects (e.g., Boy Scouts, Girl Scouts, Habitat for Humanity, etc.) engage students. Such programs also are time intensive. Hence, they often reduce the amount of time isolated from others, which often translates into less free time to ruminate about suicidal thoughts or violence plans. Encouraging students the freedom to choose community service programs they wish to become involved in seems like a helpful way to provide both service to the community and to students. Habitat for Humanity, for example, teaches students to value life and to serve. We believe that as students learn to value others and actively contribute to the well-being of others, their probability for suicide and violence diminishes.

Animal Relationships

Working at local animal shelters or with local animal groups (e.g., Save the Greyhounds, etc.) seems like a logical way of having students gain further understanding of and caring for living beings. Further investigation into possible correlations between the effects of nurturing interactions between youth and suicidal and violent behavior is warranted.

School-wide Discipline Plans

Walker (1995) states that consistent school-wide discipline plans can promote a peaceful, caring student culture that reinforces students in highly visible ways for exhibiting prosocial behaviors. Here the discipline plan ensures that students, teachers, parents, and administrators know the school rules and corresponding sanctions and rewards. Thus, school-wide discipline plans can be established in ways to decrease violent behaviors and encourage prosocial interactions.

Removal of Punishment-Oriented Policies

It is clear that students need rehabilitative services rather than punishment-oriented policies (Fitzsimmons, 1998). Those breaking established school rules need to be nurtured and moved back into prosocial behaviors. It does little good to expel students and have undereducated, underemployed, and underutilized citizens on the street. Punishment for punishment's sake, according to Fitzsimmons, does little to habilitate. Programs and policies should be designed to enhance healthy social interactions with peers and adults and to ensure successful completion of an educational plan that will lead to successful work attainment.

School Counselor Personal Threat Assessment

One neglected area over the years has been related to threats made by students toward school faculty, staff, and counselors. Juhnke has created the Danger to Me Personal Threat Assessment Scale and is currently researching this instrument to determine its potential utility with school counselors. Like the VIOLENT STUdent Scale, the Danger to Me Personal Threat Assessment Scale is founded on 10 literature-identified risk factors and provides an easy-to-remember mnemonic, "danger to me." School counselors can utilize the scale to assess and quantify potential threats engendered by students toward them (see Figure 11.3). Although the scale is in its early developmental

---

D **Delusional**, hallucinations, paranoid, diminished, or clouded reality testing.

A **Access to guns** or weapons.

N **Noted history of violence**, previous violent acts including arrests or incarcerations.

G **Gang** involvement.

E **Expressions** of harm intent (letters, poems, videos, or songs outlining violent intent).

R **Remorselessness** (lacking compunction for previous acts of cruelty or violence, etc.).

T **Traitor-Troublemaker:** A belief that the school counselor betrayed the student's trust, caused harm, or is the chief cause of the student's troubles.

O **Overt, covert, or veiled threats** of harm made directly toward the school counselor or told to others (e.g., "I'm going to kill that school counselor").

M **Myopic** or ever-increasing focus on harming others or enforcing "justice" on others.

E **Exclusion** from others (e.g., increasing isolation from others, loss of friends or family members, etc.).

Figure 11.3 **Danger to Me Personal Threat Assessment Scale**

stages, the hope is that the instrument can help school counselors better determine the immediate level of risk posed by students who present as threatening or who threaten them.

CHAPTER SUMMARY

The frequency of school suicide and violence necessitates both preventive and response policies and procedures that will likely increase the probability of safety and protection for all persons within schools. Regretfully, even the best-written or best-intended policies will not end school suicides or violence. The preparedness planning, template, and described promising future interventions serve as a place for school counselors to start. They can be modified to meet the individual characteristics of any school and should be viewed as a basic foundation for most schools. When used in conjunction with assessment and interventions described in this book, they can help create student safety and establish a collaborative, nonsuicidal, nonviolent environment both within and outside the school campus milieu. Finally, the projects suggested are merely a beginning. The time to act is now. Our youth and America's future compel us to establish new interdisciplinary and collaborative suicide intervention and antiviolence programming. Without such responses, the continued suffering, loss of innocent lives, and costs of suicide and violence will continue to wreak harm on our children and the society in which we live.

⟫⋅⟪

Appendix
Ethical Decision-Making Model

Proposed School Suicide or Violence Intervention

_____

_____

_____

_____

A. Four-Principles Approach

1. Has Respect for Autonomy been fully addressed? (If "Yes," describe how you have addressed items a–e. If "No," describe when and how you will address items a–e.)

    _____

    _____

    _____

    _____

    a. Describe the professionally acceptable and safe options that have been made available for the identified student(s) and potentially impacted others (PIOs) (e.g., parents, peer students, etc.).

        i. _____

        ii. _____

        iii. _____

        iv. _____

b. Describe when and how the identified student(s) and PIOs were allowed to select these presented options.

Date: ___/___/___

_____

_____

_____

_____

c. Describe when and how the identified student(s) and PIOs were allowed to alter the presented options, develop new professionally acceptable and safe options, or refused both.

Date: ___/___/___

_____

_____

_____

_____

d. Report when and how the counselor demonstrated respect for the identified student(s) and PIOs when the student:

   i. selected or developed a new professionally acceptable and safe option, or

  ii. selected an option that failed to fully address issues related to imminent danger and/or safety.

Date: ___/___/___

_____

_____

_____

_____

e. Has the identified student(s) and PIOs consented to participate in options that provide the necessary threshold of safety for all involved and surpass potential liability risks?

Yes: _____

No: _____ (If "No," describe the counselor's attempts to address identified student(s) and PIOs' concerns and the reason(s) why the intervention cannot be acceptably altered.)

Date: ___ /___ /___

_____

_____

_____

_____

2. Has Respect for Beneficence been fully addressed?
(If "Yes," report anticipated intervention benefits and perceived beneficiaries below.
If "No," describe when Beneficence will be fully addressed and report anticipated intervention benefits and perceived beneficiaries below.)
(DATE Beneficence will be fully addressed: ___ /___ /___)

a. List anticipated intervention benefits for the identified student(s)
   i. _____
   ii. _____
   iii. _____
   iv. _____

For the primary counselor(s)
   i. _____
   ii. _____
   iii. _____
   iv. _____

For PIOs
   i. _____
   ii. _____

iii. _____

iv. _____

Do the anticipated intervention benefits to the student(s) clearly outweigh potential benefits to the primary counselor(s) or school?

Yes: _____

No: _____ (If "No," revise the proposed intervention until the intended intervention benefits to the student(s) clearly outweigh benefits to primary counselor(s) and school.)

Does anyone benefit more from the proposed intervention than the identified student(s)?

Yes: _____ (If "Yes," revise the intervention until: (1) the identified student(s) and PIOs are not at risk of imminent danger and (2) identified students will clearly have greater benefits than those previously identified as having the most benefits.)

No: _____ (Proceed to Nonmaleficience.)

3. Has Respect for Nonmaleficence been fully addressed? (If "Yes," report potential unintended outcomes that might result from the proposed intervention. If "No," consider potential unintended outcomes that might result from the proposed intervention and report same below.

   a. List potential unintended negative outcomes that may result if the proposed intervention is implemented.

      i. Potential unintended negative physical outcomes to the identified student(s) and ways to reduce the probability or severity of same.

         (a) _____

         Ways to reduce probability or severity of same: _____

         (b) _____

         Ways to reduce probability or severity of same: _____

         (c) _____

         Ways to reduce probability or severity of same: _____

         (d) _____

         Ways to reduce probability or severity of same: _____

ii. Potential unintended negative emotional or psychological outcomes to the identified student(s) and ways to reduce the probability or severity of same.

(a) _____

Ways to reduce probability or severity of same: _____

(b) _____

Ways to reduce probability or severity of same: _____

(c) _____

Ways to reduce probability or severity of same: _____

(d) _____

Ways to reduce probability or severity of same: _____

iii. Potential unintended negative social or interpersonal outcomes to the identified student(s) and ways to reduce the probability or severity of same.

(a) _____

Ways to reduce probability or severity of same: _____

(b) _____

Ways to reduce probability or severity of same: _____

(c) _____

Ways to reduce probability or severity of same: _____

(d) _____

Ways to reduce probability or severity of same: _____

iv. Potential unintended negative academic outcomes to the identified student(s) and ways to reduce the probability or severity of same.

(a) _____

Ways to reduce probability or severity of same: _____

(b) _____

Ways to reduce probability or severity of same: _____

(c) _____

Ways to reduce probability or severity of same: _____

(d) _____

Ways to reduce probability or severity of same: _____

v. Other potential unintended negative outcomes that may impact the identified student(s) and ways to reduce the probability or severity of same.

(a) _____

Ways to reduce probability or severity of same: _____

(b) _____

Ways to reduce probability or severity of same: _____

(c) _____

Ways to reduce probability or severity of same: _____

(d) _____

Ways to reduce probability or severity of same: _____

vi. Potential unintended negative physical outcomes to the PIOs and ways to reduce the probability or severity of same.

(a) _____

Ways to reduce probability or severity of same: _____

(b) _____

Ways to reduce probability or severity of same: _____

(c) _____

Ways to reduce probability or severity of same: _____

(d) _____

Ways to reduce probability or severity of same: _____

vii. Potential unintended negative emotional or psychological outcomes to the PIOs and ways to reduce the probability or severity of same.

(a) _____

Ways to reduce probability or severity of same: _____

(b) _____

Ways to reduce probability or severity of same: _____

(c) _____

Ways to reduce probability or severity of same: _____

(d) _____

Ways to reduce probability or severity of same: _____

viii. Potential unintended negative social or interpersonal outcomes to the PIOs and ways to reduce the probability or severity of same.

(a) _____

Ways to reduce probability or severity of same: _____

(b) _____

Ways to reduce probability or severity of same: _____

(c) _____

Ways to reduce probability or severity of same: _____

(d) _____

Ways to reduce probability or severity of same: _____

ix. Potential unintended negative academic outcomes to the PIOs and ways to reduce the probability or severity of same.

(a) _____

Ways to reduce probability or severity of same: _____

(b) _____

Ways to reduce probability or severity of same: _____

(c) _____

Ways to reduce probability or severity of same: _____

(d) _____

Ways to reduce probability or severity of same: _____

x. Other potential unintended negative outcomes that may impact the PIOs and ways to reduce the probability or severity of same.

(a) _____

Ways to reduce probability or severity of same: _____

(b) _____

Ways to reduce probability or severity of same: _____

(c) _____

Ways to reduce probability or severity of same: _____

(d) _____

Ways to reduce probability or severity of same: _____

4. Has Justice been fully addressed? (If "Yes," report when and how issues of justice have been addressed below. If "No," provide the date when issues of justice will be addressed and how justice issues will be addressed.)

Date addressed: ___ /___ /___

Describe how addressed:

_____

_____

_____

If "No," when will issues of justice be addressed?

Date: ___ /___ /___

And how:

_____

_____

_____

   a. Report the date and how the proposed intervention will fairly treat identified students and PIOs without exploitation or discrimination.

   Date: ___ /___ /___

   _____

   _____

   _____

   _____

b. Report the date and how the proposed intervention will address pertinent issues to the identified student(s) and PIOs such as poverty, social stressors or awkwardness, physical or mental challenges, and family stressors.

Date: ___/___/___

_____

_____

_____

_____

B. Four Out of Five Consultations

1. Has the Four Out of Five Consultation been completed? (If "Yes," complete the information below. If "No," describe when and whom you will contact. Once the Four Out of Five Consultation has been completed, fill in the information below.) (Date of Future Contacts: ___/___/___)

   a. Names, Titles, Locations, Degrees, Licenses, and Certifications of Contacted Consultants

   i. _____

   ii. _____

   iii. _____

   iv. _____

   v. _____

   b1. In detail, describe the suggested revisions to the proposed intervention described by corresponding Consultant i above.

   Date and Time: _____

   Date and Time of Any Additional Contacts Regarding Consultation: _____

   Suggested revision(s): _____

   _____

   _____

   _____

b2. In detail, describe the suggested revisions to the proposed intervention described by corresponding Consultant ii above.

Date and Time: _____

Date and Time of Any Additional Contacts Regarding Consultation: _____

Suggested revision(s): _____

_____

_____

_____

b3. In detail, describe the suggested revisions to the proposed intervention described by corresponding Consultant iii on the previous page.

Date and Time: _____

Date and Time of Any Additional Contacts Regarding Consultation: _____

Suggested revision(s): _____

_____

_____

_____

b4. In detail, describe the suggested revisions to the proposed intervention described by corresponding Consultant iv on the previous page.

Date and Time: _____

Date and Time of Any Additional Contacts Regarding Consultation: _____

Suggested revision(s): _____

_____

_____

_____

b5. In detail, describe the suggested revisions to the proposed intervention described by corresponding Consultant v on the previous page.

Date and Time: _____

Date and Time of Any Additional Contacts Regarding Consultation: _____

Suggested revision(s): _____

_____

_____

_____

c. Final Consultant Recommendation Intervention Agreement.

Name	Intervention Agreement?	
	Yes	No
i. _____	____	____
ii. _____	____	____
iii. _____	____	____
iv. _____	____	____
v. _____	____	____

d. Final Consultant Recommendation.

_____

_____

_____

_____

C. Supervisor, School District Legal Department, and Risk Management Insurance Consultations

1. Has the school counselor informed the supervisor of the specific concerns and obtained specific directions on how to address the pressing issues? (If "Yes," complete the information below. If "No," describe when and whom you will contact. Then complete the information below regarding the supervisor's directions.) (Date of Future Supervisor Consultation:___ /___ /___)

a. In detail, describe the supervisor's directions.

Date and Time: _____

Specific Directions: _____

_____

_____

_____

b. In detail, describe exactly how you followed the supervisor's direction and any noted concerns or problems.

Date and Time: _____

Description of Implemented Intervention as Directed by Supervisor:

_____

_____

_____

_____

c. Follow-up report with supervisor.

Date and Time: _____

Describe in Detail What Occurred and Any Potential
Concerns: _____

_____

_____

_____

Seek Any Further Directives Made by Supervisor to You Regarding
This Case: _____

_____

_____

_____

2. Has the school counselor obtained the supervisor's permission to contact the school district's legal department and has the school counselor consulted with the school district's legal department to determine exactly what to do? (If "Yes," complete the information below. If "No," seek supervisor's permission and support in contacting the school district's legal department, then contact the legal department for specific directions. (Date of Future Legal Department Consultation: __/__/__)

    a. Date and Time Received Permission and Support from Supervisor to Contact Legal? _____

_____

    b. In detail, describe the school's legal department directions.

       Date, Time, Legal Department Consultant's name: _____

_____

       Specific Directions: _____

_____

_____

_____

    c. In detail, describe exactly how you followed the legal department's direction and any noted concerns or problems.

       Date and Time: _____

       Description of Implemented Intervention as Directed by Legal Department: _____

_____

_____

_____

    d. Follow-up Report with Supervisor and Legal Department.

       Date and Time: _____

       Describe in Detail What Occurred and Any Potential Concerns: _____

_____

_____

_____

Seek Any Further Directives Made By Supervisor or Legal
Department Regarding This Case: _____

_____

_____

_____

3. Risk Management Consultation with School Counselor's Professional
Liability Carrier.

Has the school counselor contacted the risk management staff of
the school counselor's professional liability carrier and consulted
with the risk management staff? (If "Yes," complete the information
below. If "No," seek supervisor's permission and support in contacting
the school district's legal department, then contact the legal department for specific directions.) (Date of Future Legal Department
Consultation: __/__/__)

a. Date, Time, and Risk Management Person Spoken to:

_____

b. In detail, describe risk management's directions.
Specific Directions: _____

_____

_____

_____

c. In detail, describe exactly how you followed risk management's direction and any noted concerns or problems.

Date and Time: _____

Description of Implemented Intervention as Directed by Risk
Management: _____

_____

_____

_____

d. Follow-up Report with Risk Management.

Date and Time: _____

Describe in Detail What Occurred and Any Potential
Concerns: _____

_____

_____

_____

Seek Any Further Directives Made by Risk Management Regarding
This Case: _____

_____

_____

_____

4. Contact National or State Professional Counseling Association Ethics
Board or State Licensing Board Ethics Panel for Further Information.
Should the school counselor continue to have unanswered concerns
despite following the previously indicated ethical decision-making
processes and consultations and ongoing supervision input from the
clinical supervisor and direct administrative supervisor, the school
counselor should consider contacting national or state professional
counseling associations or state licensing board ethics panels for further
consultation(s).

a. Date, Time, Counseling Association/State Licensing Ethics Board,
and Person Spoken to: _____

_____

b. In detail, describe risk management's directions.
Specific Directions: _____

_____

_____

_____

c. In detail, describe exactly how you followed these directions and any noted concerns or problems.

Date and Time: _____

Description of Implemented Intervention as Directed: _____

_____

_____

_____

d. Follow-up Reports

Date and Time: _____

Describe in Detail What Occurred and Any Potential Concerns: _____

_____

_____

_____

Seek Any Further Directives Regarding This Case: _____

_____

_____

_____

Sources: Principles of Biomedical Ethics, 6th ed., by T. L. Beauchamp andJ. F. Childress, 2009, New York: Oxford University Press; and _Principles of Health Care Ethics_, by R. Gillon and A. Lloyd, 1994, Chichester, England: John Wiley & Sons.

References

Adams, J. R., & Juhnke, G. A. (2001). Using the Systems of Care philosophy to promote human potential. *Journal of Humanistic Counseling, Education & Development, 40*, 225–232.

Adams, J., & Juhnke, G. A. (1998, November). *Wraparound services with school children and their parents.* Presented at the North Carolina School Counselors Association Conference. Winston-Salem, NC.

American Academy of Child & Adolescent Psychiatry. (2005). http://www.aacap.org

American Association of Suicidology. (1998). School suicide postvention guidelines. Washington, DC: Author.

American Association of Suicidology. (2006). Warning signs for suicide. Retrieved from http://www.suicidology.org/web/guest/stats-and-tools/warning-signs

American Counseling Association. (2005). *Codes of ethics.* Retrieved from http://www.counseling.org/Resources/CodeOfEthics/TP/Home/CT2.aspx

American Foundation for Suicide Prevention, American Association of Suicidology, and Annenberg Public Policy Center. (n.d.). Reporting on suicide, recommendations for the media. Retrieved from www.afsp.org

American Medical Association. (2008). Code of medical ethics: Current opinions with annotations 2008–2009. Chicago: American Medical Association.

American Psychiatric Association. (2000). *Diagnostic and statistical manual of mental disorders.* Arlington, VA: Author.

American School Counselor Association. (2004, June 26). *Ethical standards for school counselors.* Retrieved from http://www.schoolcounselor.org/files/ethical%20standards.pdf

Ang, R. P., Chia, B. H., & Fung, D. S. S. (2006). Gender differences in life stressors associated with child and adolescent suicides in Singapore from 1995 to 2003. *International Journal of Social Psychiatry, 52*(6), 561–570.

Aseltine, R. H., Jr., & DeMartino, R. (2004). An outcome evaluation of the SOS Suicide Prevention Program. *American Journal of Public Health, 94*, 446–451.

Askew, M., & Byrne, M. W. (2009). Biopsychosocial approach to treating self-injurious behaviors: An adolescent case study. *Journal of Child and Adolescent Psychiatric Nursing, 22*, 115–119.

Austin, L., & Kortum, J. (2004). Self-injury: The secret language of pain for teenagers. *Education, 124*, 517–527.

Bailley, S. E., Kral, M. J., & Dunham, K. (1999). Survivors of suicide do grieve differently: Empirical support for a common sense proposition. *Suicide and Life Threatening Behavior, 29*, 256–271.

Beauchamp, T. L., & Childress, J. F. (2009). *Principles of Biomedical Ethics* (6th ed.). New York: Oxford University Press.

Becker, K., & Schmidt, M. H. (2005). When kids seek help on-line: Internet chat rooms and suicide. *Reclaiming Children and Youth, 13*, 229–230.

Berman, S. L., Kurtines, W. M., Silverman, W. K., & Serafini, L. T. (1996). The impact of exposure to crime and violence on urban youth. *American Journal of Orthopsychiatry, 66*, 329–336.

Bongar, B. (2002). Risk management: Prevention and postvention (pp. 213–261). In B. Bongar (Ed.), *The suicidal patient: Clinical and legal standards of care* (2nd ed.). Washington, DC: American Psychological Association.

Bowen, N. K., & Bowen, G. L. (1999). Effects of crime and violence in neighborhoods and schools on the school behavior and performance of adolescents. *Journal of Adolescent Research, 14*, 319–324.

Braddock III, C. H., Edwards, K. A., Hasenberg, N. M., Laidley, T. L., & Levinson, W. (1999). Informed decision making in outpatient practice. *JAMA, 282*, 2313–2320.

Brausch, A. M., & Gutierrez, P. M. (2010). Differences in non-suicidal self-injury and suicide attempts in adolescents. *Journal of Youth & Adolescence, 39*, 233–242.

Brock, S. E. (2003). Suicide postvention. In S. E. Brock, P. J. Lazarus, & S. R. Jimerson (Eds.). *Best practices in school crisis prevention and intervention* (pp. 553–576). Bethesda, MD: National Association of School Psychologists.

Brown, S. A. (2009). Personality and non-suicidal deliberate self-harm: Trait differences among a non-clinical population. *Psychiatry Research, 169*, 28–32.

Cable News Network. (2009). Conviction in MySpace suicide case tentatively overturned. Retrieved from http://www.cnn.com/2009/CRIME/07/02/myspace.suicide/index.html

CACREP (2009). The 2009 CACREP standards. Retrieved from http://67.199.126.156/doc/2009%20Standards.pdf

Campfield, D. C. (2009). Cyber bullying and victimization: Psychosocial characteristics of bullies, victims, and bully/victims. ProQuest Information & Learning, US. *Dissertation Abstracts International: Section B: The Sciences and Engineering, 69*(9), 5769.

Capuzzi, D. (1994). *Suicide prevention in the schools: Guidelines for middle and high school settings.* Alexandria, VA: American Counseling Association.

Capuzzi, D., & Gross, D. R. (2004). The adolescent at risk for suicidal behavior (pp. 275–303). In D. Capuzzi, & D. R. Gross (Eds.), *Youth at risk: A prevention resource for counselors, teachers and parents.* Alexandria, VA: Pearson Education.

Carter, L. (2002). A primer to ethical analysis. Office of Public Policy and Ethics, Institute for Molecular Bioscience, University of Queensland, Australia. Retrieved from http://www.uq.edu.au/oppe

Cassidy, W., Jackson, M., & Brown, K. N. (2009). Sticks and stones can break my bones, but how can pixels hurt me? Students' experiences with cyber-bullying. *School Psychology International, 30*(4), 383–402.

Centers for Disease Control and Prevention. (2010). Choking game awareness and participation among 8th graders—Oregon, 2008. *Morbidity and Mortality Weekly Report.* Retrieved from http://www.cdc.gov/mmwr/preview/mmwrhtml/ mm5901a1.htm

Centers for Disease Control and Prevention. (2008). Youth risk behavior surveillance—United States, 2007. Retrieved from http://www.cdc.gov/mmwr/ preview/mmwrhtml/ss5704a1.htm#tab21

Centers for Disease Control and Prevention. (2007). *Web-based Injury Statistics Query and Reporting System (WISQARS).* Retrieved from www.cdc.gov/injury/ wisqars/index.html.

Centers for Disease Control and Prevention, Department of Health and Human Services (2000). *School Health Policies and Programs Study.* Retrieved December 14, 2005, from http://www.cdc.gov/HealthyYouth/SHPPS

Children's Mental Health Screening and Prevention Act, H.R. 2063, 108th Cong. (2003).

Chiles, J. A., & Strosahl, K. D. (2005). *Clinical manual for assessment and treatment of suicidal patients.* Washington, DC: APA.

Cho, H., Guo, G., Iritani, B. J., & Hallfors, D. D. (2006). Genetic contribution to suicidal behaviors and associated risk factors among adolescents in the U.S. *Prevention Science, 7*(3), 303–311.

Doll, B., & Cummings, J. A. (2008). *Transforming school mental health services: Population-based approaches to promoting the competency and wellness of children.* Thousand Oaks: CA: Corwin Press and jointly published by the National Association of School Psychologists.

Dougherty, D. M., Mathias, C. W., Marsh-Richard, D., Prevette, K. N., Dawes, M. A., Hatzis, E. S., Palmes, G., & Nouvion, S. O. (2009). Impulsivity and clinical symptoms among adolescents with non-suicidal self-injury with or without attempted suicide. *Psychiatry Research, 169*, 22–27.

Downs, M. (2005). The highest price for pleasure. MedicineNet.com. Retrieved from http://www.medicinenet.com/script/main/art.asp?articlekey=51776

Dwyer, K, Osher, D., & Warger, C. (1998). *Early warning, timely response: A guide to safe schools.* Bethesda, MD: National Association of School Psychologists.

Emanuel, E. J., Wendler, D., & Grady, C. (2000). What makes clinical research ethical? *JAMA, 283*, 2701–2711.

Etzersdorfer, E., & Sonneck, G. (1998). Preventing suicide by influencing mass-media reporting. The Viennese experience 1980–1996. *Archives of Suicide Research, 4*, 67–74.

Everly, G. S., Jr., Flannery, R. B., Jr., & Mitchell, J. T. (2000). Critical Incident Stress Management (CISM): A review of the literature. *Aggression and Violent Behavior, 5*(1), 23–40.

Federal Emergency Management Agency. (2003). *Integrating manmade hazards into mitigation planning.* Web release 10. Washington, DC: Author. Retrieved November 11, 2009, from http://www.fema.gov/library/viewRecord.do?id=1915

Fitzsimmonds, M. K. (1998). *Violence and aggression in children and youth.* ERIC Digest. (ERIC Document Reproduction Service no. ED429419.)

Florida Department of Health. (2009, December 12). Licensure requirements. Retrieved from http://www.doh.state.fl.us/mqa/491/soc_lic_req.html#Mental%20Health%20Counseling

Franklin, C., Harris, M. B., & Allen-Meares, P. (2006). *The school services sourcebook: A guide for school-based professionals.* New York: Oxford University Press.

Friedman, R. M., & Drews, D. A. (2005, February). Evidenced-based practices, Systems of Care, and individual care. Tampa, FL: Research and Training Center for Children's Mental Health.

Garbarino, J. (1999). *Lost boys: Why our sons turn violent and how we can save them.* New York: Free Press.

Gillon, R., & Lloyd, A. (1994). *Principles of health care ethics.* Chichester, UK: John Wiley & Sons.

Gould, M. S., Marracco, F. A., Kleinman, M., Thomas, J. G., Mostkoff, K., Cote, J., & Davies, M. (2005). Evaluating iatrogenic risk of youth suicide screening programs: A randomized controlled trial. *Journal of the American Medical Association, 293*(13), 1635–1643.

Granello, D. H. (2010). A suicide crisis intervention model with 25 practical strategies for implementation. *Journal of Mental Health Counseling, 32*(3), 218–235.

Granello, D. H. (2010). The process of suicide risk assessment: Twelve core principles. *Journal of Counseling and Development, 88,* 363–371.

Granello, D. H., & Granello, P. F. (2007). *Suicide: An essential guide for helping professionals and educators.* Boston: Pearson/Allyn & Bacon.

Gurian, M. (1999). *A fine young man: What parents, mentors, and educators can do to shape adolescent boys into exceptional men.* New York: Jeremy P. Tarcher/Putnam.

Harris, K. M., McLean, J. P., & Sheffield, J. (2009). Examining suicide-risk individuals who go on-line for suicide-related purposes. *Archives of Suicide Research, 13,* 264–276.

Heath, N. L., Toste, J. R., & Beettam, E. L. (2006). "I am not well-equipped": High school teachers' perceptions of self-injury. *Canadian Journal of School Psychology, 21,* 73–92.

Helms, J. F. (2003). Barriers to help-seeking among 12th graders. *Journal of Educational and Psychological Consultation, 14*(1) 27–40.

Hinawi, S. S. (2005). A model screening program for youth. *Behavioral Health Management, 25,* 38–44.

Jacobson, C. M., & Gould, M. (2007). The epidemiology and phenomenology of non-suicidal self-injurious behavior among adolescents: A critical review of the literature. *Archives of Suicide Research, 11,* 129–147.

Jacobson, N., & Gottman, J. (1998). *When men batter women: New insights into ending abusive relationships.* New York: Simon and Schuster.

Jenkins, E. J., & Bell, C. C. (1994). Violence among inner city high school students and posttraumatic stress disorder (pp. 76–88). In S. Friedman (Ed.), *Anxiety disorders in African Americans.* New York: Springer.

Jimerson, S., Brock, S., & Pletcher, S. (2005). An integrated model of school crisis preparedness and intervention: a shared foundation to facilitate international crisis intervention. *School Psychology International, 26*(3), 275–296.

Joe, S., & Bryant, H. (2007). Evidence-based suicide prevention screening in schools. *Children & Schools, 29,* 219–227.

Juhnke, G. A. (1997). After school violence: An adapted Critical Incident Stress Debriefing model for student survivors and their parents. *Elementary School Guidance & Counseling, 31,* 163–170.

Juhnke, G. A., & Liles, R. G. (2000). Treating adolescents presenting with comorbid violent and addictive behaviors: A behavioral family therapy model (pp. 319–333). In D. S. Sandu & C. B. Aspy (Eds.), *Violence in American schools: A practical guide for counselors.* Alexandria, VA: American Counseling Association.

Juhnke, G. A., & Shoffner, M. E. (1999). The family debriefing model: An adapted Critical Incident Stress Debriefing for parents and older sibling suicide survivors. *Family Journal: Counseling and Therapy for Couples and Families, 7,* 342–348.

Kadushin, A. (1983). *The social work interview* (2nd ed.). New York: Columbia University Press.

Kaffenberger, C. (2006). School reentry for students with chronic illness: A role for professional school counselors. *Professional School Counseling, 9,* 223–230.

Kalafat, J. (2003). School approaches to youth suicide prevention. *American Behavioral Scientist, 46,* 1211–1223.

Kalafat, J., & Underwood, M. (1989). *Lifelines: A school-based adolescent suicide response program.* Dubuque, IA: Kendall & Hunt.

Katzer, C., Fetchenhauer, D., & Belschak, F. (2009). Cyberbullying: Who are the victims? A comparison of victimization in internet chatrooms and victimization in school. *Journal of Media Psychology: Theories, Methods, and Applications, 21*(1), 25–36.

Kelson vs. the City of Springfield, Illinois, 767, F.2d 651 26 Ed. Law Rep. 182 No. 84-4403. United States Court of Appeals, Ninth Circuit. Argued and Submitted July 9, 1985. Decided Aug. 2, 1985.

Kim, Y. S., & Leventhal, B. (2008). Bullying and suicide. A review. *International Journal of Adolescent Medicine and Health, 20*(2), 133–154.

Kim, Y. S., Leventhal, B. L., Koh, Y., & Boyce, W. T. (2009). Bullying increased suicide risk: Prospective study of Korean adolescents. *Archives of Suicide Research, 13*(1), 15–30.

Kiriakidis, S. P. (2008). Bullying and suicide attempts among adolescents kept in custody. *Crisis: The Journal of Crisis Intervention and Suicide Prevention, 29*(4), 216–218.

Klonsky, E. D. (2007). The functions of deliberate self-injury: A review of the evidence. *Clinical Psychology Review, 27,* 236–239.

Klonsky, E. D., & Muehlenkamp, J. J. (2007). Self-injury: A research review for the practitioner. *Journal of Clinical Psychology, 63,* 1045–1056.

Koocher, G. P., & Keith-Spiegel, P. (2008). *Ethics in psychology and the mental health professions: Standards and cases* (3rd ed.). New York: Oxford University Press.

Kress, V., & Hoffman, R. M. (2008). Non-suicidal self-injury and motivational interviewing: Enhancing readiness for change. *Journal of Mental Health Counseling, 30,* 311–329.

Krill, W. E., Jr. (2009). Encopresis and enuresis in stress disordered children. Retrieved November 13, 2009, from http://hubpages.com/hub/Encopresis-and-Enuresis-in-Stress-Disordered-Children

Lazear, K., Roggenbaum, S., & Blase, K. (2003). Youth suicide prevention school-based guide. Retrieved from http://theguide.fmhi.usf.edu/pdf/Overview.pdf

Leis, S. J. (2003). Do one-shot preventive interventions for PTSD work? A systematic research synthesis of psychological debriefings. *Aggression & Violent Behavior, 8*(3), 329–337.

Maine Youth Suicide Prevention Program. (2009). Maine youth suicide prevention, intervention, and postvention guidelines. Retrieved from http://www.maine.gov/suicide/

McEvoy, M. L., & McEvoy, A. W. (1994). *Preventing youth suicide: A handbook for educators and human service professionals.* Holmes Beach, FL: Learning Publications.

McWhirter, J. J., McWhirter, B. T., McWhirter, E. H., & McWhirter, R. J. (2007). *At risk youth: A comprehensive response for counselors, teachers, psychologists, and human services professionals* (4th ed.). Belmont, CA: Thomson Higher Education.

Miller, D. N., & DuPaul, G. J. (1996). School-based prevention of adolescent suicide: Issues, obstacles and recommendations for practice. *Journal of Emotional and Behavioral Disorders, 4,* 221–230.

Minnesota Board of Behavioral Health. (2009, December 12). LPC applications. Retrieved from http://www.bbht.state.mn.us/Default.aspx?tabid=1149.

Mishna, F., Saini, M., & Solomon, S. (2009). Ongoing and online: Children's perceptions of cyber bullying. *Children and Youth Services Review, 31,* 1222–1228.

Mitchell, J. T. (1994, February 24–25). *Basic Critical Incident Stress Debriefing.* University of North Carolina at Chapel Hill. Chapel Hill, NC.

Mitchell, J. T., & Everly, G. S. (1993). *Critical Incident Stress Debriefing (CISD): An operations manual for the prevention of traumatic stress among emergency services and disaster workers.* Ellicott City, MD: Chevron Press.

Muehlenkamp, J. J. (2006). Empirically supported treatments and general therapy guidelines for non-suicidal self-injury. *Journal of Mental Health Counseling, 28,* 166–185.

Muehlenkamp, J. J., & Gutierrez, P. M. (2007). Risk for suicide attempts among adolescents who engage in non-suicidal self-injury. *Archives of Suicide Research, 11,* 69–82.

Muehlenkamp, J. J., & Gutierrez, P. M. (2004). An investigation of differences between self-injurious behavior and suicide attempts in a sample of adolescents. *Suicide and Life-Threatening Behavior, 34*, 12–23.

Muehlenkamp, J. J., & Kerr, P. L. (2009). Untangling a complex web: How non-suicidal self injury and suicide attempts differ. *Prevention Researcher, 17*, 8–10.

Muehlenkamp, J. J., Walsh, B. W., & McDade, M. (2010). Preventing non-suicidal self-injury in adolescents: The Signs of Self Injury program. *Journal of Youth & Adolescence, 39*, 306–314.

Murray, B. (1999, July/August). Boys to men: Emotional miseducation. *American Psychological Association Monitor, 1*, 38–39.

National Association of School Psychologists. (2006). *Supporting student success: Remedying the shortage of school psychologists.* Retrieved from http://www.nasponline .org/advocacy/personnelshortages.pdf

National Association of School Psychologists. (n.d.). *Preventing youth suicide: Tips for parents and educators.* Retrieved from http://www.nasponline.org/resources/ crisis_safety/suicideprevention.aspx

National Board of Certified Counselors. (2005). Code of ethics. Retrieved from http://www.nbcc.org/AssetManagerFiles/ethics/nbcc-codeofethics.pdf

National Center for Education Statistics. (2009). *Documentation to the common core of data state nonfiscal survey of public elementary/secondary education school year 2007–2008.* Retrieved from http://nces.ed.gov/ccd/stnfis.asp

National Center for Injury Prevention and Control, Division of Violence Prevention. (2008, August 4). *Suicide prevention: Youth suicide.* Retrieved October 12, 2009, from http://www.cdc.gov/ncipc/dvp/suicide/youthsuicide.htm

National Child Traumatic Stress Network and National Center for PTSD. (2006, July). *Psychological first aid: Field operations guide* (2nd ed.). Retrieved June 6, 2009, from www.nctsn.org

National Crime Prevention Council. (2007). *Teens and cyberbullying: Executive summary of a report on research.* Retrieved from http://www.ncpc.org/resources/ files/pdf/bullying/Teens%20and%20Cyberbullying%20Research%20Study.pdf

National Institutes of Health. (2001). *Bullying widespread in U.S. schools, survey finds.* Retrieved from http://www.nichd.nih.gov/news/releases/bullying.cfm

National Strategy for Suicide Prevention: Goals and Objectives for Action. (2001). U.S. Dept of Health and Human Services, Pub No. 02NLM: HV 6548.A1. Rockville, MD.

Nixon, M. K., & Heath, N. L. (2009). *Self-injury in youth: The essential guide to assessment and intervention.* New York: Routledge.

No Child Left Behind (NCLB) Act of 2001, Pub. L. No. 107–110 §115, Stat. 1425 (2002).

Nock, M. K. (2009). Suicidal behavior among adolescents: Correlates, confounds, and (the search for) causal mechanisms. *Journal of the American Academy of Child & Adolescent Psychiatry, 48*, 237–239.

Nock, M. K., Prinstein, M. J., & Sterba, S. K. (2009). Revealing the form and function of self-injurious thoughts and behaviors: A real-time ecological assessment study among adolescents and young adults. *Journal of Abnormal Psychology, 118*, 816–827.

North Carolina Board of Licensed Professional Counselors (2009, December 12). Licensed professional counselor. Retrieved from http://ncblpc.org/LPC.html

Northouse, P. G. (2006). *Leadership: Theory and practice.* Thousand Oaks, CA: SAGE.

O'Donnell, I., Farmer, R., & Catalan, J. (1996). Explaining suicide: The views of survivors of serious suicide attempts. *British Journal of Psychiatry, 168,* 780–786.

O'Hara, D. M., Taylor, R., & Simpson, K. (1994). Critical Incident Stress Debriefing: Bereavement support in schools developing a role for an LEA education psychology service. *Educational Psychology in Practice, 10,* 27–33.

Ohio.gov. (2009, December 12). Counselor licensing. Retrieved from http://cswmft.ohio.gov/clicen.stm

Pellegrino, E. D., & Thomasma, D. C. (1993). The virtues in medical practice. New York: Oxford University Press.

Perry, B. D. (2002). Stress, trauma, and Post-traumatic Stress Disorders in children: An introduction. Online booklet from the Child Trauma Academy. Retrieved from www.childtrauma.org on November 11, 2009.

Peterson, J., Freedenthal, S., Sheldon, C., & Andersen, R. (2008). Nonsuicidal self injury in adolescents. *Psychiatry, 5*(11), 20–24.

President's New Freedom Commission on Mental Health. (2003). *Achieving the promise: Transforming mental health care in America* (Pub. No. SMA 03–3832). Rockville, MD: Author. Retrieved from http://www.mentalhealthcommission.gov/reports/reports.htm

Reis, C., & Cornell, D. (2008). An evaluation of suicide gatekeeper training for school counselors and teachers. *Professional School Counseling, 11,* 386–394.

Richters, J., & Maxtinez, P. (1993). The NIMH community violence project: I. Children as victims of and witnesses to violence. *Psychiatry, 56,* 7–21.

Roberts-Dobie, S., & Donatelle, R. J. (2007). School counselors and student self-injury. *Journal of School Health, 77,* 257–264.

Robinson, R. (2004). Counterbalancing misrepresentations of Critical Incident Stress Debriefing and Critical Incident Stress Management. *Australian Psychologist, 39*(1), 20–34.

Rose, S., Bisson, J., & Wessely, S. (2003). A systematic review of single-session psychological interventions ("Debriefing") following trauma. *Psychotherapy & Psychosomatics, 72*(4), 176–184.

Scott, M. A., Wilcox, H. C., Schonfeld, I. S., Davies, M., Hicks, R. C., Turner, J. B., & Shaffer, D. (2009). School-based screening to identify at-risk students not already known to school professionals: The Columbia Suicide Screen. *American Journal of Public Health, 99,* 224–339.

Shaffer, D., Scott, M., Wilcox, H., Maslow, C., Hicks, R., Lucas, C. P., Garfinkel, R., & Greenwald, S. (2004). The Columbia Suicide Screen: Validity and reliability of a screen for youth suicide and depression. *Journal of the American Academy of Child & Adolescent Psychiatry, 43,* 71–79.

Sharaf, A. Y., Thompson, E. A., & Walsh, E. (2009). Protective effects of self-esteem and family support on suicide risk behaviors among at-risk adolescents. *Journal of Child & Adolescent Psychiatric Nursing, 22,* 160–168.

Shields, L. B. E., Hunsaker, J. C., & Stewart, D. M. (2008). Russian roulette and risk-taking behavior: A medical examiner study. *American Journal of Forensic Medicine and Pathology, 29,* 32–39.

Shneidman, E. S. (2005). How I read. *Suicide and Life-Threatening Behavior, 35*(2), 117–120.

Silverman, E., Range, L., & Overholser, J. (1994–95). Bereavement from suicide as compared to other forms of bereavement. *Omega, 30,* 41–51.

Simon, T. R., Swann, A. C., Powell, K. E., Potter, L. B., Kresnow, M., & O'Carroll, P. W. (2001). Characteristics of impulsive suicide attempts and attempters. *Suicide and Life-Threatening Behavior, 32*(Suppl.), 49–59.

Stephan, S. H., Weist, M., Kataoka, S., Adelsheim, S., & Mills, C. (2007). Transformation of children's mental health services: The role of school mental health. *Psychiatric Services, 58,* 1330–1338.

Stillion, J. M., & McDowell, E. E. (1996). *Suicide across the lifespan: Premature exits* (2nd ed.). Washington, DC: Taylor & Francis.

Texas Department of State Health Services. (2009, December 12). Texas State Board of Examiners of Professional Counselors apply for a new license—requirements. Retrieved from http://www.dshs.state.tx.us/counselor/lpc_apply.shtm

Thompson, R. (1990). *Post-traumatic loss debriefing: Providing immediate support for survivors of suicide or sudden loss.* Greensboro, NC: ERIC Clearinghouse on Counseling and Student Services. (ERIC Document Reproduction Services No. ED 315 708).

Toste, M. A., & Heath, N. L. (2009). School response to non-suicidal self-injury. *Prevention Researcher, 17,* 14–17.

Tuckey, M. R. (2007). Issues in the debriefing debate for the emergency services: Moving research outcomes forward. *Clinical Psychology: Science and Practice 14*(2), 106–116.

U.S. Department of Education. (2007). Office of Safe and Drug-Free Schools. Practical information on crisis planning: A guide for schools and communities. Washington, DC.

U.S. Department of Health and Human Services. (2001). *National Strategy for Suicide Prevention.* Rockville, MD: Public Health Service.

Vacc, N. A., & Juhnke, G. A. (1997). The use of structured clinical interviews for assessment in counseling. *Journal of Counseling & Development, 75,* 470–486.

van Emmerik, A. P., Kamphuis, J. H, Hulsbosch, A. M., & Emmelkamp, P. M. (2002). Single session debriefing after psychological trauma: A meta-analysis. *Lancet, 360,* 766–771.

VanDenBerg, J. E., & Grealish, E. M. (1996). Individualized services and supports through the wraparound process: Philosophy and procedures. *Journal of Child and Family Studies, 5,* 7–21.

Walker, D. (1995). *School violence prevention.* Ann Arbor, MI: ERIC/CAPS. (ERIC Document Reproduction Service No. ED 379 786).

Walsh, B. W. (2006). *Treating self-injury: A practical guide.* New York: Guilford Press.

Warner, J. (2009). Some docs in the dark about choking game. *WebMD.* Retrieved from http://www.webmd.com/parenting/news/20091214/some-docs-in-the-dark-about-choking-game

Washington County Department of Public Health & Environment. (2001). *Adolescent depression and suicide opinion survey.* Retrieved from http://www.co.washington.mn.us/client_files/documents/FHL-teensurv.pdf

Weekley, N., & Brock, S. E. (2004.) Suicide: Postvention strategies for school personnel. Helping children at home and school: Handouts for educators, S-9, 45-47. Retrieved from http://www.aamentalhealth.org/SCHOOLPERSONNEL_000.pdf

Weist, M. D. (1999). Challenges and opportunities in expanded school mental health. *Clinical Psychology Review, 19,* 131–135.

Whalen L. G., Grunbaum J. A., Kinchen S., et al. (2005) *Middle School Youth Risk Behavior Survey 2003.* U.S. Department of Health and Human Services. Retrieved from http://www.cdc.gov/healthyyouth/yrbs/middleschool2003/pdf/fullreport.pdf

Whitlock, J., Lader, W., & Conterio, K. (2007). The Internet and self-injury: What psychotherapists should know. *Journal of Clinical Psychology, 63,* 1135–1143.

Whitlock, J. L., Powers, J. L., & Eckenrode J. (2006). The virtual cutting edge: The Internet and adolescent self-injury. *Developmental Psychology, 42,* 407–417.

Willard, N. (2007). Cyberbullying and cyberthreats: Responding to the challenge of online social aggression, threats, and distress. Champaign, IL: Research Press.

Williams, J. M. G., Duggan, D. S., Crane, C., & Fennell, M. J. V. (2006). Mindfulness-based cognitive therapy for prevention of recurrence of suicidal behaviors. *Journal of Clinical Psychology: In Session, 62,* 201–210.

Wyke v. Polk County School Board, United States Court of Appeals, Eleventh Circuit. Nos. 95-2799, 95-3653., Nov. 19, 1997.

Wyman, P. A., Brown, C. H., Inman, J., Cross, W., Schmeelk-Cone, K., Guo, J., & Pena, J. B. (2008). Randomized trial of a gatekeeper program for suicide prevention: 1-year impact on secondary school staff. *Journal of Consulting and Clinical Psychology, 76*(1), 104–115.

Young, R., Van Beinum, M., Sweeting, H., & West, P. (2007). Young people who self-harm. *British Journal of Psychiatry, 191,* 44–49.

Zenere, F. J. (2009, October 1). Suicide clusters and contagion. *Principal Leadership Magazine.*

Index